2002

Mapping the Cultural
Space of Journalism

Mapping the Cultural Space of Journalism

How Journalists Distinguish News from Entertainment

SAMUEL P. WINCH

Foreword by David Bocyink

PRAEGER

Westport, Connecticut
London

Library of Congress Cataloging-in-Publication Data

Winch, Samuel P.
    Mapping the cultural space of journalism : how journalists
distinguish news from entertainment / Samuel P. Winch ; foreword by
David Boeyink.
        p.   cm.
    Includes bibliographical references and index.
    ISBN 0–275–95763–2 (alk. paper) —ISBN 0–275–96467–1 (pbk.)
    1. Television broadcasting of news.   2. Sensationalism in
television.   3. Sensationalism in journalism.   I. Title.
    PN4784.T4W56   1997
    070.1'95—DC20   96–33190

British Library Cataloguing in Publication Data is available.

Library of Congress Catalog Card Number: 96–33190
ISBN: 0–275–96467–1 (pbk.)

First published in 1997

Praeger Publishers, 88 Post Road West, Westport, CT 06881
An imprint of Greenwood Publishing Group, Inc.

Printed in the United States of America

The paper used in this book complies with the
Permanent Paper Standard issued by the National
Information Standards Organization (Z39.48–1984).

10 9 8 7 6 5 4 3 2 1

To Paula and Bridget,
who fill my life with love and smiles.

Contents

Tables and Figures

Foreword

David Boeyink

Tabloid newspaper headlines scream out from the checkout stand of the supermarket. Tabloid news shows fill television screens every night. But little serious attention is given to these non-traditional forms of news by media critics and scholars. Tabloid journalists aren't part of the classic studies of American journalists by David Weaver and Cleveland Wilhoit; video news archives collect only network television programs, not Inside Edition or Hard Copy. Finding a copy of the National Enquirer at an academic library is about as likely as finding an academic journal at the local newsstand.

Samuel Winch's study explores the reasons for this neglect of non-traditional media. More accurately, he opens our eyes to the ways in which journalists construct and defend boundaries between what they believe is news and what they reject as entertainment, or simply bad journalism. Winch dissects a series of case studies in which journalists and non-journalists struggle to create boundaries: What is news and what is not? What is good journalism and what is not? In the process, they struggle to distinguish information from entertainment, acceptable journalistic practices from unacceptable ones, news from trash.

Using Thomas Gieryn's methodology, Winch's cases illustrate sharply the range of strategies used to draw these boundary lines, including epistemological, functional, methodological, and organizational differences. For example, in the controversy over

---

David Boeyink is an associate professor at the Indiana University School of Journalism. He served as the dissertation advisor for the thesis on which this book is based.

Gennifer Flowers and Bill Clinton, Winch shows how some journalists argued that Flowers' unproven allegations were not news, but only rumor (an epistemological difference). Yet in a delicious bit of casuistry, many mainstream journalists also argued that once the charges were reported in tabloids, the reports themselves were news, justifying the reporting of the charges.

In short, Winch demonstrates the difficulty of sustaining the boundary between what is news and what is not. For example, he documents in great detail how the government, despite numerous attempts, was unable to define the boundary between news and entertainment.

Of equal importance is Winch's insight that the very standards used to create the boundaries expose the permeability of those boundaries. When journalists claim that only the tabloids pay for sources, cases of source payment surface in mainstream media. The more news is distinguished from entertainment, the more entertainment values can be seen as driving news coverage. Differences are only matters of degree, especially close to the boundary line.

Having shown how news boundaries are socially constructed, Winch has opened the way for more serious study of the neglected half of the news spectrum: tabloids. With readership in the millions and increasing popularity on prime time television, the tabloids deserve more serious attention from all those interested in how news is created and the function it plays in a democracy. After all, the boundary isn't that tough to cross.

Preface
and Acknowledgments

Before beginning this study, I noticed that many journalists were complaining that the "boundaries of journalism were being crossed." I wondered what those boundaries might be and how they became known. Professor Holly Stocking of Indiana University alerted me to the work of sociologist Thomas Gieryn (1995; 1992; 1983), who studies a similar issue in the sociology of science: How do scientists construct and maintain public perceptions of boundaries between what they do and what non-scientists do? In the interest of parsimony of social theory, it makes sense to use this same *sensitizing concept* to help us understand how similar social actions operate in journalism.

This was a really fun project to do, even though it consumed me for the better part of three years, and it took forever to become a true social constructivist.

A lot of people deserve thanks for helping me. Above all, my dissertation advisor, Dave Boeyink, and my wife Paula Winch deserve halos. My father, the Rev. Bill Winch, helped out too, as did the great editors at Greenwood Publishing Group: Lynn Zelem, Marcia Goldstein, and Nick Street.

I also want to thank the rest of my wonderful dissertation committee (my dream team): Holly Stocking, Tom Gieryn, and Don Agostino. My colleagues at Bowling Green State University—particularly Ray Laakaniemi and Catherine Cassara—were helpful and supportive, as were the rest of my extended family and friends. Finally, I want to thank my brother Steve for drawing the cartoon facing the Foreword.

Mapping the Cultural
Space of Journalism

The Cultural Space of Journalism

Once, the borders were clear and inviolate: Newspapers, newscasts and newsmagazines covered serious events; pop culture entertained us. But in the past generation, the culture sparked by rock & roll, then fused with TV and mutated by Hollywood, ran riot over the traditional boundaries between straight journalism and entertainment.

—Jon Katz
"Rock, Rap and Movies Bring You the News"

INTRODUCTION

Many journalists like Jon Katz today feel that the boundaries between news and entertainment are blurring, particularly in the television medium. In this book, I examine these boundary concepts and attempt to answer a few complicated questions, such as: Why and how are journalism's boundaries socially constructed? How are they negotiated by different groups of people with interests in mass communications? And—perhaps most importantly—how do journalists breach these boundaries and then respond to the breaches through boundary-maintenance exercises? I hope to recover some of the messiness of the boundaries through this inquiry. The impetus for this study are the numerous observations and arguments that network television news and tabloid television entertainment programs are converging in style and content into a new genre called "reality-based programming." This study will examine some of these arguments, looking for how this phenomenon is described, the explanations given for it, as well as the explanations for why it has become an issue. As analyst, I will not be in a position to reach a definitive conclusion about the boundaries of these categories. Rather, I will describe how interested players draw the boundaries. It is important to note that boundary work is committed within the day-to-day work of journalism as well as in the latter representations and reconstructions of journalism content and practice.

To accomplish these goals, I will examine three case studies—specific instances of boundary construction, negotiation, and maintenance in journalism. Most of the emphasis will be on how these boundaries affect television journalism, but other journalism media are also examined. According to Justin Lewis (1991), television is arguably the greatest culture-producing machinery on earth (pp. 5–7). For that reason, and because many conceive of television as primarily an entertainment medium, most of the attention in this study will be focused on television journalism boundaries.

SIGNIFICANCE OF THE PROJECT

As Peter Dahlgren (1992) says (perhaps understatedly), "Journalism's centrality in politics and culture, as well as its vested economic and occupational interests, make questions regarding its boundaries, uses and contingencies of more than idle concern" (p. 4). Some of the questions along this vein that demand our attention include: How have journalists been able to demarcate their area of mass communication from other types of mass communication? What do they gain from such work? Do journalists maintain control over the production and evaluation of news? How are journalists able to maintain the public perception that they are authoritative or credible? How do journalists convert cultural authority into other opportunities, such as jobs, political influence, and prestige? How do journalists respond to threats or challenges to their cultural authority? Admittedly, this study is just a start in this line of research.

Journalists assert that they have the authority to perform an important function in our democratic society: to truthfully report the news and to inform the public. This authority depends on the trust of the publics that the news media serve. American journalists say the defining characteristics of their work are that it is true, accurate, and in the interest of the audience—yet these are irrelevant unless audiences believe in the truthfulness and accuracy of journalistic accounts. If the public believes in the accuracy of journalism, then journalists gain authority—the authority to tell the news.

Other culture-producing mass media institutions, such as the advertising, public relations, and entertainment industries, also communicate to the masses. When these institutions and industries produce messages that appear similar to journalism, journalists interpret these events as threats to the boundaries and authority of journalism (Hallin, 1992). The cultural authority of the institution of journalism depends on the ability of people to distinguish between it and other kinds of mass communication.

It is useful for us to examine what sociologists of science call *boundary-work rhetoric:* the rhetorical strategy of one group wishing to distinguish itself from another (Gieryn, 1983). For example, medical doctors draw a boundary—within their discourse and routine practices—between what they do and what faith healers do. Likewise, journalists who consider themselves mainstream draw boundaries between what they do and what other mass communicators do. As I will show, these other communicators include people such as entertainment talk show hosts and tabloid journalists. When the public does not notice the difference between a faith healer and a doctor, either the doctor, the faith healer, or both will engage in boundary-work rhetoric; socially constructing a boundary in order to protect the authority to do their work. Likewise, journalists engage in boundary-work rhetoric because they want the public to be aware of the differences between news work and entertainment work.

RESEARCH QUESTIONS

The main questions I examine in this study are: How and why have television journalists and others defined "television news" and the goals, norms, and ideologies of television journalism as they have? How have the boundaries between entertainment and news been constructed and negotiated as they have; and what rhetorical moves do journalists and others make to distinguish between the two? What are the differences in the uses of distinguishing characteristics between those within the journalism profession and those outside the profession? In effect: Who does boundary work, and how do different groups do it differently? And finally, how do the interests and strategies of boundary-work rhetoric along the news/entertainment boundary compare to the interests and strategies of rhetoric uncovered along other boundaries, such as science/non-science; and what is it about the news/entertainment boundary that makes these strategies different—or similar?

To understand the significance of these questions, we must first examine some of the concepts that seem to be at stake here, such as authority, jurisdiction, and autonomy.

THE AUTHORITY AND SELF-DEFINITION OF JOURNALISM

The institution of American journalism has earned a mantle of authority in American society. The mere fact that many historians rely on newspaper and magazine accounts as primary source material indicates in a small way how journalism and the work of journalists become authoritative. As purveyors of facts and interpretation, journalists use this authority to describe events and everyday life to the public. Gieryn and Figert (1986) describe this kind of authority as social power: "'Cognitive authority' is the legitimate power (in designated contexts) to define, describe or explain bounded realms of reality" (p. 67). The public entrusts journalists with this cognitive authority to the extent that they believe in journalists and their work. When the authority is threatened, journalists respond to consolidate their power.

Paul Starr (1982), in his studies of the medical profession, calls this power *cultural authority*. He says "cultural authority entails the construction of reality through definitions of fact and value" (p. 13). Starr distinguishes cultural authority from social authority, which he says "involves the control of action through the giving of commands." Cultural authority, on the other hand, is derived from performing a service and from the ability to determine the *needs* of clients. If journalists perform the service of informing public debates, then they determine which cultural conversations people need to be aware of and engaged in. The cultural authority of journalists, therefore . . . is based on the dependence of the public on the ability of journalists to present important information in a coherent and reliable fashion, or at least make it seem that way. This authority is reproduced in and through the everyday practices of journalists as well as later through boundary-work rhetoric. Starr says the cultural authority of medical doctors rests on three aspects of legitimacy: collegial, cognitive, and moral (p. 15). For journalistic cultural authority, these same aspects of legitimacy are appropriate: 1. The collegial legitimacy of the journalist—the acceptance by others in their profession; 2. the cognitive legitimacy of the journalistic product—it is perceived to be based on rational, objective methods; and 3. the moral legitimacy of the journalist—journalists' judgments are expected to be oriented toward altruism and public service (Merton & Gieryn, 1982).

Threats to cultural authority of an institution or profession do not always come from outside the institution or profession. A well-publicized case of fraud or fakery is perhaps the prime example of an internal threat to the cultural authority of a social institution or profession (Gieryn & Figert, 1986, pp. 67–68). Such turmoil is publicly discussed and thereby constructed as an issue or problem. The discussion of the issue occurs as discourse within journalistic media by journalists who control the content and topics of the medium. For example, in 1980, *Washington Post* reporter Janet Cooke fabricated a news story about an imaginary eight-year-old heroin addict (Cooke, 1980, p. 1) and was on the verge of accepting a Pulitzer Prize for it when the deception was revealed. The *Post's* subsequent analysis of the deception argued that the problem was not organizational, the problem was that Cooke was an aberration—a compulsive liar (Green, 1981). As Dahlgren (1992) notes, one of the distinctive aspects of turmoil within the institution of journalism is that those within the institution "strive to maintain discursive control over such turmoil. Among other things, this helps to consolidate and legitimate professional practices and identity (by) . . . retain(ing) definitional control of the field, its problems and potential solutions" (p. 2). Definitional control of the boundaries of journalism is also accomplished by journalists when they do things like formulate definitions of news and news work. It is also accomplished through the selection of news topics.

Defining news is not a simple task. A 1965 textbook for journalists admits, "To recognize news is easier than to define it" (Harris & Johnson). Yet the primary role of journalists is to determine what is newsworthy, that is, to define news. In defining news, journalists also define what it is they do. This study shows how journalists often define journalism in relation to its neighboring professions.

SOME BACKGROUND ABOUT "THE PROBLEM"

Many journalism critics have recently argued that American journalism is undergoing a profound change because it now regularly mixes entertainment with the news (for example, Bernstein, C., 1992; Briller, 1989). Critics typically argue that this entertainment is in the form of sensationalistic celebrity-scandal. In fact, there is a long history of sensationalism in American journalism, a fact documented by several journalism historians (for example, Shaw & Slater, 1985; Stevens, 1991). But the main point of contemporary critics is that sensationalism and tabloid-style techniques, which were always present on the fringes of journalism, are now becoming the norm in American journalism, and are being adopted by so-called "mainstream"[1] media as part of economic survival strategies in the cutthroat business climate of American mass media (for example, Bogart, 1991; Hallin, 1992). These contemporary critics typically argue that there should be a rigid boundary between mainstream journalism and other kinds of mass communication such as tabloid journalism. The critics imply that one kind of communication is more legitimate in certain contexts than the other, and even that tabloid journalism is not journalism at all but is instead entertainment (for example, McClellan, 1992; Rowe, 1992). As noted above, one of the claims made by mass media critics is that journalism just recently got worse. But this may be a perennial complaint.

A quick review of journalism criticism reveals that the argument that journalism used to be better but just recently got worse is common throughout the history of journalism. The critiques usually say that journalism used to make bold distinctions between news and entertainment but now combines the two. These critiques construct the logical conclusion that journalism has steadily decreased in quality over many years. Taken together, the criticisms add up to the conclusions that the people who used to do journalism were better and had higher standards than those of today and that the distinctions between news and entertainment used to be greater. Examples of this critique can be found in even the earliest discussions of American journalism.

For instance, critics panned Benjamin Day's *New York Sun* of the early 1830s because it often contained humor and sensational news of suicides. Similarly, some critics hated James Gordon Bennett's *New York Herald* of the mid- to late-1830s because it contained entertaining, satirically written police court reports, as well as in-depth crime stories. Bennett pioneered the "human-interest story" or feature story, when he wrote in vivid detail in 1836 about the grisly murder of the prostitute Helen Jewett, quoting her madam and describing Jewett's apartment in minute detail (Hughes, 1940). Bennett's day-by-day narrative of the ensuing sensational trial reminds us of how journalism and entertaining literature have been combined for many years to make newsworthy stories "more palatable for consumption." Bennett was soundly criticized by his competitors and others for blurring the boundary between journalism and entertainment. His detractors, many of them his competitors, waged what they called a "Moral War" in the late 1830s against Bennett and his enjoyable but sensationalistic newspaper. They maintained that Bennett was a "deviant" journalist because he blurred the boundaries of journalism by making his newspaper entertaining and popular. Those running the "Moral War" against Bennett were unsuccessful at running him out of the journalism business, but they did seriously wound his business.

In the 1920s, many journalists were labeled "yellow journalists" because they sensationalized and twisted the news by appealing to prurient interests and base instincts.

In 1962, philosopher Jürgen Habermas argued that the boundaries between news and entertainment are blurring because people prefer "entertaining" news and its immediate rewards:

Public affairs, social problems, economic matters, education and health . . . 'delayed reward news'—are not only pushed into the background by 'immediate reward news' (comics, corruption, accidents, disasters, sports, recreation, social events, and human interest) but, as the characteristic label already indicates, are already read less and more rarely. In the end the news generally assumes some sort of guise and is made to resemble a narrative from its form down to stylistic detail (news stories); the rigorous distinction between fact and fiction is ever more frequently abandoned. News and reports and even editorial opinions are dressed up with all the accouterments of entertainment literature, whereas on the other hand the belletrist contributions aim for the strictly 'realistic' reduplication of reality "as it is" on the level of clichès and thus, in turn, erase the line between fiction and report.

The integration of the once separate domains of journalism and literature . . . brings about a peculiar shifting of reality—even a conflation of different levels of reality. Under the common denominator of so-called human interest emerges the *mixtum compositum* of a pleasant and at the same time convenient subject for entertainment that, instead of doing justice to reality, has a tendency to present a substitute more palatable for consumption and more likely to give rise to an impersonal indulgence in stimulating relaxation than to a public use by reason. (pp. 170–171)

Habermas, in making the observation that literature and news were "once separate domains," is doing, in 1962, journalism/entertainment boundary work.

An example of a similar critique of journalism boundary-degradation—but attributed to a different root cause—is the melodramatic opening paragraphs of Ron Powers' 1977 book *The Newscasters*, which says the sea-change in journalism happened in the 1970s:

The biggest heist of the 1970s never made it on the five o'clock news.
The biggest heist of the 1970s *was* the five o'clock news.
The salesmen took it. They took it away from the journalists, slowly, patiently, gradually, and with such finesse that nobody noticed until it was too late.
By the 1970s, an extravagant proportion of television news—local news in particular—answered less to the description of "journalism" than to that of "show business." This transformation, carried out by the sales-oriented station managers in an unbounded quest for profits, bore the profoundest implications in the way Americans were to receive information and perceive political choices. Many local newscasts ceased serving the public (at best, they served the public only incidentally) and bequeathed their primary allegiance to the advertisers. (p. 1)

Powers blames the quest for profits, instead of journalistic values, for the swing toward show business techniques and content. Similarly, Edwin Diamond, in 1975, notes that the potential for profits associated with high ratings points for news programs led to the downfall of journalistic control in local television newsrooms around the country. The responsibility of controlling the news process was relinquished to news consultants who had no knowledge of journalism but who were well-versed in audience survey techniques and behavioral psychology. In other words, they knew how to design a local news program that would attract a mass audience but not one that would inform it:

Up until a few years ago, television news was in the hands of professional news directors and producers, traditionally trained in newspaper or magazine work or broadcast journalism. It still is at the networks. But local station management has not had the same professional approach, especially since the local stations began discovering that their news times could be highly salable, often cheaper to run than straight entertainment shows, and attractive to many advertisers. Not only has television news become longer . . . [it] has become too important to be left to the newspeople. Audience research has been perceived as the key to ratings success. (pp. 91–92)

For Diamond, "professionals" are those trained in journalism, especially in newspaper and magazine journalism, areas where audience research has not been pursued as thoroughly as in television. In taking control away from the professionals, journalism has taken a back seat to superficiality, and news judgments are now made by managers skilled in audience research. Powers' and Diamond's critiques of television journalism are quite similar to the critiques that were raised throughout the early history of the television medium. They seem to argue for a monopolization of authority and protection of autonomy for journalists. In other words, Powers and Diamond would like to see journalists maintain control over all aspects of journalism and keep others from controlling any aspects of it.

Recently, Steven Stark (1995), a commentator on popular culture for National Public Radio, wrote that the root cause of increased sensationalism in radio and television news is the advent of all-news channels in the 1980s, such as CNN. He says the increased demand for news around the clock has caused journalists to become irresponsible:

Unlike the old days, when there were, at most, two news cycles a day, there is now a 24-hour demand for information. That means the network news and newspapers have to provide a different product than they once did, because they assume people get their headlines elsewhere.

The result has been a considerable broadening of what is considered reportable news and analysis—much of it far less objectively verifiable than in the past. We now have fields of news that didn't exist 15 years ago, such as entertainment reporting. News from the tabloids is considered fair game. Call-in shows can put forward any "expert" they can drum up, while encouraging callers to speculate and gossip. Some TV commentary itself is close to staged: *Crossfire* and *The McLaughlin Group* are to James Reston and Edward R. Murrow what pro wrestling is to sports.

Because of the incessant demand, news is also presented more quickly to the public, with the inevitable result that there's a far thinner line between fact and rumor—one reason why personal details about celebrities get reported more quickly, if not falsely—than before.

. . . This is all part of a far larger cultural pattern—the babble of a postmodern age that has seen feeling gain pre-eminence over thought, while elites collapse. (p. 7)

Stark's theory that journalists responded to the increased frequency of news "cycles" and an increased demand for news by lowering their standards for newsworthiness implies that journalists are not doing their jobs, and are, in fact, remiss in their responsibility to decide what counts as news. This is not a new critique, though the root cause selected by Stark may be a new idea.

Many other examples could be cited of journalists and others arguing that journalism is changing, moving toward more entertainment and less information. The critique is indeed perennial. As shown above, examples of it can be shown from the very beginnings of American journalism right up to the present. Journalism professor and historian Mitchell Stephens (1988) puts this kind of criticism in context:

Some of the criticism television journalism inspires is . . . shortsighted. . . . News and entertainment [did not] meet and mate for the first time on often giggly, often frivolous, local television newscasts in the United States; their affair dates back at least as far as criers and minstrels. Television news, in other words, did not inject a foreign substance—playfulness—into the news; news has been enjoyed for as long as it has been exchanged.

Like the penny papers of the 1830s, the yellow journals of the 1880s and 1890s and the tabloids of the 1920s, television has succeeded in attracting a new audience to the news. Once television sets became affordable, news became available to audiences of many millions, including even those lacking the energy, skill or maturity to read a newspaper or concentrate on a radio narrative. (pp. 284–285)

If the critique is perennial, then there must be a reason for it being so persistent. Perhaps these critiques serve an important purpose. Instead of evaluating the legitimacy of these claims and critiques, the constructivist approach to this debate focuses on how self-interested stakeholders (relevant actors) construct a conception of journalism that makes sense to them and that helps to consolidate their power and prestige. These stakeholders believe that the cultural authority of their institution depends on distinct boundaries, which, in turn, rest on concepts such as the perceived credibility and objectivity of their work. This constructivist approach to the issue helps us understand how the boundaries of journalism are constructed, negotiated, and maintained, giving us insights into what journalism means to people. To say that these boundaries are *constructed* implies that they have no firm, absolute contours. Instead, they are contextually contingent, local, and episodic, with the *potential* to become stable and widespread.

To give a brief example of boundary-work analysis, let us examine the words of the authors cited earlier in their arguments about the blurring of the news/entertainment boundary. They all imply that "real" journalism is something different from what we have now. The characteristics of "real" journalism that the various authors mentioned earlier in this section cite include distinctions such as: News is meant to inform, not entertain; it presents facts, not fiction; it does not include speculation or gossip; and it is controlled by professionals who serve the public, not by advertisers who seek only profits. These are demarcation criteria that help journalists "construct" their role in society—and help them understand the shape and contours of the *cultural space* in which journalism resides. Looking at the claims more closely, it appears that the authors mentioned earlier in this section cite the *functional* differences between news and entertainment: One informs, the other entertains. They also note *epistemological* differences: One is a factual kind of knowledge, the other contains fiction. They also cite *methodological* and *organizational* differences: One uses gossip and speculation, the other does not; and one is controlled by professionals who serve the public, the other serves less-altruistic goals.

As an analyst, I am not in a position to "solve" the debates about these issues. Instead, I look at how others solve them. In particular, I examine the apparent goals of boundary debates; how interested parties pick out the essential elements of the boundaries; and whether and how their work achieves any results.

SUMMARY

The goal of this project is to analyze how the boundaries between news and entertainment are "constructed" by relevant actors. To accomplish that goal, I look at several examples of constructions of monopoly, deviance, and autonomy as "social issues" with stakeholders in journalism. The constructivist approach to questions about what is journalism and what is not replaces the answer with the question as the thing to be studied. In other words, I do not try to find a definitive—necessarily essentialist—answer to the question "What are the boundaries of journalism?" Instead, I analyze and examine how journalists and others have attempted to answer this perplexing question, particularly when they claim that certain acts and practices are not journalism but are entertainment. In these kinds of claims, we gain valuable insight into the ways journalists make sense of what they do, and about the role of journalism in society.

Journalism, like all social institutions, is socially constructed. Questions about where journalism ends and entertainment begins are a viable field of study that up to this point, has been largely ignored. This project should begin to remedy this situation by examining what many call journalism ethics issues from a constructivist point of view. The way journalists make distinctions about acceptable behaviors, intentions, and content says a lot about culture production and how society creates and defines itself.

Throughout this study, cartographic metaphors—mapping images— are used as a way of thinking about the relationships between different institutions in American culture. Journalists map out the cultural space of journalism by specifying where the boundaries are located. As Gieryn (1995) notes, cartographic metaphors are useful when discussing the idea of a cultural space—territorial markers that people use to make sense of the world around them. He says, "cartographic metaphors offer a robust language for thinking about relations among cultural phenomena," particularly the relations between adjacent phenomena (p. 419). In the cultural space of mass media, news and entertainment appear to be adjacent phenomena. Gieryn suggests thatwe consider using cartographic terms such as "contours, landmarks, scale, orientation, coordinates, points of interest, and legend" (p. 419). These terms compel us to examine how this cultural space was slowly carved out of the cultural landscape rather than privilege journalism-as-it-is as the only logical outcome.

Some of the boundaries of journalism may be moving and flexible or perhaps blurry and indistinct. In other places they may be uncontested and easy to see. In any case, it is the players on either side of the alleged boundary (or in the middle of it) who are the primary stakeholders in constitutive rhetoric that attempts to delineate borders. That is why the primary site of this study is in the rhetoric of journalists: They have the most to gain or lose by such rhetoric about the boundaries of journalism.

NOTE

1. When talking about the "mainstream" dominant forms of the news media, we are (doing some boundary work ourselves) referring to daily and weekly newspapers (not the kind sold at supermarket checkout stands), television programming produced by local and network *news divisions*, cable television news programming, wire news services, and national news magazines such as *Newsweek* or *Time*. Obviously, this is not a monolithic block with perfectly similar attributes. Still, there is evidence that there are areas concerning content

and practices that the vast majority of those working in these media would agree constitute "newsworthiness," or standard operating procedures. It is the area between news and entertainment—where the differences seem slight—that is the primary interest of this project.

The Boundary-Work Approach

Journalists . . . come together by creating stories about their past that they routinely and informally circulate to each other—stories that contain certain constructions of reality, certain kinds of narratives, and certain definitions of appropriate practice. Through channels like informal talks, professional and trade reviews, professional meetings, autobiographies and memoirs, interviews on talk shows and media retrospectives, they create a community through discourse.

> —Barbie Zelizer
> "Journalists as Interpretive Communities"

Believing, with Max Weber, that man is an animal suspended in webs of significance he himself has spun, I take culture to be those webs, and the analysis of it to be therefore not an experimental science in search of law but an interpretive one in search of meaning.

> —Clifford Geertz
> *The Interpretation of Cultures*

CONSTRUCTIVISM

The main thesis of this project is that the boundary between news and entertainment is socially constructed, created through discourse intended to demarcate between similar mass communicated products and the professions that make them. Because it is socially constructed, the boundary does not rest on any essential elements.

Those who come up with demarcation criteria are essentialists—they argue that there are essential qualities of journalism that distinguish it from other types of mass communication. These kinds of arguments are what is known as "boundary-work rhetoric," because they have the apparent goal of constructing or maintaining perceived boundaries between cultural spaces. Constructivists, on the other hand, analyze, examine, and interpret the boundary work of essentialists. For a constructivist, the boundary work done by essentialists is motivated by professional and structural interest in enhancing cultural authority and professional power. This study examines boundary-work rhetoric located in several sites, focusing on cases where boundaries have been obviously threatened, or where they appear to be crumbling, blurring, or moving.

By making the distinction between essentialist and constructivist perspectives, I have opened the issue of whether there could be *any* essential differences between news and entertainment. Surely a case could be made that there are "pure" forms of entertainment that do not contain any news, and perhaps even vice versa. For example, the videotape, "Video Fireplace," which consists solely of an image of logs burning in a fireplace, complete with crackling noises, is perhaps an example of pure entertainment. The columnar listings of stock market prices in the newspaper, on the other hand, might be an example of pure news. Surely some will disagree with these essentialist assessments. Perhaps it is more instructive to think of news and entertainment as two intersecting spheres, and the area of intersection is what I have chosen to examine, partly because its messiness makes it a more interesting site. Within this gray area, players commit boundary work when they construct and describe essential differences between news and entertainment. The cultural space of journalism is contested in here, so analyses of how this area is mapped are of more importance than of how relatively uncontested areas are mapped. Still, the attributes of clearly uncontested areas are important to this examination because they show how news and entertainment are essentialized—the rock-bottom essential attributes as conceived by interested players. Generally, however, social institutions are defined through socially-constructed differences that occur where one institution "pushes up" against adjacent institutions. Often, it seems that cultural spaces are described in negative terms: For Dorothy, being in Oz is equated with being "not in Kansas anymore."

The constructivist approach to social issues emerged when sociologists became dissatisfied with the standard objectivist approach to social issues and problems, which assumes that issues *are* issues or differences *are* differences because groups of people say they are. Constructivists argue that the process of making something an issue is a subjective pursuit—something they call *claims-making*. The constructivist approach requires an examination of the claims-making rhetoric of those who claim something is an issue, a problem, or a difference (for example, Best, 1989, pp. 243–253; Geertz, 1973; Radway, 1984; Schwandt, 1994; Spector & Kitsuse, 1977). Diana Fuss (1989) says constructivists "are concerned above all with the *production* and *organization* of differences, and they therefore reject the idea that any essential or natural givens precede the process of social determination" (p. 3). In this study, I examine the production and organization of differences between news and entertainment.

Constructivism is not without its critics. One might ask: "Are there no essential traits of journalism?" To a constructivist, the answer is much more than a mere "yes or no." A better question is: "Are there any maps of journalism that are impossible?" A likely answer is "Yes, but I can't describe them (construct them) for you."

Several authors have recently attacked constructivism for rendering researchers impotent in their ability to comment on or improve society (for example., Collins, 1991; Goodheart, 1995; Murphy, 1994; Scott, Richards, and Martin, 1990; and Winner, 1993). Because constructivist researchers must remain relativists who merely interpret what others construct, they are not supposed to "privilege" one construction over another. This can have unintended consequences, such as giving as much weight to knowingly "false" data as to "true" data or giving "underdog" theories as much credence as the dominant paradigms. Some of these same critics complain that constructivist studies tend to be case studies that focus only on tiny, localized episodes that occur during brief periods of time. In other words, they offer little in the way of "generalizable" data.

I hope this study will not provoke these kinds of criticisms. Because I examine the first two decades of television news as well as three case studies from different periods in modern journalism, the resulting mosaic gives me a chance to formulate some generalizations about how boundary-work constructions are done in contemporary journalism. And although I cannot advocate changes in the way the boundaries of journalism operate in modern society, I trust that those reading these analyses will decide for themselves whether the claims made by relevant actors are troublesome or even credible.

JOURNALISM AND THE CONSTRUCTIVIST APPROACH

The constructivist approach is not new to mass communications research. For example, journalism and mass communications scholars have used the constructivist perspective in many other types of studies regarding the definition of legitimate news practices and content. Gaye Tuchman (1978) studied how newsworthiness is determined or constructed by journalists according to a privileged "frame" through which they "see" the world. Herbert Gans (1979) examined how news values

and socializing practices help determine which events are covered as legitimate news stories, as well as which events are not covered. Michael
Schudson's (1978) social history of American newspaper journalism
shows how an expectation for "objective" news was constructed during
the penny press era of the early nineteenth century (and which lives on
today). Todd Gitlin (1980) examined how a political fringe group
managed to induce the news media to cover it and how the news medi-
a's expectations shaped the kind of coverage the group received.

Some authors have suggested that other influences, such as literary
conventions, popular formula, and professional socialization, shape
how news is gathered, assembled, and manufactured, and how the
practices of journalism are socially constructed (for example., Cohen &
Young, 1981; Darnton, 1975; Henry, 1981; Newcomb & Alley, 1983;
Nord, 1980; and Zelizer, 1990).

These studies have not examined how work at the periphery of
journalism provokes jurisdictional disputes about the boundaries of
journalism and leads journalists to engage in particular kinds of
rhetoric designed to give shape to those boundaries.

In a study closer to the goals of this project—which is to examine
the construction and maintenance of the *cultural space* of journalism—
Margaret Morse (1986) examined how personality is used as a device
in television news to increase the credibility of news reports. She says
the widespread belief that mainstream news has special qualities is socially constructed:

The news is a privileged discourse, invested with a special relation to the
Real. . . . In critical discourse, only the journalistic, objective model of the
news is legitimized, while news in a subjective mode is generally considered
nothing but an aberration or degradation of news values, deplored as "show
biz," "glitz," and "glitter" atypical of the news profession. (pp. 55–56)

Her essay concludes that the use of personality in television news
programs has fundamentally changed the way people perceive the credibility of journalism. In the era before television news, when print journalism was the primary journalistic medium, Morse says credibility was
based on objectivity and thoroughness, but now, in television news, the
subjective personality of a few key anchors and star reporters in large
part determines the perceived credibility of the journalistic work.

Bird and Dardenne (1990), meanwhile, while evaluating the sensational dimension of news, argue that the concept of sensationalism is a
constructed one:

The function of serious news, we are told, is to inform, to provide a window on
important events in the world. To be 'sensationalist,' on the other hand, is to

produce news accounts that elicit an emotional or sensual response in the audience, the implicit assumption being that such responses are incompatible with a reasoned, informed understanding of events. (p. 33)

Bird and Dardenne show how journalists' conceptions of sensationalism are reactionary and typically do not examine the beneficial aspects of this storytelling dimension; journalists do not give sensationalism a chance. The line between a sensationalist and a vivid emotional story is a very fine one. It is a line constructed by journalists for a reason: maintenance of cultural authority.

Barbie Zelizer's (1993) recent study of how journalists' shared discourse helps them form an *interpretive community* is also instructive because it points to one of the themes in this study: that the rhetoric of journalists discussing the ways journalism is done gives shape to the cultural space of journalism and helps journalists understand their role in society.

The underlying theory of these constructivist approaches to the study of journalism is that attitudes, beliefs, and assumptions about journalism are things constructed, negotiated, and maintained by journalists as they make sense of their roles in society. One goal of this project is to use the constructivist approach in a relatively new way for mass communications research—to show how claims of news/ entertainment distinctions are tools for mapping some of the cultural space of journalism.

BOUNDARY WORK

Boundary work is a *sensitizing concept* (Blumer, 1954) developed by those studying the differentiation between science and non-science. Because it is a relatively new approach, the majority of the research using it has focused on these boundaries of science. As Gieryn, Bevins, and Zehr (1985) note, boundary-work rhetoric serves important needs for professionals in a given field:

Erection of social boundaries around a niche in the division of labor aids professionalization in two ways: (1) Boundaries create demand for a distinctive commodity by demarcating the professional's services from similar—but in crucial ways dissimilar—services provided by outsiders. (2) Boundaries serve to exclude providers of "similar" services who falsely claim (according to insiders) to be within the profession. Both are essential steps toward the monopolization of a profession's market, for the boundaries can be used to deny expertise, authority and thus employment and material resources to potentially competitive outsiders. (p. 393)

Boundary-work rhetoric, then, should be seen as a natural survival response common to all professions and disciplines, simply because the definition of expertise and control of each profession generally expands to abut other professions, so the boundaries are refined and mapped out through contests and disputes. In fact, Andrew Abbott, in *The System of Professions* (1988), offers a convincing argument that a large part of boundary work consists of what he calls "jurisdictional disputes" between neighboring professions. Abbott says many actions located in the process of professionalization can create changes in jurisdiction:

One competing group raises its standards or organizational efficiency and thereby threatens the public and perhaps legal jurisdiction of its environing competitors. Such structural change may be the initial move in an external attack, as with the apothecaries and the solicitors of England. (p. 97)

It is not hard to envision the process of journalists organizing into professional organizations—and adopting ethics codes along the way— as a strategy of jurisdictional warfare being waged against entertainment products that look like news products.

Abbott's main point is that neighboring professions must be examined together as a system, because within the jurisdictional disputes between professions are the mechanisms for constructing and understanding the differences between them. He also offers some insight into specific rhetorical strategies used by professionals in jurisdictional disputes. For example: *reduction*—"An attacking move made by secure professions, this argument shows some new task to be reducible, in principle, to one of the attacker's already-secure jurisdictions"; *agency*—legitimacy of jurisdiction based on the utility of practices; *metaphor*— "extends one profession's models of inference to others"; and *gradient*— "those who hold jurisdiction of the extreme versions of a problem should also hold jurisdiction of the mild ones" (Abbott, 1988, pp. 98–101; Gieryn, 1995, p. 410).

BOUNDARIES OF JOURNALISM

The process of journalists and others distinguishing television news from entertainment is the primary site of this research. Other than early drafts of some of these chapters (Winch, 1994; 1996), the social construction of the boundary between television entertainment and news has basically remained unexamined. However, many scholarly authors have taken the essentialist approach, decrying the blurring of distinctions between journalism and entertainment and noting the differences they would like to maintain (in other words, many have done boundary work). Often the critiques hold that so-called "tabloid journalism" is really a form of entertainment. No one, however, has analyzed how these boundaries are socially constructed, negotiated, and maintained. The act of doing boundary work helps journalists make sense of their world, and boundary-work rhetoric among outsiders to journalism indicates a desire of outsiders to make sense of the role of journalism in society. Boundaries between professions are flexible, constantly changing, and being constructed and reconstructed both in the day-to-day work of the profession, in education and research, and in the latterly representations of journalism work as described in criticism, fiction, and other discussions of the profession. Although these kinds of processes have been examined in other social institutions and professions (for example., Gieryn, 1995; Gieryn & Figert, 1986; Gieryn, Bevins & Zehr, 1985; and Gieryn, 1983), they have not, until now, been analyzed as they apply to the journalism/entertainment boundary.

Some authors, most notably Patricia Dooley (Dooley & Grosswiler, 1995; Dooley, 1994), have described jurisdictional disputes between journalists and politicians over political communication. Dooley's work does not, however, inform questions about the strategies of journalism boundary-work rhetoric—about how journalism boundaries are constructed or maintained—nor does it help us understand why and how such jurisdictional disputes accomplish anything other than jurisdictional control over specific occupational roles in political communication. In contrast, this study is an examination of news/entertainment boundaries that sheds light on questions about why and how boundary work is done, the rhetorical strategies used by those who do it, and what this rhetorical work accomplishes in terms of giving shape to the cultural space of journalism.

This study requires an examination of the edges of journalism, the areas that some journalists tend to disavow and that they claim are located on the boundaries between journalism and entertainment.

GENERAL DESCRIPTION OF METHOD

In this study, I analyze the boundary-work rhetoric along the news/entertainment border. I embrace an integrative approach, utilizing theoretical and methodological foundations established in the sociology of professions, cultural anthropology, and rhetorical analysis. These fields all employ methodologies that require the researcher to interpret the symbolic actions of stakeholders to understand how the actions create meaning. Symbolic acts, generally in the form of rhetorical discourse, are taken to be signifiers of how people make sense of their lives and the social institutions they know. Boundary-work rhetoric is designed to carve out an area in the cultural landscape.

Previous studies in boundary work offer models upon which to begin the analysis: Gieryn, Bevins, and Zehr (1985), in their study of two evolution/creationism trials, examined the testimony of scientists who were asked by defense attorneys to write about the theory of evolution (p. 396). These researchers examined boundary-work rhetoric, "a rhetorical style common in 'public science,' in which scientists describe science for the public and its political authorities, sometimes hoping to enlarge the material and symbolic resources of scientists or to defend professional autonomy" (Gieryn, 1983, p. 782). Gieryn, Bevins, and Zehr inductively identified five different boundary-distinguishing dimensions in the boundary-work rhetoric of those scientists arguing for the right of educators to teach Darwin's theory of evolution in public schools: epistemological differences, functional differences, methodological differences, ontological differences, and social or organizational differences. In this project examining the news/entertainment boundary, the dimension of ontology does not seem to fit—there is no question these media operate in the physical realm—but the other four dimensions or boundary-defining characteristics are helpful in understanding how and why the news/entertainment boundaries are constructed, negotiated, and maintained the way they are.

Epistemological Differences: News and Entertainment are Different "Kinds" of Knowledge

Traditionally, journalists who consider themselves mainstream have made much of the epistemological differences between conjectural rumor and verifiable fact, holding to a strict division between the two and arguing that rumor should never be reported. If a rumor is verified by several independent sources, then it becomes a different kind of knowledge, namely, fact. These distinctions along a fact/fiction boundary illuminate the two different kinds of knowledge.

Another area where epistemological differences have been cited is within the criticism by journalists of semi-historical movies that "rewrite" history to make for better entertainment. Some journalists— who say they are dedicated to the pursuit of objective truth (realizing that it may never be attained) —argue for a strict division between entertainment and information (for example., Matusow, 1986; Shaw, 1985). The furor among journalists over the mixture of historical truth and fiction in movies such as *JFK*, and more recently, *Forrest Gump*, is an example (Swislow, 1989). These journalists are implying that there are *epistemological* differences between history and entertainment—that these are different *kinds* of knowledge, as empirical fact is to literary fiction. The standards for judging something as true and accurate differ for different kinds of knowledge. As Bird and Dardenne (1990) argue:

News styles are both a reflection and reinforcement of prevailing epistemological paradigms, and in accord with the trends that have dominated history and the social and behavioral sciences, the preferred 'rational' mode is designed to 'inform' rather than to engage the senses of the reader. Following scientific paradigms, the news genre is perceived to incorporate a stance that stresses the role of the journalist as independent observer, gathering information to be impartially presented to the audience as fact. (p. 34)

Functional Differences: They Perform Different Functions

Some tabloid journalists believe that there are functional differences that create a boundary between the genres of mainstream and tabloid journalism. They say that their work serves an entertainment function, and mainstream news outlets serve an information function (Bird, 1990). Most mainstream journalists also seem to agree with this assessment. Journalism ethicists often argue that journalism is supposed to be an altruistic enterprise that serves the public by giving citizens information they need to know (not necessarily want to know) to facilitate the operation of the democracy. Mass media research and theories dealing with journalism have generally focused on three areas of theory: the processes and effects of journalism, how audiences use journalistic messages, and influences to journalistic message content. These theories often restate the traditional ideology of journalism in a democracy—as a social institution that functions as an unbiased provider of factual information, and as noted earlier, one that operates altruistically. James Carey (1989) argues that the true role of the news media is to "activate inquiry" by getting people interested and engaged in debate and discussion. He writes that the news media should be "an agency for carrying on the conversation of our culture" (p. 82).

Entertainment has a different function: It is a purely commercial business enterprise that seeks the largest possible audiences—the best ratings—and, therefore, the greatest profitability. It gives people what they want.

The functions of entertainment depend on your point of view. For an audience, entertainment functions to satisfy its desires by providing people with stimulation and relief. If you are in the broadcasting network business, entertainment serves the function of filling an allotted time slot, delivering a large audience to advertisers, and therefore, a means of accomplishing a business goal: competing with the other networks and staying profitable.

Methodological Differences: They Employ Different Tools and Methods

Others argue that the differences between entertainment and journalism are purely *methodological*—mainstream journalists work with different professional values and rules of practice than do entertainment providers (Menaker, 1976; Thomas, 1990). One example of this is the common belief within the journalism profession that tabloid journalists pay sources for stories whereas mainstream journalists do not. Others, particularly tabloid journalists, have argued that they use essentially the same methods as traditional mainstream journalists (Bird, 1990, pp. 378–380).

Organizational Differences: They Operate under Different Organizational Structures

The business distinction between news and entertainment divisions or companies is perhaps a superficial structural way to distinguish the two areas and the boundaries between them. But these organizational differences have important consequences in mass media research. For example, in most studies of American journalism, researchers completely ignore tabloid journalism and the workers that produce it because directories of journalists and journalism institutions ignore tabloid journalism institutions and tabloid journalists. The reason for the omission is presumably because tabloid journalists are not recognized as existing within news business organizations. For example, journalism researchers David Weaver and G. Cleveland Wilhoit, in a recent survey of American journalists (1992; Weaver, 1993), drew their sample from the *1991 Editor & Publisher International Yearbook*, a national directory of newspapers that does not include supermarket tabloids; the *1991 Gale Directory of Publications and Broadcast Media*, which excludes supermarket tabloids and television tabloid production companies; and the *Summer 1991 News Media Yellow Book of Washington and New York*, which excludes supermarket tabloids and television tabloids (p. 15). In 1991, these supermarket and television tabloid companies were evidently considered entertainment organizations—organizationally different from legitimate news companies.

ANALYSIS AND INTERPRETATION

In this study, interpretations of rhetoric regarding news/entertainment boundaries explain why and how this kind of rhetoric helps people make sense of these social institutions. Arguments supporting these interpretations—by nature fallible and assailable—are as strong as can be made. If this study were based on a single example of boundary-work rhetoric, or even a single body of rhetorical responses to a threatened boundary, the interpretation would be far more ambiguous and assailable. Because several dimensions of boundary-work rhetoric are examined in a variety of specific cases, the resulting mosaic reduces the uncertainty of the basic interpretations.

SELECTION OF SITES AND DATA COLLECTION

Boundary-work rhetoric occurs when boundaries are threatened, expanded, constricted, and defined. As Gieryn and Figert have noted, responses to cases of fraud and fakery in science are one good place to look for boundary-work rhetoric in science, because they show how boundaries are constructed, repaired, and maintained by those with interests within the scientific community. Likewise, the cases I selected for Chapters 4, 5, and 6 are examples of intense and sustained responses to threats to the boundaries between news and entertainment. All of the cases selected precipitated large volumes of rhetoric, and they all involve different schemes to clarify the news/entertainment boundary.

The data for Chapters 4, 5, and 6 are the total published output—the public rhetoric—of journalists and others concerned with each of the cases in question. All of the written rhetoric is naturally occurring; it was not prompted by any requests for comments from the author, so there is no chance they were designed to influence the findings of this analysis. This rhetoric was found in the written or spoken comments of people initiating or responding to the discourse of others concerned about the same events. I did not conduct focus groups, interviews, or surveys and then analyze the answers to questions, because those kinds of methods produce data that is artificially induced, contrived, and therefore, suspect (Schrøder, 1994, p. 341). Analysts of boundary-work rhetoric examine naturally-occurring rhetoric that occurs either within the rhetor's work, within professional education or research, or within the latterly representations of their work in critical articles, textbooks, and other media representations.

Some of the standard methods of gathering social science data—interviews, surveys, focus groups, and participant observation—are of little value, because they cannot represent the way boundaries are actually constructed, rather how respondents would construct boundaries when prodded by researchers. In this study I examine some of the cultural artifacts of journalism found mainly in reflexive rhetoric *about* journalism. These data speak to larger issues in journalism, so they deserve the kind of interpretive care that ethnographers such as Geertz (1973) practice.

Rhetorical analysts speak a different language from that of traditional social science researchers, and many of them may seem to be less than forthcoming about the methodologies they employ, probably because they do not hesitate to use all the critical faculties at their disposal. Kenneth Burke, for instance, uses his knowledge of philosophy, religion, psychoanalysis, and history in his rhetorical analyses (Nichols, 1952). And Burke has acknowledged as much: "The main ideal of [rhetorical] criticism, as I conceive it, is to use all that there is to use" (1941, p. 23).

Much of the rhetorical analysis methodology in this study is patterned after the work of Kenneth Burke and his successors in rhetorical studies. Burke (1969) argues that every analysis of rhetoric must answer five questions regarding act, scene, agent, agency, and purpose: "what was done (act), when or where it was done (scene), who did it (agent), how he [sic] did it (agency), and why (purpose)." This kind of analysis gives the researcher a "thick" description of the rhetoric being studied and places it in the proper context of patterns of social action leading to culture.

Similarly, rhetoricians Martin Medhurst and Thomas Benson (1984) say that rhetorical analyses examine "how people choose *what to say* in a given situation, *how to arrange or order* their thoughts, *select the specific terminology* to employ, and decide precisely *how they are going to deliver their message*" (p. vii) [emphases in original]. The main idea is that public messages are made with specific social goals and interests that may not be immediately apparent and it is up to the rhetorical analyst to interpret these connections and interests, as an anthropologist interprets the body language and customs of a native tribe. In this study, I interpret the culture of journalism as it is made public in written discourse.

Chapters 3 through 6 deal with case studies of boundary-work rhetoric. In Chapter 3, I examine the evolution of television news during its first two decades, 1948–1968, concentrating on public discourse that highlighted the epistemological, functional, organizational, and methodological dimensions of the boundaries of television journalism. In addition, I take a look at a significant text from early television journalism, the 1958 CBS handbook, *Television News Reporting*.

Chapter 4 is an analysis of how governmental workers attempted to define "legitimate" journalism in the context of certain broadcast regulations. The study by Gieryn, Bevins, and Zehr (1985) of public rhetoric by scientists during the Scopes and McLean evolution versus creationism trials is somewhat instructive for this chapter because it shows how rhetoric is used to distinguish between different kinds of pursuits—namely, religion and science. Chapter 4 shows how governmental workers sought to distinguish between entertainment and news by attempting to identify the essential elements of journalism.

In Chapter 5, I examine rhetoric that closely follows what Harold Garfinkel (1956) calls a status degradation ceremony, wherein a group ritually removes a deviant member. This chapter is heavily influenced by Gieryn and Figert's (1986) study of the status degradation ceremony of Sir Cyril Burt, a British hereditary scientist who engaged in scientific fraud and was ritually removed, posthumously, from the scientific community. I examine how Michael Gartner, as president of NBC News, was blamed for a fraud perpetrated by an NBC News program. The journalism community ritually "kicked" Gartner out and made him an outcast.

Gieryn and Figert's (1990) study of the news coverage of Richard Feynman during the Challenger disaster inquiry is a useful model for Chapter 6. In that study, the authors examined press accounts of the Nobel laureate physicist doing rudimentary science in front of television cameras, publicly demonstrating in layman's terms exactly why Challenger exploded. Feynman clamped a piece of rubber in a small c-clamp, immersed it in a glass of ice water, pulled it out and showed how unresilient rubber becomes when it is cold—explaining why the o-rings of the rocket boosters were ill-equipped to handle the cold on the day of the doomed Challenger launch. Gieryn and Figert show how Feynman "made" science out of something many scientists and engineers considered far less than scientific. In Chapter 6, I show how Gennifer Flowers and the supermarket tabloid *The Star* "made" news out of something many journalists considered to be less than newsworthy and less than reliable.

The methods used by these different researchers are not mutually exclusive—none of them adhere to monism. According to Chesebro (1992), in communication studies monism is "the tendency to find a single and coherent center or commonality which characterizes human communication." Chesebro criticizes monism because it is reductionist, encourages oversimplification, and de-emphasizes diversity while making broad generalizations.

Clearly there is a gap in the research. Although there have been a few isolated studies that have attempted to essentialize the boundaries between news and entertainment, no one has examined how these distinctions are "made" in the first place. This study is a first step in filling that void.

The Evolution of Television News: Growing Up in an Entertainment Medium

Some of our critics have flatly refused to concede value of any kind to the presentation of news on television. They talk in terms of television as a hybrid monstrosity derived from newspapers, radio news and the newsreels, which inherited none of the merits of its ancestors. However, those of us who have been engaged in television journalism for a number of years believe that television news has something to say, and has frequently said it interestingly, convincingly and, sometimes, eloquently. . . .

There were, in a sense, forerunners of television news: the theatrical newsreel, the radio news broadcast and the picture magazine. Television borrowed from all three, but the television news organization as it now exists and the product it delivers are something entirely new in journalism.

—Sig Mickelson
"Growth of Television News, 1946–1957"

INTRODUCTION

Television journalism evolved within a medium designed for entertainment—something from which journalism has traditionally tried to separate itself. Journalists and others familiar with that tradition struggled to map out the contours of this boundary. At the same time, a boundary developed between television journalism and the more traditional forms, such as newspapers. These boundaries were helpful for those trying to understand the strengths and weaknesses of the various forms of communication, as well as the links between them. This chapter is an analysis of certain of these rhetorical struggles and of the evolution of television journalism. Specifically, I examine how the entertainment roots of television influenced conceptions of television journalism as it was first developed. The primary data for this analysis is contained in the naturally occuring public rhetoric—speeches and writings—of television and print journalists who worked during the first two decades of television journalism, 1948–1968. This public discourse between interested parties reveals how those within the institutions of television and journalism perceived themselves and the role they believed they played in society. It is a revealing look at the intersecting spheres of—and struggles among— traditional forms of journalism, television journalism, entertainment, commerce, and public service. Like many social issues, a recurring element of this struggle has been a conflict between competing interests: business profits versus "public interest."

The technological innovation of television was developed and financed by large radio broadcasting companies—broadcasting networks and receiver manufacturers—who received advice and consent from the Federal Communications Commission. Television developers were in it for one thing: to make money. The FCC helped them do this in an organized way. But the FCC had an additional mandate: to require television to operate in the public interest, because the limited spectrum of radio waves "belonged" to the public. Much of the rhetoric examined here was made by those who felt broadcasters should operate more clearly in the public interest—a perennial complaint that television inherited from radio.

Television is primarily a direct descendant from radio: It is essentially controlled by capitalist commercial interests and their attendant economic realities, which dictate the degree of governmental regulatory interference. In addition to radio, television also adopted production techniques from movie and newsreel production companies. The early history of television news, when people were trying to define what it was and what they wanted it to be, is a ripe source for boundary-work rhetoric simply because television was a brand-new medium, with no established ground rules or set expectations. People expected all sorts of different things from television. Within the networks, television entertainment and news interests competed for airtime and resources. Television news producers also dealt with an internal struggle— whether to adopt entertainment-style methods, workers, and values or to adopt the methods and personnel of traditional forms of journalism, such as newspaper journalism. The rhetoric of these struggles served the purpose of helping television journalists understand their role in society.

This chapter is organized into four parts. First I present a brief history of television news which outlines some of the historical context in which it emerged. Next I analyze boundary-work rhetoric produced by journalists and others who were involved with television news during its first two decades, 1948–1968. Then I analyze a single significant text, a handbook for television news producers that was published by CBS in 1958. It is significant because it shows how the dominant television news network considered the norms of television journalism when it was just a decade old. Finally I integrate my findings into some conclusions.

A BRIEF HISTORY OF TELEVISION NEWS

Before Television: When Radio Set the Tone

Early radio manufacturers such as RCA thought of radio as an ordinary household appliance and initially believed that the most money to be made in radio was in the manufacturing of receivers. Much later, the gold mine of advertising became apparent (Leonard, 1987, p. 58; "Television: A $13,000,000 If," p. 54). RCA's David Sarnoff, for instance, said in 1926 that he thought of radio broadcasting "as a public institution in the same sense that a library, for example, is regarded" (Horton, 1960, p. 14). He also said he was opposed to "direct advertising on the air," believing that radio manufacturers would probably contribute money for programming.

The first radio programs, however, were financed by stations as a means of sustaining an audience. Broadcasters quickly developed a taste for the revenues possible from advertising, and within a short time, direct advertiser sponsorship of a program was practically a necessity for the program to be broadcast. By the 1930s, segments or slots of radio time were auctioned to advertisers who themselves oversaw the development and production of programs. Nearly all sponsored programs were designed to appeal to the largest possible audience, which maximized the profits for broadcasters and, theoretically, maximized the impact of advertising. Rating services sprung up to scientifically measure the audience size of individual programs. Advertising rates were determined by the ratings and were based on CPM, or cost per thousand, for reaching audiences. If a program lost its sponsor and could not find another, it was generally dropped by the broadcaster. Pollsters soon discovered that entertainment programs drew the largest audiences—of people who saw their radios primarily as tools of leisure . . . not of education. This disappointed those who had different hopes for the medium. Popular radio commentator Hans V. Kaltenborn wrote in 1931, "Today radio's chief purpose is to make money for those who control and use its mechanical devices. It threatens to prove as great a disappointment as the moving-picture for those who sense radio's undeveloped power as an agency of education, culture, and international good-will."

Even though entertainment was the dominant form of radio programming, the owners and controllers of the radio medium discovered that broadcast journalism could be captivating—even entertaining—when it conveyed the reality and immediacy of an unfolding story. The first demonstration of this phenomenon on radio happened by accident in 1930, when a broadcast of a prison orchestra concert in Columbus, Ohio, turned into a spot news broadcast when disgruntled prisoners staged a riot, setting a fire that raged out of control (Persico, 1988, p. 126). A prisoner grabbed the microphone and described the horror, as the fire ravaged the prison, killing 335 men. CBS threw the switch that put this microphone live on its entire radio network—with the sounds of the fire crackling and men screaming in the background—so that practically the entire country was able to take part in witnessing the spectacle as it happened.

Soon afterward, NBC and CBS decided to increase the strength of their radio news programming. Newspaper publishers fought the increase in radio news by persuading the wire services in 1933 to deny membership to the networks. This forced the networks to begin gathering news themselves. The American Newspaper Publishers Association fought this development by asking its members to stop printing CBS's daily programming schedule. In December 1935, the radio networks capitulated during a meeting with the AP, UP, and ANPA at New York's Biltmore Hotel, agreeing to several cutbacks in radio news: CBS dissolved its news gathering unit, and NBC agreed not to start one; they both limited their news programs to two five-minute news digests a day; and they agreed to broadcast only second hand news—stale items that newspapers had already been given the chance to print (Persico, 1988, p. 127).

The Biltmore agreement did not last long. Within a year large advertisers like Esso and Standard Oil paid wire services to break the embargo and supply the networks with unlimited news. Newspapers realized they could not fight; many bought radio stations instead (Barnouw, 1968, pp. 18–22; Persico, 1988, p. 127).

The Regulatory Environment: Communications Act of 1934, and the "Blue Book"

To understand the regulatory atmosphere into which television was born, it is important to examine some of the conflicts brewing between the radio industry and the government regulators in the years before television.

After his election in 1932, President Franklin D. Roosevelt let it be known that he wanted a new set of regulations to replace the Radio Act of 1927 that would combine telephone and broadcasting jurisdiction under one agency. The telephone industry was then regulated by the Interstate Commerce Commission, which was busy enough with railroad problems (Barnouw, 1968, p. 23).

Educational broadcasting allies saw this as an opportunity to press their case for increased frequency allocations to nonprofit entities. In 1934, Senators Robert F. Wagner (N.Y.) and Henry D. Hatfield (W.V.) sponsored an amendment to pending legislation that would require 25 percent of all station licenses to be allocated to nonprofits (*Congressional Record*, 1934, pp. 8828–8843; *Hearings on H.R. 8301*, 1934). The amendment was rejected, but in the final version of the Communications Act of 1934, a provision was inserted to direct the newly formed Federal Communications Commission to study ways in which nonprofits could gain a stronger role in broadcasting. The 1934 act essentially repeated existing broadcasting rules verbatim, which directed the broadcast regulatory commission to consider the programming of broadcasters only during license renewals, at which time they were to consider whether the station was operating in the "public interest, convenience, and necessity." In their first report on recommended steps to ensure a greater role for nonprofit organizations in broadcasting, the FCC argued that no new regulations needed to be written, and instead that the commission would undertake steps to require commercial broadcasters to cooperate with such groups (*Report of the FCC Pursuant to Sec 307*, 1935).

By the late 1930s, however, the FCC had gradually eased into the practice of routinely renewing radio licenses where engineering reports were satisfactory, without considering whether the stations were operating in the public interest. FCC Commissioner Clifford J. Durr became alarmed that many stations were ignoring the public interest programming promises they had made when applying for licenses. FCC Chairman Paul Porter suggested in March 1945 that it was "time to start comparing promise to performance" (Barnouw, 1968, p. 228). He ordered a report and analysis of the situation; and this report, entitled *Public Service Responsibility of Broadcast Licensees,* was published in March 1946. It was a 60-page soft-cover pamphlet with a blue cardstock cover, which soon became known to the industry as the "Blue Book." The Blue Book report begins with numerous examples of radio stations that had promised to broadcast live local talent programs, educational programs, religious programs, provocative social commentary, and uplifting cultural entertainment such as orchestras and operas but had broadcast instead only pre-recorded popular music punctuated by commercials. These "bad examples" were used to justify the report's conclusion that stations need to deliver what they promise.

One of the examples cited in the report concerns WTOL-AM, a station in Toledo, Ohio, which in 1938 applied for a license to extend its broadcast hours through the night (p. 6). In its application, WTOL said that it would devote 84 percent of these evening hours to local live-talent and that the Toledo Council of Churches, the American Legion, the YMCA, and other worthwhile organizations would be given airtime. The application was approved in 1939. In analyzing the actual evening broadcast performance during a week in November 1944, the FCC discovered that instead of 84 percent, "WTOL devoted only 13.7 percent of its time to such programs. . . . No evening time whatever during the week was given to the Toledo American Legion, YMCA, Boy Scouts, or any other local organizations which, according to the representations, desired time over the station at night" (p. 6).

The Blue Book was an admission by the FCC that it had not been doing its job in examining the performance of radio stations. The FCC called for industry leaders to come up with standards and proposed to examine the time devoted by stations to "sustaining programs, to local live programs, to discussion of public issues, and to the station's ability to resist advertising pressures" (Barnouw, 1968, p. 231). One of the effects of this new emphasis was that news programming was now a practical requirement for radio stations. CBS Chairman William Paley and others came to realize that news production was one of the prices a broadcaster paid for holding a broadcasting license (Schoenbrun, 1989, p. 78). By the time television was ready for commercial development, those in charge of the broadcast industry were resigned to the fact that news was a necessary requirement for maintaining their government-sponsored monopoly.

Early Television

One of the common themes in the various contemporary published histories of television is that it was not designed for journalistic purposes. In a Federal Radio Commission report on the development of television technology in 1932, it is clear that television was being developed with the assumption that it was an entertainment medium. The report said people were just getting used to "talking pictures," and television fell "far short of what the public has been led to expect in the way of entertainment" (Federal Radio Commission, 1932, pp. 42–43). The reason television was deemed inadequate was that in 1932 television was still technologically primitive: The images were difficult to watch because they were coarse, grainy, and low-resolution. By the late 1930s this problem was solved. RCA's David Sarnoff first demonstrated television to the public with great fanfare in 1939 at the World's Fair in New York. Early commercial developers of television, such as Sarnoff, promoted the medium as a great teaching tool—informing and educating the public, and perhaps elevating the public taste for drama the way radio's broadcasts of classical music had raised the musical taste of the American radio listening public (Sarnoff, 1939, p. 324).

Because of World War II, the development of the television industry was curtailed by order of the U.S. government, and new station applications were put on hold. The FCC settled on a national standard for television receivers in early 1947, and soon after started granting new television station licenses. Network television journalism began in earnest in 1947 and 1948 with the introductions of NBC's *Camel News Caravan*, hosted by John Cameron Swayze, and CBS's *Television News With Douglas Edwards*. Both were nightly 15-minute shows (Barnouw, 1982, p. 102). By the early 1950s, as television stations and receivers became more widely distributed around the country, these nightly network news broadcasts were beginning to be noticed by a large segment of the population (see Table 3.1).

Before commercial television began in earnest in 1948, it was already a settled point that the development of the new medium would be financed through advertising revenues and that the best way to maximize advertising revenues was through entertainment programming (Bogart, 1980, p. 209). Television's developers practically salivated at the prospects for advertising revenues with the new medium. Sarnoff noted in 1941, well before television began to penetrate a significant number of American households, that "A properly conceived television advertising program is believed by some advertising experts to be much more effective in sales influence than any other method heretofore employed" (p. 148). The ratings services had proven conclusively that the biggest drawing radio broadcast programs were entertainment shows, so television's developers, armed with this information, set about to devise programs for television that would attract large audiences.

Table 3.1
Television Quickly Permeates the U.S.

	% Households with TVs	% Households w/color TVs
1950	9 %	-
1955	65 %	0.2 %
1960	87 %	0.7 %
1965	93 %	5 %
1970	95 %	39 %
1978	98 %	78 %

Sources: Trager, 1992; and Lichty & Topping, 1975, p. 522.

This domination by advertiser-supported entertainment programming had a tremendous impact on the way television journalism began and how it evolved. Magazine and newspaper journalists were accustomed to being in charge of their respective media. In broadcasting they were simply an added attraction in media controlled by advertisers who favored entertainment content.

The commercial potential of television advertising became clear in the early 1950s when those in broadcasting began to hear stories such as the one about how, in three months, November 1953 to February 1954, Dow Chemical increased the sales of Saran Wrap from 20,000 cases a month to 169,000 cases a month, solely through the use of national television advertising ("Agency credits TV," 1954).

Television stations were also incredibly profitable. A popular saying was that television is "a license for making money" (Schoenbrun, 1989, p. 78). WTVE in Elmira, New York, reportedly paid off all of its start-up debts within the first month of operation ("In the black in 30 days," 1953). It is not hard to imagine why journalists from other media began to feel threatened by television. It had a momentum of gigantic proportions. Suddenly, the older forms of mass media seemed old-fashioned.

The first television journalists were transferees from the radio divisions of the networks. Some felt it was their birthright, as radio broadcasters, to control the new broadcast medium. Here, John Houseman (1950), "a producer of plays, motion pictures, and radio programs," describes how radio workers felt:

Ask a radio man about TV. You will find that he regards it as his own legitimate territory, by right of direct succession. He is convinced that television, in its general lines, will follow the existing pattern of commercial radio, with certain inevitable changes in production methods to suit the new medium. (p. 18)

Time-Based Medium

One of the problems early television stations ran into was that the medium required lengthy—and expensive—programming to fill the time. This should not have surprised transferees from the radio medium, but in radio, it was easy to fill time by playing records. In television, it was not so easy. Bill Leonard, who worked his way up the ranks of CBS, eventually to become president of CBS News, notes in his autobiography (1987): "In the early days of television before time was golden, the problem was this: How does one *fill* time? What does one put before the camera that will *consume* time? *Lots* of it. . . . There was, of course, no videotape. So live events, *long* live events, were the thing" (p. 59). Sporting events such as football and baseball games were popular for this very reason.

The use of sporting events and other lengthy events to fill the time on television had an impact on the way people thought about television—as a diversion rather than as a vital link to news and reality. Religious leaders such as Reinhold Niebuhr worried that "much of what is still wholesome in our life will perish under the impact of this new visual aid" in which "prize fights seem to be the best subjects" ("The Rumblings," 1949, p. 70).

Generally, the first purchasers of television receivers were cafe, bar, and tavern owners who used the sets to draw crowds of sports enthusiasts (for example, "Edward R. Murrow of CBS," 1953, p. 40). A June 1947 article in *Newsweek* illustrates this phenomenon:

Gil's Bar, on Eighth Avenue in New York, was almost deserted one afternoon last week. In the same block three other taverns were packed close to their shiny brass rails with beer-drinking patrons. Ed Abbott, bartender at Gil's, knew why. "Our television set is busted," he explained. "Soon's we get a new one, people'll drift back in again. The other places got their sets working. Meanwhile we lose 20, maybe 30 bucks this afternoon—and with a double-header on out at the Polo Grounds too!" ("Television in the Tavern," p. 64)

Some critics argued that the reason sports were the preferred programming of television during the late 1940s and early 1950s was precisely because of the number of bars and taverns that owned receivers (Seldes, 1949, p. 35). Television news steadily increased in influence during the 1950s, partly because of presidential campaign coverage in 1952 and 1956 (Mickelson, 1957, p. 304). These were long live events that filled a lot of programming time for the networks. For the first time, Americans were able to see and know their politicians in action.

Television news became more popular as people began to experience the sensation of dramatic social struggles as they were happening—with the feeling of having a front-row seat. The violent confrontations of the civil rights movement were one of the first national dramatic struggles to be regularly televised.

Television News Comes of Age

Harry Reasoner (1981) and more recently, Eric Burns (1993) argue that the first real demonstration of the power of television journalism was during the civil rights movement in the South in the late 1950s and early 1960s. Reasoner was a reporter for ABC-TV in Little Rock, during the forced integration of Little Rock Central High School, over the protests of Governor Orval Faubus:

The thing about Little Rock is that it was where television reporting came to influence, if not to maturity. As in the case of the Vietnam war a decade later, things might have been very different if it weren't for the new impact of television news: you could not hide from it. . . . It took television to show you the war in Vietnam relentlessly every night to force a democracy to make a democratic decision about a war—a democratic decision in which the citizens themselves made up their minds on something very like first-hand evidence. It was like that in Little Rock, and by and large the young men of television did a better job than the people of the printed word—with, of course, notable exceptions on both sides. (pp. 58-59)

Burns, a television reporter for 20 years, says in his autobiographical assessment of the television news business that television journalism was never taken seriously before the civil rights movement,

But then came Mobile and Montgomery and Oxford, Mississippi: southern whites turning on blacks and beating them and jeering at them and blasting them with fire hoses. . . . The civil rights movement of the sixties, and footage of such power and eloquence that newspapers suddenly seemed a relic from the age of Gutenberg and radio a mere talking box. (pp. 76–77)

In 1963, CBS and NBC both expanded their nightly news programs to 30 minutes in length; ABC, which had always been a distant third in news, followed suit in 1967. Television's eloquence in bringing the civil rights and Vietnam conflicts to the American public sealed the fate of the television industry as a major provider of news.

EVOLUTIONARY BOUNDARY WORK

The boundary-work rhetoric of journalists and other critics familiar with journalism during the early years of television highlights the differences between, and similarities of, traditional journalism, television journalism, and entertainment. By highlighting the similarities along these boundaries, critics hoped to change the situation; they believed that these boundaries were blurred in certain areas and should be made more distinct. The rhetoric cites differences and similarities that can be categorized into four general arguments: that there are epistemological, organizational, functional, and methodological differences and similarities between television journalism and television entertainment as well as between traditional journalism and television journalism.

Following is a rough outline of the major recurring arguments found within the boundary-work rhetoric examined here. Following that is an in-depth analysis of each of these various boundary-work strategies.

I. Epistemological differences—*television news is a different kind of knowledge*

A. *News is foreign to television:* Television news exists in a medium designed for entertainment, which by its nature cannot avoid blurring fact and fiction.

B. *Immediate and unpredictable:* Television news can be immediate and unpredictable, unlike entertainment, which is staged, predictable, and frequently taped or filmed in advance; and unlike traditional forms of journalism.

C. *Intimate nature of television:* Unlike traditional forms of journalism, television news makes audiences feel like they are part of the action, like "being there" when things happen. Television news is similar to television entertainment in this respect.

D. *Audiovisual, time-based nature requires passivity of audiences:* All television—news and entertainment—requires a passivity on the part of the audience: People do not need to envision in their minds what is happening because they can see it, and they are required to follow the stories at the pace set down by the producers. Television news is unlike earlier printed forms, because people cannot sit and study a picture or phrase, they must digest television news at the rate it comes to them.

II. Organizational differences—*television operates under a different kind of organizational structure*

A. *Hierarchy of authority:* In the organizational hierarchy of television, news occupies a lower rung than entertainment. In traditional journalistic media, journalists ascended to the highest ranks in the organizations.

B. *Advertiser influence:* Like other television programming, advertisers influenced television news. This was a foreign concept in traditional journalism.

C. *Celebrity:* In broadcast journalism, a "star system" developed wherein certain individual journalists became larger-than-life personalities whose presence was necessary to draw an audience. Again, this was a trend usually associated only with entertainment.

III. Functional differences—*television serves a different kind of function*

A. *Social function: Abbreviated, entertaining news:* Television news mainly serves as a headline service, not as a source of in-depth information. In a way, it is entertaining news. Moreover, television news caters primarily to the less educated segments of society who are not inclined to read newspapers and news magazines.

B. *Industrial function: Regulatory obligation:* Television broadcasters are forced by the FCC to provide public service programming, and one of the primary ways they fulfill this requirement is through news programming. Television news serves a specific business interest of television broadcasters: It is perceived as a necessary price they pay for a broadcasting license.

IV. Methodological differences—*television uses different methods*

A. *Superficiality:* Television news utilizes "slick" production techniques borrowed from entertainment, and it hires people based on their style of delivery and stage presence rather than on their editorial judgment or writing ability.

B. *Amateurish and unprofessional:* Television news is typified by a lack of expertise and professionalism, and television journalists often demonstrate a lack of journalistic expertise or judgment. Television journalists hesitate to investigate stories until their print media counterparts do so, essentially relegating to print journalism the task of legitimizing the news value of stories, at the same time reinforcing the view that television journalism is more entertainment than news.

Epistemological Differences

News Is Foreign to Television

One of the fundamental problems of television news was summed up by John F. Day, director of news for CBS, in a talk he gave to the University of Minnesota School of Journalism and Mass Communication in February 1956:

Television has been cut to a pattern that says, "Television is an entertainment medium; therefore television news must entertain."

Who says television HAS to be an entertainment medium? Some broadcasting officials act as though they have been handed holy writs saying, "This is your air and your electronic gadget; you're to use them solely for the purpose of making money and amusing the morons." (1968, p. 315)

This was a difficult issue for journalists who were used to the idea that they should inform not entertain. If the entire television medium was designed for entertainment, then how could journalism exist within such a medium? Television journalists soon learned that they would have to learn certain tricks to maintain their news audiences; the same tricks that entertainers use to appeal to audiences.

For instance, the consumption of television news is paced by the producers, not the consumers. People can take their time reading a newspaper. Because of this difference, pacing in television news is very important for both keeping people awake—not boring them—and not going too fast and confusing them. Radio has the same time-based dimensional problems. But people watching television must give it their undivided attention. With radio they can be doing something else, such as driving a car or reading a newspaper. Because of this, pacing was much more important in television. By capturing an audience's undivided attention, television transported the audience to the time and place of the program.

Jack Gould, television critic for the *New York Times*, summed up in 1947 the apparent strengths of television: "Television's effectiveness in covering sports and special events already has been proved beyond serious doubt—the sense of being in two places at once is very real" (p.

34). In a sense, then, television took people places—it was a sort of transport mechanism to another dimension of reality.

Marya Mannes in 1957 noted how this phenomenon was a problem because it caused boundaries to blur and caused people with discerning tastes (snobs, she calls them) to tune out:

I think what we—the snobs—want of television is either the immediacy of reality, which it is superbly equipped to convey in its intimate observation of people and places and situations, or the stimulation of real imagination, which it rarely achieves. We want our stuff straight, the lines clear, and the areas separate. We want television that can be adult for ourselves and childlike for our children—but at different times. And I further believe that the reason why commercial television may lose us in the long run to some other television system is that its survival depends on blurring all these lines. (p. 20)

To Mannes, the blurring of the distinctions between fact and fiction is a required element of all television programming. Mannes implies that this is an epistemological problem that will never allow commercial television to be a serious journalistic medium. Journalists had never before been called upon to use entertainment-style techniques such as pacing to maintain their audiences and gearing the content for children and adults at the same time.

Immediate and Unpredictable

The advantage of the immediacy of television journalism was often mentioned as a strength by critics, but also as a weakness when the news was old or complicated. Newspaper journalism is stale by the time it reaches the viewer, whereas television journalism coverage can be immediate.

Before television was developed, there were many speculations about what sorts of uses the medium would have. In one such speculative article published in 1939, Alva Johnston predicted that television advertisers would take advantage of television's strength of creating interest in events where the outcome is in doubt:

One advertising account that television expects to have in time is that of automobile manufacturer who, in order to show how safe his car is, sends it at high speed into an obstacle. The car turns three or four somersaults and lights on its four wheels. The driver steps out and takes a bow. Once in a while, however, the car lands on its side or loses a wheel. Occasionally, the driver comes out a little the worse for wear. The theory is that interest in this act would be multiplied in television because something might go wrong. (p. 107)

Although it is clear that people understood that audience interest is heightened with spontaneity, it is equally clear from Johnston's speculation that some early prophets had no idea how television would use this strength. Jack Gould, television and radio critic for the *New York Times*, wrote in 1951 concerning television's strengths and weaknesses: "The athletic contest, where the outcome is in doubt, is the best ready-made spectacle of all" (p. 22). Gilbert Seldes, who worked on the development of television for CBS from 1937 to 1945 wrote in 1954, "When it delivers a report after the event, TV is operating below its full capacities, so there is always the tendency to turn news reporting into newsreel." The newsreel was a weekly summary of events captured on movie film, edited with a narrative sound track, and presented between features at movie theaters—not a spontaneous form of information like television. An early handbook for television directors and producers echoes this point about the importance of spontaneity in television entertainment:

The television audience will not only accept, but even enjoy, a production error or a comedian who blows his lines and admits it, or who asks his straight man to feed him a cue once again, so that he can make another try at getting the gag to come out right. This leniency on the part of the audience is caused by the increased feeling of spontaneity and immediacy which minor crises create. (Stasheff & Bretz, 1956, p. 22)

Many entertainment shows were filmed ahead of time, so these methods of implying spontaneity were often contrived in entertainment yet unavoidable in live news programs.

By the 1960s, network news divisions began to market the sponsorship of spontaneous news bulletins that interrupted other programs when exciting events happened. According to an article in a broadcasting trade magazine, Gulf Oil signed a deal worth over $1 million with NBC-TV in 1960 to make it the sponsor of unscheduled news bulletins. Paul Sheldon, advertising coordinator at Gulf said, "This is the kind of vehicle we have been looking for. We believe it to be the most exciting area of television" ("Excitement," p. 34). As part of the deal, Gulf stipulated that over half of the "unscheduled" interruptions would occur during prime time, which might make one wonder just how spur-of-the-moment they really were. In a sense, advertisers discovered that news *was* entertaining and exciting—and therefore "sponsorable"—when it was spontaneous, breaking news.

The spontaneous nature of televising news as it happens was a break from traditional journalism primarily in the aspect that people could now see events happening, not just hear them as they had been doing with live radio newscasts. Newspapers printed special "extra" editions when significant events warranted, but they were no match for the spontaneity of broadcast news.

Intimate Nature of Television

Millard Faught noted in 1950, "As one housewife put it, 'Turning on the television set is just like inviting the entertainers and other people on the programs right into my living room. . . . Some of them are welcome but some others have already worn their welcome out'" (p. 8). In contrast, newspaper journalists were, for the most part, faceless names to their readers (with a few notable exceptions, such as Walter Lippmann and Scotty Reston). Most importantly, audiences could not feel personal connections to newspaper journalists the way they could with television journalists.

In their handbook for entertainment writers, directors, and producers, Stasheff and Bretz advise writers to remember that "The approach to the audience must be intimate and friendly, instead of formal and 'stagey'" (p. 65).

Another argument about the intimate proximity of the television set in the average household was that its accessibility—as an appliance or piece of furniture common to every living room—lowers the qualitative expectations of those who watch it, simply because it was effortless compared to going to a movie theater (Bernard Smith, 1948, p. 37).

Television sets are located in living rooms and have mixed audiences of children and adults, who feel like they are interacting with the personalities on the television programs. According to some television journalists, entertainment and news both capitalize on this intimate relationship with the audience by highlighting the personalities of those in their programs and by targeting their messages to the entire family.

In a television news handbook published by the Medill School of Journalism at Northwestern University in 1953, several of the contributors note that giving the news "a personality—the direct contact between speaker and viewer, the feeling of personal acquaintance" is a vital tool for attracting audiences to news programs (Ray, 1953, p. 5). Evidently, this was a practice borrowed from radio news (Allen, 1953, p. 46).

Television news audiences were comprised of the entire family, whereas with newspapers, younger members of the family were not expected to be a part of the audience. Certain topics, such as violent crimes, were more easily discussed in the matter-of-fact style and less intimate nature of newspaper journalism. The National Association of Radio and Television Broadcasters, concerned about the content of television programs, drew up a Television Code in 1952 to help guide television broadcasters. The preamble to the second edition of the code, written in March 1954, highlights the perception of the intimacy of television: "It is the responsibility of television to bear constantly in mind that the audience is primarily a home audience, and consequently that television's relationship to the viewers is that between guest and host." In contrast, newspaper journalism is often described as a more neutral type of relationship: messenger and audience. The intimacy of television—through individual personalities and through its proximity to the inner sanctums of family life—was something shared by news and entertainment programs, and at the same time was very different from the relationships between newspaper journalism and its readers.

Audiovisual, Time-Based Nature Requires Passivity of Audiences

The television medium is a very active medium that requires a passive audience; newspapers are a passive medium that require readers to make choices. For instance: Newspaper readers decide which headlines are important, which stories to read, and how long to spend on them. Newspaper readers decide if an advertisement is interesting enough to look at, and if it is, they can examine it with a magnifying glass for hours. In television, according to those involved in it, these decisions are made for the audience, the action is fleeting—a product dances onto the screen with sound and music, and then disappears all by itself—and the audience must sit passively and watch these commercials before being fed additional news items, all in an order and duration scientifically designed to keep viewers tuned in.

The audiovisual/action and sequential linearity of the television medium lead to different news judgments and news values for television journalism. Many argued that the nature of television causes audiences to have shorter attention spans, so showmanship—exciting presentation—is important in all types of television programming, including news.

Marya Mannes wrote in 1957 that television viewers "are characterized perhaps more than anything else by their passivity. For those who are passive through age or through illness, through boredom or fatigue or lack of will, television is an unparalleled boon" (p. 20).

In-depth stories with intricate detail are difficult to convey on television journalism programs. Newspaper reporter Stan Opotowsky observed: "Television coverage is at its best when the entire event takes place before the camera . . . all there for the viewer to behold. Television coverage is at its worst when the news is complicated" (p. 180).

Television waves are broadcast to your home whether you want them or not. With the minimal effort of turning a few dials and sitting down at the proper time, a television audience member can participate in television news. Newspaper journalism requires a heftier investment: Newspapers cost money and require the audience member to participate by making decisions about which items to read, which to skim, etc.

To sum up the epistemological distinctions of television news: Some believed that news is foreign to television, a medium designed for family entertainment that blurs the distinctions between fact and fiction and between adult and kids' fare. Like other television programs, television news was paced for the consumers, was designed to keep their interest (keep them from turning the channel), and required little investment or energy—watching television is a passive activity. And at the same time, television journalism could be spontaneous, immediate, and intimate—which traditional journalism could not.

Organizational Differences

Hierarchy of Authority

Television news programs at the national level are produced by network news divisions, which are small parts of large corporations organized to make money for the stockholders. The way to make money in television is to increase ratings and therefore, the value of advertising time. At newspapers, the editorial personnel—those in charge—are perceived to have the most prestige. At television networks, the entertainment personnel (such as actors and producers) and the advertising personnel are perceived to have more power and prestige than the journalists, simply because they are more responsible for bringing in revenues than are journalists.

New York Times television critic Jack Gould wrote in 1951,

As a means of disseminating information and education, television does not yet have its heart in its work. Since programs in these classifications seldom produce revenue, they are regarded by the broadcasters as of secondary importance and often as a nuisance. (p. 23)

Television journalists got the message from the rest of the network that their work was not the vital work of the network. Reuven Frank (1991), former president of NBC News tells how in the early 1960s he once gave a private screening to RCA chairman David Sarnoff of a documentary on which he had been working. Sarnoff was impressed with the work and said that he would make sure it was aired. Frank says it took almost a year for the piece to be broadcast. Frank wrote that "News was so little regarded by the people who really ran the network that Sarnoff's approval was barely enough to get the program produced and shown at all" (p. 82).

Television journalists felt like second-class citizens in their organizations. At a convention of broadcasters in 1958, Edward R. Murrow described the control structure of the television networks:

The top management of the networks, with a few notable exceptions, has been trained in advertising, research, sales, or show business. But by the nature of the corporate structure, they also make the final and crucial decisions having to do with news and public affairs. Frequently, they have neither the time nor the professional competence to do this.

Murrow's solution was to put a journalist in charge of the network—probably an impossible goal. Murrow says evidence of the organizational hierarchy of the network is apparent in the priorities for different kinds of programming when more than one kind seeks to fill airtime. Murrow's producer, Fred Friendly (1967), who went on to head CBS-TV's news division in the mid-1960s, tells how, when faced with interrupting a network entertainment program for a news bulletin, the news division was instructed to not interfere with scheduled commercials: "Even on big entertainment shows, instructions to the news division were that if we had to interrupt the program for a news bulletin, deletion of the commercial should be the last resort. The standard order of procedure was to sacrifice the plot but not the revenue" (p. 267). David Schoenbrun (1989) offers a similar example in his memoirs:

When [James] Aubrey was calling the shots for the TV network, in 1962, I was in Washington, as chief correspondent and bureau chief. . . . I was shocked to be told that Aubrey had ordered news to stop pre-empting entertainment shows, even for the most important newsbreakers, even a threat of war or the thrilling conquest of space. His talking horse, Mr. Ed, and "Gomer Pyle" were more important to Aubrey than the Cuban missile crisis, when the world teetered on the brink of nuclear war. (p. 135)

Television journalists felt that their work was not appreciated by the rest of the network personnel. This created a level of distrust and professional jealousy among journalists—wishing that they were in charge and wishing that their work was more valued by their organizations. Given the frustration of powerlessness and feeling unappreciated, it is not surprising the number of instances of journalists—television and other media—who criticized the organizational hierarchy and political economy of the television networks. Print and radio journalists joined in the chorus because they felt that their television brethren were being mistreated. Newspaper reporter Stan Opotowsky (1961), who investigated the workings of television after the quiz show scandal of 1959, says he found that "the network news directors who plead for higher budgets are always reminded by the boss that they represent the tail, not the dog, and that television is primarily an entertainment medium. The news shows, like the movies' newsreels, are just an added attraction" (p. 10).

Opotowsky makes it clear that he does not like the underclass status of television journalism. Television journalists often came from the print media ranks, and they belonged to some of the same professional organizations, such as the Society of Professional Journalists, or Sigma Delta Chi, as it was known back then. It was paradoxical, then, for journalists like Opotowsky—used to being in control of a mass medium, such as magazines and newspapers—to see journalists relatively powerless in the television organizational hierarchy.

The reason given by network executives for the low status of television journalism was because it was not the money-making arm of the network. Leonard Goldenson, who had headed United Paramount Theatres and who took control of ABC in 1956, wrote in his memoirs (1991) about his struggle to make ABC competitive (as it had always trailed a distant third behind CBS and NBC):

CBS and NBC dominated broadcast news. . . .

We had so much to do to make ABC a competitive third network—and such limited resources—that I decided to concentrate our funds and talent on building entertainment programming. That was, I felt, the surest way to attract bigger audiences and better affiliates. We put development of our news department on the back burner for a time. . . .

There was a period of about a year, for example, in the mid-1960s, when our evening news wasn't on a single station in the state of Ohio. (pp. 273–274, 293)

Goldenson admits that because entertainment was the money-making engine for his corporation, it got the most attention. His mentions of ABC News are extremely brief in his memoirs—signaling the relative importance of journalism to him. Goldenson once said that showmanship was the most important principle in television—even in news— and would be his topic of discussion if he were invited to be the keynote speaker at the National Association of Broadcasters annual convention, which he was not (Goldenson, 1963).

Showmanship and calling attention to yourself is something journalists have difficulty with, because it resembles entertainment, advertising, promotion, and public relations publicity—hardly neutral or disinterested activities. Most journalists argue that they should not be involved with such activities, but some broadcast journalists use the "you can't preach to an empty church" argument when explaining the importance of ratings and attracting an audience (McManus, 1994). In other words, you cannot do a public service for people if they are not watching and listening. For instance, CBS vice president Richard S. Salant told Ohio broadcasters in 1958, "Broadcasters should get off the defensive and come right out and say they're in business—that they can't serve the public interest unless they get audiences and advertisers in the first place" ("Salant tells broadcasters," 1958). Salant implies that journalists should do what they can—perhaps even varying presentation or content—to build audiences. Almost twenty years later, after the occasion of the death of Elvis Presley, Salant was singing a different tune in regard to making program decisions calculated to improve ratings. Av Westin (1982), a coworker of Salant's, tells how Salant and ABC News' Roone Arledge had a discussion about how the importance of news stories is determined. The top story on ABC on the day Presley died was Presley's death. On CBS, it was presidential candidate Ronald Reagan's statement of his intention to not honor then-President Jimmy Carter's Panama Canal Treaty—an expected statement.

It was a decision that conformed to Salant's dictum in the CBS News Standards Book. "We in broadcast journalism cannot, should not and will not base our judgments on what we think the viewers and listeners are 'most interested' in, or hinge our news judgment and our news treatment on our guesses (or somebody else's surveys) as to what news the people want to hear or see, and in what form." In 1976, Salant told Ron Powers, the Pulitzer Prize-winning television critic, "I take a very elitist position. Our job is to give people not what they want but what we decide they ought to have. That depends on our accumulated news judgments of what they need." To Arledge now, Salant added: "Our job is not to respond to public taste. Elvis Presley was dead—so he was dead." Any deviation from the choice of "importance" over "interest" was pandering to the audience in search of ratings. (p. 64)

Salant's change in attitude could be interpreted as living proof of the moral development of television journalism during the period. In 1958, he encouraged broadcast journalists to make news decisions based on audience appeal, but close to 20 years later he denied any connection between news decisions and audience appeal. For Salant, the boundary had changed.

Richard Goedkoop, in his recent analysis of local television news calls these competing interests *permissivism vs. parentalism* (1988, p. 19). He argues that a news broadcaster who follows the correct virtue, parentalism, gives a viewer what they need rather than what they want. This points to one of the differences often cited in the rhetoric distinguishing news from entertainment: News does not care whether it appeals to people—that is, whether it is profitable—because it is good for them, like a spoonful of cod liver oil.

In the early years of television news, showmanship and audience appeal were qualities judged by many journalists to be as important as newsworthiness. This reflected the organizational hierarchy—advertising and entertainment on top, news on the bottom. This was an uncomfortable position for journalists used to being in charge at more traditional journalistic media.

Advertiser Influence: Avoiding Controversy

It was a common perception that advertisers maintain a degree of control over television journalism program content unlike the separation between editorial and advertising at most newspapers and magazines. Television treated news and entertainment the same way—as programming—which bothered journalists who saw news as something of a higher calling than mere entertainment.

What really bothered a lot of television journalism critics was the impression that advertisers were able to influence not only entertainment, but also news and the subjects journalists would cover, as well as which journalists would appear on their programs. Programs that were controversial in the slightest were dropped by advertisers. This trend began in radio and was documented in the FCC's Blue Book: "In 1935, to take an extreme example, Alexander Woollcott's 'Town Crier' broadcasts were discontinued when the sponsor complained Mr. Woollcott had criticized Hitler and Mussolini, and might thus offend some listeners" (*Public Service Responsibility*, 1946, p. 17).

Bernard Smith, a prominent New York attorney specializing in broadcast law, wrote in 1948, "If we have learned anything from our experience with commercial radio, it is that the advertiser is less interested than is the professional radio broadcaster in providing the public with news, information, education, or distinguished drama. His interest is in attracting a mass audience—a guaranteed mass audience" (p. 40). Albert N. Williams, described as a "radio writer, director and critic," wrote an essay in 1948 that discusses the intent of broadcasting—whether broadcasters using the publicly-owned airwaves truly intend to serve the public, or whether their actual intent is solely to make money by appeasing advertisers:

Everybody knows the intent of a manufacturer. It is to sell as much of his product as he can. And the turning over of a selected thirty minutes of broadcast time to a manufacturer and his advertising agent without retaining the reins of constant responsibility is surely a clear clue as to the broadcaster's intention. It is to make as much money as possible.

Proprietors of the older media of mass communications, the more sober business men and thinkers in the field of journalism, long ago consigned to the ash-heap the advertising throw-away. The editors and publishers get out their paper without the help, advice, or direction of the advertisers, and even edit the advertising copy on occasion. It is traditional that the good magazines and the good newspapers, those that have survived the test of readership decade after decade, abhor even the vaguest suggestion concerning news content or feature make-up from advertisers and their agents. . . .

The networks and the stations—in concert, or even singly—can take back from the advertisers the duties and privileges of broadcasting. They can decide, in the light of their broader experience, demagnetized of allegiance to a particular brand of soap, what the public interest and necessity really is, and they can become experts in radio instead of advertising specialists, relegating the sale of products to the same importance that it has in journalism—the back of the book.

Williams's 1948 essay was directed at radio broadcasters. But it could just as easily have been directed at television broadcasters, because both kinds of broadcasting were organized similarly, owned by the same network companies, and dominated by the same advertising agencies. It is a clear indication that the precedent for allowing advertisers to have control over broadcast content during the time periods they sponsored—even during journalism program times—first started in radio.

In 1955, E. B. White noted: "The most puzzling thing about TV is the steady advance of the sponsor across the line that has always separated news from promotion, entertainment from merchandising. The advertiser has assumed the role of originator, and the performer has gradually been eased into the role of peddler." White seems concerned that journalism's cultural authority to define reality was being handed over to advertising people who did not follow the same altruistic principles as journalists. These critics charged that advertisers and broadcasters were more concerned with serving people whatever they are interested in, rather than serving the difficult-to-define concept of "the public interest." In 1959, "The president of CBS, Frank Stanton, said of the new quiz show [*The $64,000 Question*] and the others to follow it: 'A program in which a large part of the audience is interested is by that very fact . . . in the public interest'" (Kendrick, 1969, pp. 382–383).

Sig Mickelson, a vice president of CBS and general manager of CBS News, addressed the Texas Association of Broadcasters and the Texas State Legislature on April 13, 1959, in which he discussed the problem of getting people interested in the news. He said that broadcasters should not be expected to interest people in political affairs and news. Passing the buck, Mickelson argued that "the schools, the home, the churches, the clubs, the lodges and public meetings have responsibility too, a responsibility for creating a climate in which information is welcomed; indeed, demanded" ("News complexity," 1959).

Statements by broadcast executives often implied that the relative organizational value of any given element of the television kingdom was solely determined by ratings points, and that a general lack of interest in news was a social problem that television was unequipped to solve. Opotowsky (1961) found that workers in television felt trapped by the "system" of television—the way it was financed through advertising—and the dependence on ratings points and mass audience appeal:

I found that most of the people in television are quick to concede the industry's shortcomings, and just as quick to explain why these shortcomings are inescapable. They often feel trapped by a system, and their despair occurs because they cannot conceive an alternative to that system. . . . They are convinced that it is "the system" that produces the mediocrities, and they consider themselves as much the victims as anyone else with a set in the living room. (p. 11)

The "system"—whereby programs survive only if they achieve high ratings, no matter the social or cultural value—results in the virtual requirement that all programming appeal to the widest possible segment of people. This requirement translates into special demands on journalists to make their programs more appealing, that is, more like entertainment programs. This was a dilemma for some journalists who considered the insulation of news from outside influences to be like the separation of church and state. Any breaks in this separation could affect perceived credibility and, therefore, cultural authority. Statements such as this testimony before the Federal Communications Commission in March 1960 by Frank K. Kelly of the Fund For The Republic illustrate the fear that all television was advertiser-controlled:

Industry spokesmen contend that broadcasting's responsibility to the public is harmonious with its responsibility to the advertisers. The assumption in such a statement is that the broadcasters are adequately serving the public by renting out their channels at prime viewing hours to those who have enough money to buy time. . . .
    In terms of freedom of expression, broadcasting is certainly entitled to equal standing with the other media. But there is a notable difference between broadcasting and the press: in the print-media, advertisers do not as a matter of settled policy hold control of the placing and presentation of non-advertising matter. The press, with all its faults, inherently has far more independence of commercial forces and a more direct responsibility to the mass of paying customers who are its audience. (Kelly, 1960, p. 4)

Clearly, to those used to the older forms of the news media, television seemed too controlled by advertisers and, therefore, too consumed by profits. Because television was free to the audience (not counting the value of their time spent watching commercials), critics argued that television executives treated advertisers as their main constituents—and why not?—they held the purse strings. In 1960, Robert L. Foreman, executive vice president of B.B.D.O., a large New York advertising agency, admitted, "I think this is the only advertising medium

today in which the advertiser has any say over editorial content"
(Horton, 1960, p. 20).

Advertiser and affiliate reaction to Edward R. Murrow's broadcast,
"Harvest of Shame," a *CBS Reports* documentary broadcast on
November 25, 1960, which revealed the mistreatment of migrant
workers, caused CBS Chairman William Paley to reconsider producing
controversial news investigation programs, because the program of-
fended southern station owners and sponsors. According to
Schoenbrun (1989), one of Murrow's colleagues at CBS:

Paley had had more than enough of Murrow's championing of controversial
causes. . . . Critics raved about it, social science professors acclaimed Murrow,
but southern affiliates refused to carry the program and sponsors canceled
commercials. Paley told friends, "CBS is not the Ministry of Justice, not an
avenging angel. We are a big business and we are being hurt." (p. 129)

Television journalists learned that controversy must be avoided to
maintain advertisers. Gilbert Seldes said in 1954 that television stations find it difficult to do programs that might offend the sponsors. In
fact, he said, "I have never heard any daily TV newscaster editorialize
on a subject that was controversial in the sense that the word is used
politically." Barnouw (1970) says television documentary producers
discovered early that documentaries cannot be done on unpopular or
uninteresting topics because they are unsponsorable (p. 337).

Television critics lamented the cancellation of Murrow and Fred
Friendly's *See It Now* in the spring of 1958, because it was a program
that had regularly taken on very controversial subjects, such as the
"Communist-infiltrator" scare tactics of Sen. Joseph McCarthy, Jr., of
Wisconsin. Television critics such as John Crosby of the New York
Herald Tribune cynically mourned the loss of the program: "*See It Now*
was born in the early days of television when it was thought that TV
was a tremendous medium for the exchange of information and ideas"
(quoted in Friendly, 1967, p. 94). In a way, Crosby's remarks seem cu-
riously out of place: Previous critics argued that even in the early days
television news was dominated by advertiser and entertainment influences, and that the news/entertainment boundary was blurred. His remarks indicate that such a conclusion is too simplistic; that certain
dominant personalities, like Murrow, were able to give the television
entertainment/television news boundary sharp delineations, if only
temporarily.

Although television critics like Crosby—and many others—loved *See
It Now*, sponsors were uneasy about Murrow and Friendly's knack for
stirring up controversy, and they knew that mass-appeal, but mindless,
programs such as the quiz shows were a far safer vehicle for advertising.

In a 1962 book warning about excessive television advertiser influence, Gail Smith, advertising director for General Motors, was quoted: "We have elected to avoid being concerned with matters that are controversial, and we endeavor to see that the programs with which we are associated do not become involved in controversial matters" (Roe, 1962, p. 129). This precluded the giant automotive manufacturer from sponsoring controversial public service documentaries or news analysis programs. Television critic Yale Roe gives many other examples of major advertisers who held similar policies (pp. 128–131).

The boundary between news and entertainment was blurred, according to these critiques, because before broadcast media came along, only entertainment was controlled by advertisers. With these new media, news and entertainment were treated equally by advertisers: as things to shape into mass market and mass appeal vehicles for their advertising. By bringing attention to the blurring of these boundaries—making it a problem to be fixed—these authors worked to consolidate the professional power and authority of journalism. Critiques such as the one by Crosby show that the boundaries could be made clearer by certain dominant personalities like Edward R. Murrow.

Celebrity

An organizational similarity between news and entertainment is that in television, news and entertainment programs are all organized around star celebrities. This is due to the intimate nature of the medium, and is rather ironic, considering how the process of the production of television journalism programs is probably much more collaborative than the corresponding newsgathering process at newspapers. As Ernest Rose noted in 1961, "With the development of the cult of news 'personalities' we have come to regard our commentators as much entertainer as oracle." Barbara Matusow (1983), in her historical study of the network anchor system, notes that the anchor system was a personality-driven attraction—a means to interest people in the news:

This emphasis on the personality of the newscaster, which had its antecedents in radio, is uniquely American. . . . In the United States . . . broadcast news grew up as an offshoot of large entertainment corporations whose real business is promoting the sale of products, and personality turned out to be the greatest selling device ever discovered. Personality was the key to radio's phenomenal success, and no one saw any reason to change the formula on TV, whether the program format was comedy, variety, or news. (p. 51)

In Great Britain, television news "readers" are not even identified—the British de-emphasize personality. Av Westin (1982) says the "star system" of television first really surfaced when Chet Huntley and

David Brinkley were paired to cover the 1956 national political conventions. Suddenly people were apparently tuning in to the news solely because the special dynamic between the two contrasting personalities of Huntley and Brinkley added a sense of drama to the news (p. 37).

Some argue that certain journalists with a flair for show business were hired in order to bring more drama and, hence, to interest audiences. For instance, the hiring of Mike Wallace by CBS in 1963 was criticized because he came from show business beginnings rather than work his way up through the journalism profession. Schoenbrun (1989), one of "Murrow's Boys"—CBS radio reporters recruited by Murrow primarily from newspapers and wire services during World War II—describes the hiring of Wallace as a symptom of a slip in the tradition of serious news at CBS:

Another headliner joined CBS in that turning-point year, 1963, and it was yet another indication of how CBS policy had changed. CBS News signed a big contract with Mike Wallace. Many at CBS were surprised. They did not consider Wallace to be a CBS-style class act. He was dynamic, had a following, but was more aggressive, brash, tough than CBS tradition. Most did not realize how CBS had changed. Wallace was the kind of newsman that [James] Aubrey liked, a showman. (p. 157)

The fact that Wallace was hired for ostensibly his showmanship skills irritated other CBS News staffers like Schoenbrun. According to some critics during this time, the policy of hiring news personalities based on looks and showmanship was even more prevalent at the local level. In a 1962 article in a television advertising trade magazine, various broadcast news executives were asked to answer the question: "Does tv/radio news need the star system?" Lee Hanna, the director of news and special events at WNEW in New York said:

"If we mean by 'star' a man who delivers the superficial virtues of a serious mien and stentorian tones as a substitute for lucid thinking, solid writing, and honest, trustworthy presentation of the facts, then the answer must be no," Hanna insisted. "We have too many of them. Today, in too many cases, the 'star' newsman's only close association with the news is the proximity of his office to the newsroom." (pp. 32–33)

Opotowsky (1961) argued that "The man you see reading the news on television seldom knows any more about it than you do. His dispatches are written, edited, and selected by the behind-the-scenes news department, and his pictures were taken by the station photographer" (p. 178). True, legitimate journalists were those who came from newspapers, wire services, or radio, who knew how to write, and who had done time in the field covering war, like Murrow, Schoenbrun, and the rest of the Murrow Boys. Wallace and others who had crossed over to television journalism from interview shows and other entertainment shows were generally held in lower regard by their colleagues within the journalism community.

Star celebrity-journalists were one tool for organizing the television news business to make the news more interesting and more watched by audiences. The underlying message in the rhetoric about organizational differences between media reiterates the dilemma of the economic imperatives of television conflicting with the public service imperatives of journalism. Unlike other forms of news media, the primary imperative of television (including television journalism) is economic. In other words, television news is *organized* to get high ratings and, therefore, increased advertising revenues. By contrast, an imperative often cited by traditional forms of news media is altruism—that journalism is *organized* to serve the public interest. In an op-ed piece written by Edward R. Murrow in 1949 for the *New York Times* which was never published, Murrow asked: "Will television regard news as anything more than a salable commodity?" (Kendrick, 1969, pp. 318–319). It was a question many still pondered at the end of the first two decades of television.

Functional Differences

Social Function: Abbreviated, Entertaining News for the Lower Classes

Early researchers and journalists argued that the television medium, and therefore television news, serves a different segment of society: people on the low end of the socioeconomic scale. The implication is that the rich and educated leaders of society—the people who really need to be informed—get their news elsewhere (that is, from newspapers, radio, and magazines). This argument reveals the perception of a different social function for television news—as an abbreviated, entertaining form of news for the lower classes of society.

Bernard Smith, a critic of the for-profit broadcasting system in the United States, said in 1948: "Studies made of the financial status of purchasers of television sets indicate conclusively that a majority of them come from families with incomes of less than five thousand dollars" (p. 35).

In 1955, Thomas Coffin, manager of NBC's research office, published an article in a professional psychology journal summarizing the results of 60 research studies done on the effects of television and the adoption of television technology by Americans. Coffin says the usage of, and the opinion of, television "tend to be highest in lower-income and large families, lowest in high-income, high-education families." He notes that one study found that TV owners knew less about current affairs, and another found that TV owners "have a penchant for passive, spectator recreation . . . and show less participation in community organization."

In 1964, Dr. Leo Bogart of the Bureau of Advertising, was asked by *Editor & Publisher*, a newspaper trade magazine, to comment on a survey of Americans by Elmo Roper and Associates, commissioned by the Television Information Office, which found that television is considered a more believable and important news source than newspapers. Bogart cited socioeconomic class-based differences between the consumers of the two different media:

Surveys conducted over the past 30 years, Dr. Bogart said, consistently demonstrate that reliance on newspapers is greatest at the upper end of the educational and socio-economic scale, while reliance on broadcast media as a source of news is greatest at the lower end.

Entertainment, he said, is of relatively greater importance to those farther down.   In other words, he pointed out, newspapers are most relied on as a source among those people for whom news is most important.

"The two media." Dr. Bogart said, "perform different news functions." ("Dr. Bogart," 1964, p. 13)

All these authors show that the people who watch television, including television journalism programs, are less intelligent, are less educated, are poorer, and have little imagination or inclination to significantly participate in society. The television set is a pacifier, it lowers people's expectations and desires. And yet it became a common feature of the landscape of every American household—an appliance, a piece of furniture, a part of every household, particularly among the lower classes. Millard Faught (1950), a New York management consultant who wrote about television, noted that

In the first six months of 1950 upward of 3,000,000 sets were sold at an average price of $300 each. An estimated six out of ten sets are sold on credit, with the poor crowding the rich away from the counters. It is already a significant issue in some cities as to whether a family should be dropped from the relief rolls for buying a television set. (p. 7)

In 1962, Roe noted that "more families have television sets than have telephones, or vacuum cleaners. Furthermore, they watch those television sets from five to six hours a day" (p. 14). Researchers during the Great Depression found that people were more willing to give up their iceboxes and bedsprings than their radios (Matusow, 1983, p. 45).

Many of those producing broadcast news believed it only served as a headline or bulletin service—a supplement to the newspaper. Joseph

Persico (1988) says it was common in the early days of radio for radio news announcers to tell listeners "For further details, consult your local newspaper" (p. 246). In his memoirs (1991), Reuven Frank, an early television news writer, tells how he thought of television news:

Like any human institution, television news, too, had begun in innocence. When I was writing the *Camel News Caravan* we assumed that almost everyone who watched us had read a newspaper that day, that our contribution, our adventure, would be pictures. The people at home, knowing what the news was, could see it happen. And it was the lure and excitement of picture that had enticed me to television; for words, I could have stayed with the newspaper. To be sure, television also had the bulletin function that was the heart of radio, the ability to dispense news immediately, without waiting to set it into type, print it, and get the finished newspaper to the street. (pp. 95–96)

Opotowsky argued that the reason television news was so brief was that advertisers—and therefore network executives—believed that longer news programs would bore the audience: "TV has a stock answer to complaints about [short news programs]: The audience won't sit still for any more news. And, as usual, it goes to the rating services as proof of this contention" (p. 178).

In 1963, Dallas Townsend, a journalism educator, wrote about his worry that people think they're getting all the information they need on television, when actually they are getting very little depth. He said people get a "relatively small number of sentences . . . about a relatively small number of events," and many news programs "seem to be built around commercials" (p. 285). In 1965, after CBS and NBC had doubled their evening newscasts to a half-hour, CBS-TV News anchor Walter Cronkite discussed the impossibility of presenting all the news in a half-hour television news program:

Whether we cover the news is a sticky question. I don't think so. I don't think we could. The front page of the *New York Times* couldn't go in half an hour. The highest function we serve is showing the news in the form of pictures on the air and taking the viewer to where the news is being made. We couldn't cover all the news in one hour but that brings up the problem of whether we could keep the people with us for an hour. We cover as much news as the people can see and listen to easily. (Tarzian, 1965, p. 58)

There is just not enough time to do a thorough job of telling the news, according to Cronkite, but it is an impossible dilemma because the audience will not watch any more than a half-hour news program— in theory, anyway. The real reason the networks did not try longer news programs was because they received a lot of pressure from their affiliates when they extended the nightly news programs to a half-hour in length, so they were reluctant to extend it any further.

Edward Barrett, Dean of Columbia University's School of Journalism, tells how at a 1964 broadcasters convention, a local affiliate executive told him he was angry at NBC for putting so much news on the television: "We lose audiences every time we have to put that stuff in place of entertainment. Take that nonsense of extending the Huntley-Brinkley program from fifteen minutes to a full half hour. That alone cost us way over $100,000" (p. 18). Barrett concludes— echoing the critique of the FCC's Blue Book— that managers of local stations "do not bother to pay lip-service to the public-information pledges they made at the time of license applications," and compared to network executives, are much less concerned about what he envisions as television's "mission to inform" people.

Clearly those in charge of television news believed that their television audiences came from the lower socioeconomic segments of society, had low expectations for the content of television, and would accept no more than cursory, abbreviated news programs that kept them entertained. This may have become a self-fulfilling prophecy.

Institutional Function: Regulatory Obligation

Similar to radio news, television journalism programming was one of the methods for television station licensees to fulfill the public service programming requirements set forth by the FCC. In effect, news was necessary to maintain a government license, so it served a specific function for the owners of a station or a network. David Schoenbrun (1989) describes how Chairman William Paley felt about CBS news in the 1950s:

In the extraordinary decade of the fifties . . . the company was smaller, devoted only to broadcasting, news was bigger, more important. Paley did not care how much news spent, for it was a relatively small sum for the giant returns it brought. The network was a gold mine, a license for making money, and Paley felt that news was the license fee he had to pay for that privilege. (p. 78)

A CBS executive told Marya Mannes in 1957, "Our public affairs programs are usually a dead financial loss, since most of them are unsponsored. . . . There is no law that says we have to put on these shows. We do it because we feel we owe it to a section of our audience" (p. 21). More likely, CBS did news because they felt they owed it to the FCC.

Some within the FCC also felt that way about news—that it was the fee for owning a governmental franchise. Lee Loevinger, an FCC commissioner, said in a 1963 speech to journalism educators:

It seems clear that the most significant public interest served by broadcasting, and the end that most clearly justifies the spectrum allocations made to it—is the performance of the journalistic function and its contribution to the maintenance of a political democracy and a free society. This conclusion provides a guide to the proper role of government in relation to broadcasting. (1968, p. 326)

A year later, Loevinger said "The kind of social license I would exact from broadcasters . . . is not that broadcasting serve me the kind of entertainment I want . . . It's that broadcasting provide news" ("Only the title," 1964, p. 80).

Television executives understood this, and they often seemed eager to note that the networks supplied a lot of free time to unsponsored, "sustaining" television journalism programs, and that running a news division was very expensive. For instance, William R. McAndrew, executive vice president, NBC News, said at FCC hearings in January and February 1962: "[U]nrecovered NBC News costs in 1961 allocable to the NBC television network amounted to almost $12,000,000, or 81% of the total cost, and we expect those unrecovered costs to be even more in 1962" ("Television Stepping Up," 1962, p. 44). McAndrew's point was that news programming loses money for the networks, and the only reason they do it is to provide a public service. Network executives believed that news was a vehicle for increasing the prestige of a network. William Paley wrote in his memoirs (1979) about his perception of the social value of CBS's network-produced radio news; his comments probably equate to his feelings about CBS's network television news:

At CBS, my associates and I recognized radio news as a unique service we could provide to the public, and we realized early that the prestige of our network would depend to a considerable extent upon how well we could provide such service. . . . It must be remembered that when I came to CBS in 1928, radio was looked upon by most people as a gadget, a toy, an amusing instrument of light entertainment. (p. 118)

Paley believed that news programming was useful because it made people take radio seriously, to see it as more than a mere toy. Later, he followed the same belief in his television network, encouraging CBS-TV News to become the early leader in television journalism. Paley believed that news—unlike entertainment—was a powerful, positive public relations tool for the network. A critical answer to these arguments is that the true reason networks and local stations provided news of any kind was the regulatory pressure they felt from the FCC, which required them to operate in the public interest.

Methodological Differences

Superficiality

Television news was very similar to entertainment programming in the methods employed to attract viewers: It tended to dwell on superficial subject matter that was uncontroversial, easy to understand, and often characterized by flashy visual elements. Edward R. Murrow felt that television journalists' news judgment was clouded by the pictorial value of a given story: "What seems to concern television isn't the horror of the atomic bomb, but the unique picture it makes," he said (Kendrick, 1969, p. 341). Opotowsky (1961) says the early television "recruits from radio . . . were fascinated by the new dimension of sight. They preferred to show water skiers at Cypress Gardens to an announcer reading a dispatch from the Supreme Court" (p. 178). Murrow and Opotowsky (and many others) were concerned about this superficial tendency of television news, and they believed that the blurred news/entertainment boundary in this methodological dimension was something that needed to be made more distinct.

Many critics argued that television journalism was typified by many kinds of slick production techniques borrowed from television entertainment, principally drama, presumably in an effort to build ratings. Robert MacNeil, who started with NBC-TV in 1960, says television journalists, much like drama writers, always look for "'the right bit,' the most violent, the most bloody, the most pathetic, the most tragic, the most wonderful, the most awful moment. Getting the effective 'bit' is what television news is all about" (1982, p. 129).

Television journalists felt that they also needed to add excitement and interest to their programs. One way they did this was through the use of lively music and sound effects. A 1953 manual for television journalists suggests that the addition of musical soundtracks and sound effects is an effective method for increasing interest in news programs (Fentress, 1953, p. 67).

Journalists use drama skills to conduct reenactments, and perhaps more subtly, to express sorrow and indignation (or whatever emotional response seems appropriate), when interviewing the subjects of news. Mike Wallace, who was the host of a news interview program in New York called *Nightbeat* in the mid-1950s, says he "occasionally came near to vaudeville when I resorted to the piercing, rather than the penetrating question. . . . The piercing question was instituted purely for shock value—like a telegraphed punch" (Downs & Wallace, 1967, p. 168). Wallace also admits that the studio staging and lighting for *Nightbeat* were designed to give a feeling of starkness to his interviews (pp. 168–169).

William Benton, former U.S. senator (D-Conn.) and former vice president of the University of Chicago and Assistant Secretary of State, wrote in 1953 that he feared American television was taking the "road to trivialization—with our TV stations devoting their good viewing hours to vying with a few salable program stereotypes, for the same lowest-common-denominator of audience interest, all in behalf of fifteen or twenty big sponsors."

Similarly, Dallas Townsend complained in 1963 that in television news, visual action is more important than news importance or social significance: "A minor ship sinking in the Atlantic may be given bigger play and more space than the fall of a government in Asia" (p. 286). This critique has also been leveled against newspapers, however. A sensational picture always seems to get into journalistic media. But television, because it depends so heavily on visuals, may give these kinds of pictures even more significance in the news determination process.

In television journalism, as well as in other forms of journalism, entertaining content can be seen as a form of relief from the tedium of depressing (bad) news. Some say entertaining news is the glue that keeps the audience from turning away in disgust. Sociologists, for instance, have long theorized that entertaining news on television served the function of reducing audience anxiety from too much bad news (Wright, 1960, p. 620). In newspapers, editorial cartoons, feature sections, and the comics pages serve as the entertainment. Marya Mannes complained in 1957 that intelligent programming was avoided by television producers because they did not want to "penalize" the majority of viewers who, evidently, prefer less-complicated news:

One of the most creative and intelligent network officials, a producer of public-affairs programs, remarked the other day that no network in its right mind would present a *See It Now*, for example, at the same time a rival network was showing a star-studded variety program. "We can't penalize the majority," he said, "for the sake of the minority."

The word "penalize" was an interesting choice, since it apparently meant "force the majority to think" or "bore"—implying, indeed, that the two were synonymous. (p. 19)

Superficial methods of presentation—superficial in the sense that they contribute little to the informational value of the medium—were one way to distinguish between traditional forms of journalism and television journalism. Traditional forms of journalism also employed certain superficial methods of presentation—such as banner headlines and sensational pictures of relatively unimportant events—but according to many critics, they did not employ such methods to the same degree as television journalism. In this regard, the television

news/television entertainment boundary was blurred. Television journalism used the same methods as entertainment programs to attract
and hold audiences.

Amateurish and Unprofessional

The rhetoric shows evidence of a pervasive impression that early
television journalism was typified by a lack of expertise and professionalism. The seductive glitter of television seemed to lower the standards
of professionalism of otherwise legitimate journalists. Ray Sherer, a
veteran television journalist, described how local television news was
done in Washington, D. C., in the late 1940s:

On television we were doing the most primitive sort of news reportage. I
started in radio, and then I worked on a local TV show with Earl Godwin. He
was a very well known radio commentator during the war, and the show we did
on TV in 1948 or '49 was on this funny little set, a sort of country store, where
Earl acted as the proprietor. He'd stand behind the counter, wearing sus-
penders, the lights reflecting off his bald head, and I would come through. I
was supposed to be the reporter for the local paper, and he'd say, "Well Ray,
what's new?" And I would say, "Well Earl, today Harry Truman fired off an
angry letter to the music critic of *The Washington Post* complaining about the
nasty review he'd written about his daughter Margaret's singing." And then
Earl would launch into a rambling sort of commentary about that. Pretty elementary stuff.
    Our facilities weren't very elaborate. Our first news camera held only 100
feet of film. We had one cameraman; he had a 16 mm silent camera. I'd clip
the morning *Washington Post*, and the *Times-Herald* . . . I'd pick out news and
feature stories, he'd go out and shoot some film. Fifty feet of that event,
twenty feet on this story—he'd bring it back, we'd assemble it all into a newsreel and run it that night with a live commentary. (Wilk, 1976, p. 97)

Sherer blames the lack of professionalism on bad facilities and lack
of a budget, but he does not explain why Godwin and he presented the
news humorously, in the fictional context of a country store, with each
of them playing an imaginary character. Presumably, they believed this
kind of dramatic presentation would be more interesting to audiences,
even if it did blend fictional scenes with factual news.

The newness of the television news field led to nonjournalists being
used to fill journalistic roles, as well as unqualified journalists being
asked to fill photojournalistic roles. For instance, a 1948 description of
how television news is produced notes that "NBC . . . uses engineers
rather than program men as cameramen. They feel it's important to
have a trained technician on the spot, to service the camera in case of
trouble, even though he may not have as keen a sense of dramatic values as the program man" (Loosbrock, pp. 122–123). Interestingly, the

author believes "dramatic values" to be more important than journalistic values.

A couple of years later, in 1950, Korean War footage was shot by radio reporters working for the networks. A 1950 article in *Newsweek* noted that CBS "handed 16-millimeter cameras to its radio men, with unexpectedly good results, although 'good reporters are not generally good photographers.' Bill Downs first handed a camera in Germany six months ago, has turned out to be a 'natural cameraman'" ("Korean Coverage," p. 48).

Leonard (1987) says "The men who filmed documentaries from the late 1950s to the early 1960s came almost without exception from the ranks of the old newsreel cameramen" (p. 82). The newsreel workers held journalistic values that differed from those of television news— tending toward what today is known as tabloid: sentimental, corny, and perhaps voyeuristic. As Harry Reasoner, a former ABC and CBS television reporter, notes in his autobiography (1981):

Before the network news programs began to stretch and feel and learn in the middle 1950's, no one had ever done news with moving pictures before. America was used to newsreels—the little stories with music, the annual sheep-shearing competitions, the fashion shows and the White House Easter Egg rolls and Lew Lehr noting that monkeys are the craziest people. Newsreels didn't cover news: there was a feeling that people didn't want the news when they went to the movies. (p. 4)

Those who worked in television journalism in the early years realized the relatively low stature their medium had among news media workers. From the very beginning, as a site for doing newswork, television was a professional ghetto—a place to be avoided if you cared about your career. According to some broadcast historians, most radio journalists resisted the move to television, sensing that it could damage their professional reputations (for example, Matusow, 1983, pp. 45, 50).

Critics argued that television journalism was methodologically different from other types of journalism because television journalists did not maintain complete control over the journalistic process—something the critics felt was unprofessional. Some of the early network news operations did not maintain complete control over newsgathering—much of it was done by newsreel companies and other free-lance subcontractors. Journalists did not like the policy. John Daly resigned in 1960 as head of news at ABC-TV because he was tired of having outside newsreel companies gather the news ("Hagerty Shooting," 1961, p. 12). Daley's replacement, James Hagerty, however, apparently did not have a problem with that policy. Their boss, Leonard Goldenson, says in his autobiography that the newsreel company subcontractors overseas were a way of saving money: "We had no film crews overseas. Instead we relied on Fox Movietone or Hearst Telenews" (Goldenson & Wolf, 1991, pp. 273–274).

Critics and television journalists seem to agree that early television journalists often did not know what they were doing, were unsure of themselves, were unprofessional, and rewrote wire copy rather than gather the news themselves. Av Westin, who wrote and produced for CBS from the 1950s to the 1970s wrote in his memoirs (1982):

In the early days of television news, there was a tendency to follow the wire services lead or to reproduce on film what the *New York Times* had reported that morning. . . . Television journalists were so unsure of their own judgment that the reinforcement of seeing something in print was an absolute requirement. (pp. 74–75)

Independent judgment of newsworthiness—an essential editorial function of journalists—was missing from television journalism, according to Westin. Similarly, Bill Leonard (1987), who worked at the CBS affiliate station in New York City, covering local news, discovered that the ability to make journalistic decisions was lacking among many network television journalists:

CBS News seemed to acquit itself of its responsibility for coverage of New York City with a quick rewrite of the front page of *The New York Times*. Its editor and executives had eyes fixed permanently on the wire machines. Al Morgan once said, "If the Mayor of New York was shot in front of 485 Madison Avenue [CBS News headquarters] and a CBS deskman saw it take place, the first thing he would do would be to rush up to the newsroom on the seventeenth floor and take a look at the AP wire to find out if it had really happened."

As I got to know more and more about CBS News . . . that original impression, going back to the forties, hung on. (p. 54)

Local television news was very often criticized for being unprofessional. For instance, in June 1959, Associated Press General Executive Louis J. Kramp, speaking at the Pennsylvania AP Broadcasters Association meeting, "urged radio-tv newsmen to help sponsor an awareness of the responsibilities of their position, to be more quality-conscious about their work. He asked station owners and managers to learn more about news practices and principles," implying that they were ignorant of the professional standards to which the rest of the journalistic community adhered ("AP's Kramp," 1959, p. 70). The Associated Press had only grudgingly accepted radio and television stations as members, and now it still did not feel that local television and radio journalists were quite up to par with newspaper journalists.

Many print and radio media reporters disliked television journalism's superficiality and unprofessional personnel, and they were not afraid to say so. It was common for newspaper reporters to try to deny television journalism's right to coexist with them, such as seeking to bar television coverage of major news events, on the grounds that the television reporters were unskilled and unprofessional. Schoenbrun, covering the Eisenhower campaign in 1952 for CBS-TV, notes that newspaper journalists had his cameras barred from a major speech in Abilene, Kansas (1989, p. 90). Newspaper reporters were evidently very upset when Eisenhower held the first televised presidential press conference in 1955 (Ferrell, 1983, p. 169). Opotowsky (1961) described the animosity between print and television journalists:

There is a constant war between the newspaper reporters and the TV reporters in the coverage of the news. Unfortunately, this comes out not as a race for scoops but as a duel of industrial jealousies. Reporters object to the presence of TV cameras in their press conference. They claim this makes them captive actors for the TV stations and that TV persists in filming these press conferences only because its own reporters don't have the experience and background to ask proper questions of their own. (pp. 179–180)

In Los Angeles during the late 1950s, the animosity between print and television journalists grew into an all-out feud:

Since TV first thrust its nose into the press-conference tent, there has been less and less room for newspapermen. . . . Last week in Los Angeles, growing antagonism between press and TV flared into open combat; newsmen on three of the city's four major dailies (holdout: the evening *Mirror-News*) were obeying standing orders to boycott press conferences rather than take any guff from TV. . . . The newspapermen's main objection: TV stations seldom send a trained reporter along with the technical crews they assign to press conferences, thus contribute nothing to the story except hot lights, silly questions and endless delays for retakes. "They should handle their own news instead of cashing in on our brains and experience," snapped Bud Lewis, city editor of the Los Angeles *Times* (whose KTTV is one of the city's busiest cashers-in). "The TV people are afraid of separate conferences, because they just don't have the trained reporters to handle them." ("Jab to the nose," 1957, pp. 90–91)

Compared to traditional journalistic media, the methods used in early television news were primitive and borrowed from show business. Many of the people who employed these methods were new to journalism—relatively untrained—and tended to re-create the media they came from, principally newsreels. They used other than journalistic criteria to determine the newsworthiness of events or subjects, tending instead to dwell on pretty faces, excitement, and action. Television journalists tended to abdicate their editorial judgment, preferring to follow the lead of the wire services or the print media. Many could not write or merely preferred to rewrite wire copy. Professional jealousies erupted when television cameras became common at press conferences. Print reporters claimed that they asked "smarter" questions than their television counterparts, whom they claimed were unskilled at covering politics. In a sense, they tried to strengthen their own professional jurisdiction over the news, while denying that authority to television journalists. Their rhetoric highlighted the differences—and the boundary—between television journalism and their more traditional version of journalism.

TV NEWS AT TEN: AN ANALYSIS OF CBS'S 1958 *TELEVISION NEWS REPORTING*

It is important to remember that radio news was dominated by the Columbia Broadcasting System in the 1930s and 40s. Radio news was important to William Paley, the multimillionaire chairman and primary stockholder of CBS. As noted earlier, he felt that news was an important prestige-building public relations tool for CBS, and in practical terms, it was also the governmental "license fee" for his broadcasting kingdom. He hired and encouraged Edward R. Murrow, who was the most respected radio journalist during World War II. Murrow's radio dispatches during the bombing of London became legendary. After the war, Murrow was promoted to vice president of CBS, and his reputation as a journalist continued to grow. CBS continued its dominance of broadcast news when commercial television was developed, and many of its star radio journalists, such as Murrow, made the crossover to television journalism.

Considering the dominance of CBS in broadcast journalism, it is significant that in 1958 CBS News published a handbook for television journalists entitled *Television News Reporting*. Its guidelines for television journalists comprise a fascinating look at the beginnings of television journalism—sort of an assessment of the constructed roles and methods of television journalism as they had been built during the first decade of television journalism—by those working in the network with the most prominent news division. Examined as a whole, the rhetoric contained in the handbook illustrates the dilemma of reconciling the competing pressures for television journalists to use entertainment-style devices to advantage yet to deny the journalistic legitimacy of news styles that depended too heavily on entertaining content, namely, the newsreels popular before television came along.

The introduction, written by John F. Day, the Director of News,

CBS News, notes the problem of doing journalism in a brand-new medium:

Television journalism is so recent an arrival in the field of public communications that there have been relatively few attempts to formulate its principles, procedures and practices. We are still exploring the breadth and the limitations of this medium, finding, for example, that the dimension of sight is sometimes so powerful that it tells too much and may even require restraining. Sometimes, on the other hand, the sight dimension does not tell enough, or tells it falsely.

We are busy trying to open up new sources of news to the eye of the camera. We are busy trying to secure public acceptance and status for television reporting. We are wrestling with the matter of translating news which is made where the camera cannot go—whether in a man's mind or in a remote corner of the earth—into meaningful visual terms.

In acknowledging the unforeseen problems of television journalism, Day implies that television journalists are focused on improvement. He indicates that the problems have not all been ironed-out, but that they are working on them and they will take care of them. This statement is calculated to engender sympathy and empathy in those reading it, as they are asked to be patient because television news is new and mysterious and is just now being explored and understood.

Day notes that the visual aspects of television journalism can be a problem, hinting that the appeal of the visual dimension overwhelms the verbal aspects of news. This was seen as a problem because the visual aspects had an inherent captivating or entertaining quality about them. He assures the reader that television journalists understand this inherent entertainment quality and that they will responsibly harness or restrain it.

In the last paragraph Day says television journalists are working to "open up new sources to the eye of the camera," and to "secure public acceptance and status for television reporting." Clearly, building status and public acceptance for television journalism is very important to Day, implying that in his estimation the status of television journalism is lower than it should be. Status-building exercises are an important part of the development of professional roles and of consolidating professional power.

Later in the handbook, the goals of television journalism are spelled out:

So let us set forth the essentials of a television news show and consider the qualities it contains, the situations it faces, the procedures necessary to get it on the air. . . . In reporting the news, it has one main job, to interpret the magnitude and complexity of each day's happenings, no matter where, into meaningful and factual terms. In its framework of accomplishing this end, television news has borrowed or improved upon techniques developed by newspapers, news magazines, and radio. . . . Every television news broadcast must bear authority, must be impartial, and must impart a sense of experience far more intimate than that offered by any other news medium; intimate because television adds the subjective to what is normally an objective business. The subjective is added when the viewer participates in the news. Persons, distinguished or corrupt, hero or villain; places as obscure as the wild hills of Afghanistan or the snow-white expanse of the South Pole—they all suddenly come to life when television news reports about them. (pp. 12–14)

In this statement, television journalists are reminded that they "borrow or improve upon" procedures and professional ideology from the print and audio journalism from which their medium evolved— such as objectivity and a devotion to facts—but they are also reminded that television imparts a sense of intimacy, and that it should use this intimacy dimension to advantage, even if it detracts from television journalism's objectivity. The implication is that intimacy is an unavoidable advantage that should be exploited. Not only "must" it be impartial, but it must exploit the intimate nature of the medium—even though intimacy is a subjective, participatory element heretofore avoided in previous types of journalism.

In the following statement, the authors note that television news evolved from newsreels, but that the subject matter of newsreels was less newsworthy and more sensationalistic and entertainment-oriented:

Before television news and its use of motion picture film, perhaps the most remarkable fact about the use of motion picture film in reporting the news was that it was limited to what can be described as showmanship. The subject area never extended beyond the limits of what was good box office. A story which fitted the general definition of entertainment took precedence over one which was plainly news. A laugh, a raised eyebrow, a shock were far more desirable than a thought.

The climate changed considerably during the Second World War. In fact, motion picture coverage assumed a balance of thought and influence along far more serious lines. (p. 15)

Evidently, according to the writers of the manual, the war had an effect on the content of newsreels, reflecting a desire for more serious subject matter among American moviegoers, and the newsreels responded by giving the people what they wanted. Before the war, they imply that all newsreels were dominated by journalistically superfluous, entertaining subject matter.

In the next selection, the writers suggest that television journalists should make the news easier to remember and follow by determining a specific theme for the news program each day, and that this is an important tool for television journalism to use to distinguish itself from newspapers and radio:

There are days in the news business when a theme seems to predominate the flow of stories. . . . In order to be different, as opposed to newspaper or radio coverage, the television handling should make possible a visual grasp of the day's news theme. Let's say it is a day of air crashes. Independently of one another, planes have crashed in the United States and abroad. There is a challenge here. Is it right to handle each story separately? No, not if you are reporting the news by television. Handling air crashes as a theme of the day's news is a potent means of adding visual dimension to it. . . .

The best thematic tag construction on a television news program appears as a part of the natural pattern of the day's news. It is presented as a logical and visual contribution. It does not appear contrived, nor is it. Nothing is easier to spot than an inferior or synthetic kind of thematic tag. The film and the running story should complement each other. They should be understood effortlessly by the viewer. No exposition should be necessary. (pp. 33–34)

This suggestion for organizing news stories by using a thematic structure is a good example of how the television news producers chose to use their own news-organizing structures—rather than the types used in traditional news media. These news-organizing structures are based on entertainment-style storytelling presentations rather than the pragmatic, factual, inverted-pyramid accounts common to most written newswriting styles. The apparent goal is to make the news easier to understand, but the implication is that television news is targeted toward people too lazy to read, must be made simple for people to follow, and requires no effort on the part of the audience.

In newspaper journalism, the customary news categories can be described as: local, national, international, editorial opinion, and features. Television network news, because it is national, does not carry local stories, nor does it usually carry editorial opinion. The news categories of newspaper journalism did not fit television's format, so television journalists felt free to invent their own methods of organizing information.

The differences between hard news and feature stories are also discussed in the handbook, with the admonition to avoid overusing features and to avoid some of the pitfalls that the theater newsreels and early television news programs fell into—pictorialism without considering content or newsworthiness:

Whether consciously or not, most television news shows segregate features from the main body of the program. The important news of consequence, filmed or otherwise, is given first. Then, as if in relief from the stress and texture of the main body of the show, the feature is presented. . . .

It is fairly safe to say that any feature which arouses a grin, or even a tear, has all the elements of a good feature. . . . Don't overdo the feature. In the beginning, television fell into the trap created by 35-millimeter coverage for theater newsreels. Anything that was pictorial was snapped up, regardless of its news importance. In some quarters, television is still suffering from the questionable reputation it gained during its early day when parades, ski spills, and beauty contests were used indiscriminately. (pp. 35, 37)

The sequencing discussed in the first paragraph—hard news first, then features—illustrates the use of techniques borrowed from drama and narrative storytelling. Devices such as conflict, climax, resolution, and comic relief were routines suitable for television news delivery. The authors first indicate that this is perhaps done unconsciously, but then they advocate the technique as a formula for success.

They also hint that one of the differences in technique between newsreels and television news is the film size. Most television news was shot using 16-millimeter cameras—inferior in picture quality, but much lighter, more portable, and much cheaper than shooting 35-millimeter film. Because 35mm motion picture cameras are so large, they tended to be used only at set-up or prearranged "news events" rather than at spontaneous news or spot news. In addition, because 16mm film was about half the size and price of 35mm, more footage could be shot at unfolding news events. The additional film meant that editing took on more importance, giving producers greater opportunity to evaluate newsworthiness during editing, which coincidentally took some control away from photographers. This explains the impression that 35mm film is less newsy and more show business.

According to the authors, television news is often compared to tabloid journalism. They take the time to examine this comparison— one they do not deny or regret. Daily tabloid newspapers were much more common then, and the term "tabloid" did not have the connotations it does today, because the "supermarket tabloid" had not yet been invented. Tabloids were newspapers that were designed in a size and format to make them easy to read and that incorporated a lot of visual elements:

[T]he television news editor spends much of his time, like the tabloid editor, fitting the hard news in and around the film available. He mentally places a priority value upon the film, marking that which is most immediate and newest with the highest value. There follows the sometimes painful job of selecting the film to be used on the show, painful because the film may have no relation to the hard news. It is a challenge to the editorial staff's wit and intelligence to fit the two—hard news and film—together logically, or amusingly, or with a thematic tag. This is not unlike the problems a tabloid faces in its make-up.

Should the television news staff find that using a film hinders a show's flow, they drop it, or place it in the back of their minds. . . . In making themselves interesting and satisfying, television and tabloid both realize that their exceptional strength lies in polished and imaginative use of pictorial material. (pp. 81–83)

Again, the problem of visual messages that have little to do with the verbal messages is discussed in the manual. For television news producers, "wit and intelligence" were necessary. It took a clever person to fit pictures and words together—especially when the two did not obviously relate to one another. It is significant that they note that "hard news and film" are diametrically opposed aspects of television news. They imply that the visual realm is by nature the opposite of "hard news."

The authors admit that the greatest strength of television, like tabloids, "lies in the polished and imaginative" use of visuals. And yet, as they noted earlier in the handbook, visuals can become overpowering, to the point of crossing the boundary to entertainment. When visuals are compelling but do not have any relation to the rest of the news, the wit and intelligence of the producer in finding a way to tie the visual to the thematic tag for the day becomes paramount.

The analysis of this handbook has illustrated how television journalists in the late 1950s perceived some of the differences between their media and older forms of journalistic media. It also shows how they believed that these differences were a proper justification for remapping the boundaries of acceptable journalistic behavior, such as using entertainment-style devices like thematic organization, personality, and intimacy in journalism programming.

CONCLUSIONS

Because television news was invented alongside other types of television programs, it was influenced by them. The rhetoric examined here shows that this disturbed many who were familiar with the responsibilities of journalism; they saw the blurring of news/entertainment distinctions as a threat to the cultural authority of journalism. Another way they expressed this was by distinguishing the differences between traditional journalism and television journalism. Some were not disturbed by the blurring of boundaries between traditional journalism, television journalism, and television entertainment at all; they saw television journalism as a hybrid form of journalism that could freely adopt practices and values to which it was suited.

Many conceived of television journalism as a hybrid that, because of its cultural location adjacent to entertainment, was justified in allowing itself to appear related to entertainment. Figure 3.1 is a graphic representation of this kind of conception of the spatial relationships between traditional journalism, television journalism, and entertainment.

Figure 3.1 Apparent Perception of the Cultural Space of Television Journalism

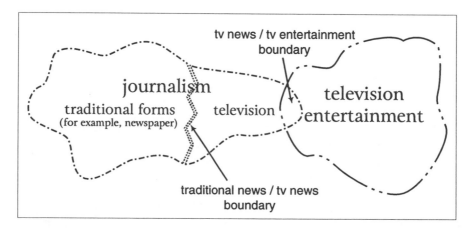

Figure 3.1 is an attempt to visually illustrate several themes discovered in the rhetoric analyzed here:

1. The television journalism/television entertainment boundary is of a different nature than the traditional journalism/television journalism boundary.
2. The cultural space of these institutions can be amorphous at times, and other times well-defined.
3. The factors that distinguish television news from traditional journalism are often different from the factors that distinguish it from television entertainment.

The spatial associations in Figure 3.1 also point to a recurring theme: On a news-entertainment continuum, television news is thought to be located somewhere between traditional news and television entertainment. These two boundaries are described through rhetoric that highlights their unique characteristics and offers clues about how they are related. For example, many critics emphasize one boundary while at the same time implying that the other boundary is indistinct or nonexistent. Others argue that television journalism is separate—distinct—from traditional forms of journalism and from television entertainment.

Television adopted the organizational and economic structures of radio, which allowed strong advertiser influence and which left television journalists near the bottom of the organizational hierarchy of the television industry. Advertisers favored mass appeal programming that consisted primarily of light entertainment. Television journalists felt strong pressure to make television news light and entertaining as well— to blur the epistemological and methodological differences between news and entertainment—and this translated into brief, superficial news programs that did not raise controversial issues and that depended on pacing, spontaneity, exciting visual action, intimacy, and strong personalities to attract audiences. Many argued that these audiences were passive consumers, from the lower socioeconomic classes, and television news programs were designed to serve this group and to keep audiences passive (that is, from turning the channel). Television organizations viewed news departments as a necessary function—a price they paid for their government franchises for a slice of the electromagnetic spectrum. Early television journalists were reluctant recruits from radio and newsreels, and they often followed the lead of newspapers and wire services, abdicating their news function as agenda setters. Newspaper journalists disliked television journalism because of professional jealousies and fear of losing jurisdiction over the news. They attempted to demarcate the boundary between television journalism and their more traditional version of journalism by noting the different levels of professional expertise—an organizational difference. Television journalists also sought to distinguish their work from that of more traditional journalism by adopting unique methods such as introducing personality, organizing a day's news around a particular theme, and sequencing stories in a particular dramatic order.

Journalists believed that the boundaries between television news and entertainment often became blurred in the early days of television, but they also believed that certain dominant personalities like Edward R. Murrow were able to sharpen the boundaries, if only temporarily.

Mission Impossible?
When Government Tries to Map
the Boundaries of Journalism

> With the press as the sole arbiter of its own defense, news-worthiness is defined descriptively, not normatively, and the judiciary is left with a strictly empirical and hopelessly tautological view of the newsmaking process: news is whatever journalists say it is.
>
> —Theodore Glasser
> "Resolving the Press-Privacy Conflict"

INTRODUCTION

This chapter is an examination of a governmental threat to the cultural authority of journalism, and responses to it by journalists. The threat here was to the autonomy of journalists who defend their authority to delineate the boundaries of the cultural space of journalism. They define this space in such specific areas as the constitutive elements of legitimate journalism content and practices, and in more general terms such as the role of journalism in society. Like other fields that are more widely recognized as professions, journalism has long practiced autonomous self-definition—a boundary-making exercise (Merrill, 1974). In the episodes examined in this chapter, outsiders—legislators and government regulators—told journalists what qualifies and does not qualify as journalism. This raised the ire of the journalism community. It is a classic case of boundary-work rhetoric, a "rhetorical game of inclusion and exclusion in which agonistic parties do their best to justify their cultural map for audiences whose support, power, or influence they seek to enroll" (Gieryn, 1995, p. 406).

In 1959, the Federal Communications Commission—a federal regulatory agency—was directed by Congress to define "bona fide news" programs, a definition broadcast journalists were to follow to be excluded from certain equal-time regulations. In the making of these regulations and in subsequent decisions made by the FCC, the government discovered the difficulty and danger in defining legitimate news and journalism.

Andrew Abbott (1988), in his examination of the process of professions defining their professional jurisdictions, says legal settings offer the clearest and most precise rhetorical maneuvers in boundary work, whereas workplace definitions are the least precise (pp. 62–68). The rhetoric contained in legal decisions is carefully crafted to advance particular arguments and to avoid ambiguity. These contests for legally sanctioned jurisdiction occur within legislative, regulatory, and judicial institutions (Abbott, 1988, pp. 62–63). In the jurisdictional disputes examined here, only the legislative and regulatory branches participated.[1] Governmental agencies and their workers—lawmakers, and administrative regulators—grappled with the delicate task of defining the essences and, therefore, the jurisdictions and proper social roles of journalism. These attempts at legal definition are an important site for this project because they highlight how outsiders to the institution of journalism perceive the differences between journalism and other types of mass communication. I focus specifically on television, where programs such as entertaining talk shows and panel discussions are considered by some to be legitimate journalistic enterprises, yet considered by others to be entertainment. I show that legislators and government regulators discovered that it is extremely difficult—and perhaps politically dangerous—to even attempt to define "legitimate" news programs (journalism), news content (newsworthiness) and news producers (journalists). In the end, this "very knotty problem," as Rep. Oren Harris of Arkansas described it in 1959 (*Congressional Record 105*, Sept. 2, 1959, p. 17778), was passed—over a period of 33 years—like a political hot potato from one level of government to another, until finally it was essentially declared unsolvable, and journalists and other mass communicators were finally allowed to define themselves, their jurisdictions, and their work.

This chapter chronologically follows the issue of legal definitions of "bona fide" broadcast news as it was worked out in two different governmental arenas: from the legislative—when Congress first wrote the exemptions to Section 315; to the administrative and regulatory applications of the law by the FCC—as they examined the boundaries of journalism within the context of Section 315. Within each of these arenas, specific episodes of boundary-work rhetoric are examined to see how different aspects of the cultural space of journalism were cited by authors wishing to promote particular definitions to serve their interests. As Gieryn notes, boundaries are local, episodic, contextually contingent, and continuously renegotiated according to the terms of the particular dispute (Gieryn, 1995, p. 405). In the episodes examined here, I show how journalism boundary-defining arguments that worked at one time and place became useless later on.

LEADING UP TO THE *LAR DALY* DECISION

The Communications Act of 1934, which guides the regulation of the radio spectrum, contains a section designed to make sure that political candidates have equal opportunity to "use" the facilities of radio and television stations. This is Section 315, known as the "equal-time" or "equal-opportunities" provisions. The stated reasons for these provisions are the same given for many of the special regulations on radio and television: The airwaves "belong" to the public, and in economic terms are a scarce resource (only so many radio or TV stations can operate in a given area). Station licensees, therefore, are required to operate in the public interest—which means in this case, they should allow a variety of political views to be heard. Because networks own stations, they are bound by the same rules in their network programming. Section 315 states that if a broadcaster lets a "qualified political candidate" make a "use" of its facilities—letting him or her appear on camera or before a microphone—then the station must also allow opposing candidates the same opportunity. In practice, the provisions came to mean that a "use" by a political candidate triggered an obligation on the part of the broadcaster to provide equal time to any opposing candidates. Congress expected the FCC to write the specific rules regarding the equal-time provision, and they expected routine news appearances by candidates to be exempted—to not be considered a "use." During U.S. Senate debate in 1926 concerning inclusion of the equal-time provision as an amendment to the Radio Act of 1927 (precursor to the Communications Act of 1934), Sen. Dill of Washington, manager of the legislation in the Senate, was asked by Sen. Fess of Ohio why specific situations—such as when politicians speak in public about newsworthy issues—were not specifically exempted from the provisions within the language of the equal-time legislation. Sen. Dill offered this explanation: "The commission shall make rules and regulations to carry out the provision. It seemed to me to be better to allow the commission to make rules and regulations governing such questions as the Senator has raised rather than to attempt to go into the matter in the bill" (*Congressional Record 67*, July 1, 1926, p. 12503). Congress trusted the Federal Radio Commission, which later became the Federal Communications Commission, to make specific rules that would carry out its wishes. Congress was also in a hurry. The legislative history shows that the bill was hurried through the Senate before the end of the session for the summer recess (*Congressional Record 67*, July 1, 1926, p. 12505). The amendment was passed in the Congress but was vetoed by pocket veto by President Coolidge.

Sen. Dill's response reflected the feeling in Congress that in the FRC they were creating an expert agency of regulators who were much better qualified to iron out the details of Congress's wishes. The legislation that replaced the FRC with the FCC, The Communications Act of 1934, was very similar to the earlier statutes, though the provisions were renumbered and rearranged, and the FCC was given regulatory control over a wider range of electronic communications areas. And this time, the equal-time provision *was* included—as Section 315(a). The text of §315(a):

If any licensee shall permit any person who is a legally qualified candidate for any public office to use a broadcasting station, he shall afford equal opportunities to all other such candidates for that office in the use of such broadcasting station: Provided, that such licensee shall have no power of censorship over the material broadcast under the provisions of this section. No obligation is hereby imposed upon any licensee to allow the use of its station by any such candidate.

For many years afterward, Congress did not make any revisions to the Equal Time provisions of the 1934 act. They left it up to the FCC to decide when a "use" of a station by a candidate occurred, letting them examine the merits of individual cases when people complained to the FCC of unfairness.

Before 1959, there were no stated exceptions to Section 315, but the Federal Communications Commission, the agency in charge of interpreting these regulations, had always held that a "use" of facilities that would trigger the provisions was only one in which the candidate had initiated the broadcast. Some examples are when a candidate pays for time to present a campaign message, or when a partisan station gives a candidate free reign to campaign on the air. In 1957 the FCC first directly addressed the question of whether news items about candidates were exempt from the equal-time provision. Allen H. Blondy, a candidate for Common Pleas Court judge in Detroit, complained to the FCC that one of his opponents, Elvin Davenport, was briefly shown and mentioned in news broadcasts on television station WWJ in Detroit. The broadcasts briefly showed Davenport with a group of other judges being sworn in, and identified him by name. Blondy thought this was unfair, so he asked for equal time from the station and was turned down. He complained to the FCC, which wrote back and told him that the news broadcasts about his opponent were not covered by the provision for several reasons:

There is no evidence before us that Mr. Davenport in any manner or form directly or indirectly initiated or requested either filming of the ceremony or its presentation by the station, or that the broadcast was more than a routine news broadcast by Station WWJ-TV in the exercise of its judgment as to newsworthy events. . . .

In our opinion . . . WWJ-TV did not permit [a "use" of its facilities] by showing and referring to Mr. Davenport in its routine newscasts. (*Letter to Allen H. Blondy*, 1957, p. 1200)

In this statement, it is clear that the FCC considered it essential for a candidate to have some part in initiating the television coverage, or for the coverage to be other than "routine news" coverage controlled by the news judgment of journalists. They implied a level of trust in the judgment of broadcast journalists to decide for themselves when something is newsworthy, saying that the equal-time provision would not be used to interfere with news judgments by qualified professionals. By highlighting the *independent judgment* of the broadcaster, the FCC drew an epistemological boundary—arguing that news is a different kind of knowledge than the politically-motivated, non-independent kind (Park, 1940).

In 1959, however, the FCC reversed course when a man named Lar Daly, running for mayor of Chicago, complained to the FCC that he had not been given equal opportunities because his opponents, Democratic candidate incumbent Mayor Richard J. Daley and Republican candidate Timothy P. Sheehan, were shown on television news reports—starting their mayoral campaigns, and participating in other televised events such as the March of Dimes campaign and greeting the president of Argentina, who was visiting Chicago. Lar Daly claimed that the television stations, in devoting this time to news reports about the other candidates and in denying equal time to him, violated Section 315. The FCC agreed, and on February 19, 1959, told the television stations to give Daly an equal amount of time before the scheduled election, February 24, 1959 (*Columbia Broadcasting*, 1959). Here the FCC seemed to reverse course, saying in effect that all mass communications about political candidates—including news—is the same, requiring balancing time for opponents. They rejected their previous ruling that indicated that special treatment should be accorded the "independent news judgment" of journalists. The decision constituted a denial of any boundaries between news and other forms of political mass communication.

The *Lar Daly* decision was termed "ridiculous" by all levels of government officials and journalists—because they feared it would force a virtual blackout of all politicians from broadcast news.[2] Politicians and broadcasters argued that television and radio stations could not afford to supply free time to all other candidates every time they showed the newsworthy happenings of one candidate. Such a decision, they argued, would tend to "dry-up" all news coverage of politicians. One of the interesting aspects about the case was that Lar Daly was not a serious candidate. He had entered many, many political races—for mayor, for Congress, and for president. In this particular mayoral race, he was on both the Democratic and Republican primary ballots. He was known as a "perennial" candidate, not a serious candidate, and one who would probably never be elected to any office. Often he dressed in a red, white, and blue stars and stripes Uncle Sam outfit and called himself Lar "America First" Daly. The fact that broadcast journalists were forced to give valuable airtime to Daly—who was considered a clown by many—angered the journalism community.

Even newspaper journalists came to the defense of their competitors in broadcast journalism. Many editorials were written around the country condemning the *Lar Daly* decision. During consideration of the House subcommittee report, Rep. William H. Avery (Kan.) noted that the committee had on file 189 editorials supporting the proposed exemptions to Section 315 (*Congressional Record 105*, 1959, p. 16225). The major point argued by these print journalists was that the *Lar Daly* decision "removes from the newscaster his *[sic]* right to news judgment" ("News is News," 1959). The independent judgment of journalists was denied—an intolerable situation for a group that cherishes autonomy.

LEGISLATION TO "CORRECT" THE *LAR DALY* SITUATION

Shortly after the *Lar Daly* decision was announced, Congress set out to correct this "ridiculous" interpretation by writing a law to stipulate that news broadcasts were exempt from Section 315. Congressional committees in both the House and Senate spent several weeks in the summer and fall of 1959 debating these provisions and, in the process, discovered the difficulty of defining "news."

Legislative records indicate that senators, during hearings on proposed legislation to correct the *Lar Daly* decision, discovered that news can include a lot of different things (*Political Broadcasting*, 1959, pp. 217–219). In particular, they focused on descriptions of different program formats. For example, the first drafts of legislation in the Senate contained the words "newscasts and special events." Later versions dropped the term "special events" and added terms such as "news interviews," "news documentaries," "panel discussions," "debates," and "news events" such as political conventions, etc. During the hearings in the House of Representatives, FCC Commissioner John S. Cross asked Congress to be precise in the language of their legislation:

If the Congress should decide to exempt newscasts, I urge that it say so in the most direct and foolproof language it can command.

If it decides to go further and exempt other programs of a similar nature, such as news interviews, news commentaries, news documentaries, on-the-spot coverage of newsworthy events, panel discussions, et cetera, I also urge that it specifically name such exempt-type programs and define them or direct the Commission to do this by rule. (*Political Broadcasts*, 1959, p. 105)

To many broadcasters, the proposed exemptions were not enough; they wanted Section 315 repealed altogether. Rex Howell, president of KREX-AM, FM, and TV, Grand Junction, Colorado, called Section 315 "the galling yoke which historically has prevented broadcasting from attaining equal status with the press. . . . We should take steps at once to insure the full freedom of the press to radio and television in exactly the same measure as is accorded to the fourth estate" (*Political Broadcasting*, 1959, pp. 222–223). Howell was one of many in the industry who believed the equal-time statute was an infringement of the journalistic autonomy of broadcast journalism. The statute put a spotlight on the unequal legal status of print and broadcast journalism.

Congress agreed that the *Lar Daly* standard stifles the free flow of information to the citizens. Rep. Paul G. Rogers from Florida said in a prepared statement to the House subcommittee:

Mr. Speaker, this [Lar Daly] interpretation of section 315 not only does violence to a basic right long enjoyed by the different communication media but also serves to stifle the fine efforts put forth by our broadcasting industry to help keep our citizens informed.

If the coverage of section 315 is extended to include regular newscasts, it is entirely conceivable that such an interpretation, if carried to its logical conclusion, might result in unwarranted Federal control over the material content of news programs. In effect, this is a situation in which the Federal Government has substituted its judgment of what is properly the subject of a newscast for the considered, good-faith judgment of radio and television news staffs. (*Political Broadcasts*, 1959, p. 21)

Similar arguments were made at numerous times during the Senate hearings—that broadcast journalists should be allowed to exercise their independent professional judgments as to what constitutes news (*Political Broadcasting*, 1959, pp. 58, 60, 80, 82, 124, 132, 196, 240–242). It bothered journalists that the responsibility of broadcasters was not assumed—the law assumes that broadcasters are irresponsible

and therefore need Congress to tell them what is fair and objective reporting. The Senate was reluctant to concede the professional judgment of journalists, simply because they did not trust the fairness of
broadcast journalists—perhaps from their own personal experiences
during campaigns. For instance, Rep. John. E. Moss (Calif.) said, "I am
not so naive as to believe we can ever legislate complete fairness"
(*Congressional Record 105*, August 18, 1959, p. 16243). Dr. Frank
Stanton, president of CBS, told the senators during the hearings:

> As I sat in the room this morning, Senator Pastore, and listened to the ex-
> change between you and some of the other witnesses, I had a rather sick feeling
> in the pit of my stomach, because I felt that you really didn't trust broadcasters
> to be honorable men and responsible people. I think you are nervous about
> whether or not we will be fair at the local level. . . .
>   Over the 30 years that we thought we had freedom for newscasts in the
> treatment of campaign news and putting politicians or candidates on the pro-
> grams, no one has ever thrown the book at us for being unfair in those periods.
> (*Political Broadcasting*, 1959, pp 106–107)

Stanton's rhetoric supplies another link in the epistemological fence
between journalism and other forms of political communication,
namely, fairness and impartiality. News is expected to be fair and impartial, whereas other kinds of political communication can be partisan
and biased and, therefore, are a different kind of information.
Lawmakers, however, did not seem to share Stanton's view that fairness was a distinguishing element of broadcast journalism.

As they grappled with the legislation, it became clear to the legislators that decisions about what is newsworthy and what is not newsworthy are decisions that only journalists are capable of making. This
bothered many. Lar Daly, for instance, came to the Senate hearings
and told the committee that broadcast journalists should not have "the
right to determine who is and who is not newsworthy" (*Political
Broadcasting*, 1959, p. 162). Senator Pastore of Rhode Island, manager
of the legislation, tried to explain to Daly why news judgment belongs
to journalists:

> We are at the mercy of these boys at the press table. . . . Sometimes we think
> what we say and what we do is so important it ought to be on the front page.
> Well, of course, a reporter or an editor, or a publisher doesn't feel that way. So
> I quite agree with you that to a large extent they are the determiners of what is
> news and what is not news. . . . But on the other hand, who is going to decide
> what is newsworthy and what is not, unless you leave it to them? (*Political
> Broadcasting*, 1959, p. 160)

In the legislation itself, however, the legislators were forced to try to pin down exactly what they felt constituted news, and once again they were faced with difficulties. An exchange between Rep. John E. Moss of California, and John C. Doerfer, Chairman of the FCC, highlights this concern, and points out the fact that everyone has a different definition of news:

MR. MOSS: How do we define news programs, news reports, news commentaries?

MR. DOERFER: I would not have too much trouble, but I can conceive of where another commissioner and I may have some difficulty and then when you multiply that and increase it to seven [the number of FCC commissioners], you might have some difficulty.

But I do think that over a period of years perhaps there would evolve some definition, some standards which today I just cannot supply. (*Political Broadcasts*, 1959, p. 62)

Doerfer wanted Congress to delegate the authority to the FCC to work out a definition of news through the process of *stare decisis*— common law through precedent. This evolutionary approach to defining news would allow the FCC to make adjustments as popular tastes and the professional practices of journalists evolve. Doerfer said substantially the same thing during the Senate hearings:

You are going to have [problems] trying to write standards as to what constitutes newscasting and how to draw the line, and you are going to have a problem trying to administer it. . . . I doubt very much whether the Commission could, before it had experience, write a standard or a definition of what constitutes pure newscast which would be acceptable to everybody . . . I think that eventually a definition, a well understood definition, and a reasonable one, and one that is acceptable will develop by a case-by-case administration. I don't think you can write it beforehand. (*Political Broadcasting*, 1959, pp. 84, 92)

Doerfer suggested that Congress trust broadcasters to police their own ranks and let them define news themselves: "I think in attempting to administer any of these very elusive standards, hard to define standards, it would be far better to entrust those who are skilled in the gathering and dissemination of news. I think it improper to assume beforehand. . . . that they are going to abuse it" (*Political Broadcasting*, 1959, p. 85). Doerfer, by the way, also advocated a complete repeal of Section 315, though the majority of the FCC commissioners did not share this opinion.

Ralph Renick, president of the Radio-Television News Directors Association, the major professional broadcast journalism association, warned the House panel not to let the FCC define legitimate news or journalism:

Mr. Chairman, we believe that this Federal agency is entering a very delicate and potentially dangerous area when it attempts to set itself up as a judge and jury over the worth of newscasts.

We think such a procedure and the threat of recriminatory action would lead to a form of censorship which would discourage radio and TV broadcasters from exercising their full responsibility in calling the shots as their news directors see them in presenting news on the air, as we have been incidentally doing up to now. . . .

We think it would be folly to attempt a definition of news programs and to leave it to the FCC to decide whether the news is being presented in the best manner possible. (*Political Broadcasts*, 1959, pp 158–159)

Renick wanted the Congress to repeal Section 315 altogether because it took the right of self-definition away from broadcast journalists and because it placed the FCC in the uncomfortable position of having to weigh the relative merits of different news programs—something he believed his organization should do by policing its ranks. In other words, Renick wanted the cultural authority to define journalism and journalism jurisdictions to remain in journalists' hands. It is not a huge leap of logic to understand Renick's position: The methods of journalism include the process of determining newsworthiness of a particular story. Definitions of news-work, that is, journalism, therefore, should also remain in the hands of journalists.

Frederick W. Ford, a commissioner of the FCC, was chosen to deliver the majority opinion of the commissioners at the House hearings on the proposed amendments and to offer the FCC's preferred version of the legislation. During one exchange between Ford and Rep. John B. Bennett of Michigan, Ford advanced the idea that a strict definition of news by Congress or the FCC might not be a good idea, that it should be left to broadcast journalists:

MR. BENNETT: What do you mean by the word "newscast"? What is a newscast?

MR. FORD: To me, and what I have intended by this word is a straight factual report of the news without interjecting opinion or interpretation on the part of the person delivering the news. . . .

Today as we see a newscast we may see the broadcaster himself describing an event and then he will flash a film clip and the candidate may say something or an individual may say something, and so it goes.

To legislate that this is a definition, that it is the only way that

> news can be presented, is to stifle the broadcasting industry and I
> would regret to see that happen. (*Political Broadcasts*, 1959, p. 98)

Ford said news does not include opinion or interpretive commentary, reinforcing the idea that news is an objective and strictly factual form of information—an epistemological distinction. But he was reluctant to see this legislated as a definition.

In the Senate report on the legislation submitted by Sen. Pastore, it is clear that senators found it very difficult to define the many varieties of news programs. Instead, they proposed to do what Commissioner Doerfer asked for—to allow the FCC to work this out on a case-by-case basis:

It is difficult to define with precision what is a newscast, news interview, news documentary, or on-the-spot coverage of news event or panel discussion. That is why the committee in adopting the language of the proposed legislation carefully gave the Federal Communications Commission full flexibility and complete discretion to examine the facts in each complaint which may be filed with the commission. . . .

The Congress created the Federal Communications Commission as an expert agency to administer the Communications Act of 1934. As experts in the field of radio and television, the Commission has gained a workable knowledge of the type of programs offered by the broadcasters in the field of news, and related fields. Based on this knowledge and other information that it is in a position to develop, the Commission can set down some definite guidelines through rules and regulations and wherever possible by interpretations. (*Equal-Time*, 1959, p. 12)

Pastore seemed to be saying that Congress was too removed from journalism to make these kinds of distinctions and that the FCC, an "expert agency," was more acquainted to the inner workings of journalism, and thus more qualified to make them.

On September 2 the House considered the conference committee report. During this discussion it was noted that the legislators decided that to be called a "bona fide newscast" meant that it was a regularly scheduled program, and that it was controlled and produced solely by broadcasters, exercising their professional news judgment (for example, remarks of Rep. Oren Harris [Ark.], *Congressional Record 105*, 1959, pp. 17778, 17781). The House wanted to make sure that partisan stations did not put together special programs featuring one candidate and then try to say that the specials were news. Thus, temporal consistency and autonomous journalistic control were the only defining characteristics that Congress recognized in legitimate broadcast journalism. They were reluctant to get any more specific.

Another concern of the legislators was that the terms "panel discussions" and "news documentaries" left the exemption wide open to abuse, so they struck these terms from the list of exempt types of programs in the final version of the bill. They emphasized that they intended programs such as *Meet the Press* and *Face the Nation* to continue to enjoy exempt status as news programs under the other categories exempted—"bona fide newscasts," or "on-the-spot coverage of news events." Although they felt they understood which kinds of programs were news, they found it difficult to describe or define the essential characteristics of these programs. Instead, they found it easier to give examples of acceptable news programs. It was a case of, "I can't tell you exactly what news is, but I know it when I see it."

Although Congress wanted to give broadcast journalists the right to exercise their "bona fide" news judgment, they also feared the consequences of giving them too little oversight. This fear was allayed somewhat by the delegation of responsibility to the FCC to be vigilant in keeping an eye on broadcasters and to refine the definitions of legitimate news through decisions and regulations on a case-by-case basis. In addition, Congress wrote into the legislation a provision threatening review of the legislation if they sensed abuse of the exemptions. Part 2 of the legislation contained the provision: "The Congress declares its intention to reexamine from time to time the amendment . . . to ascertain whether such amendment has proved to be effective and practicable" (*Congressional Record 105*, 1959, p. 17777).

On September 3, the Senate considered the conference committee bill. Senator Hugh Scott, one of the subcommittee members who worked on the legislation, explained that the difficulty of defining news required the retention of oversight by Congress:

We looked up the definition of "news," Mr. President, and one of the definitions of "news" is, "of current interest." This is a very broad definition, and therefore there remains the necessity, in our opinion, for the protection of the public by retaining supervision over the operation of this new addition to the act. This is done very wisely in section 2, where Congress declares its intentions to reexamine these provisions of the act. (*Congressional Record 105*, 1959, p. 17832)

In other words, because Congress found it impossible to precisely define news, it decided to let the FCC do it instead on a case-by-case basis, and then to review those decisions to see if the FCC could accomplish what Congress could not. Instead of leaving it to broadcast journalists, Congress decided that news is whatever the FCC says it is . . . but perhaps subject to review. By early September a conference committee bill—a compromise between the House and Senate versions—was sent to President Eisenhower for signing, which he did.

The bottom line of this legislation: News programs were now explicitly exempted from the equal opportunities provision, but the legislators had passed the buck down to the FCC—asking them to define the characteristics of "bona fide" news broadcasts. John Doerfer, chairman of the FCC, had asked for this authority, and legislators seemed to agree that the FCC was the best place for these definitions to be made. Congress had given some guidance by mentioning a few example programs and by noting the aspects of temporal consistency and autonomous journalistic control. But they genuinely struggled with these definitions and ultimately decided that the FCC was better equipped to handle them. Rhetoric contained in subsequent rulings by the FCC showed that the process of writing these definitions was not an easy task; the FCC gradually broadened the definitions of news over the next 33 years.

FCC'S DEFINITION OF NEWS

By the mid-1970s, the FCC had really discovered the difficulty of defining legitimate news programs, particularly when the programs were other than nightly newscasts—a more easily distinguishable form (for example, *Citizens for Reagan*, 1976; *Davis for Congress*, 1976; *National Broadcasting*, 1976). For instance, in 1976, the FCC restated its criteria for determining whether a television interview program is a "bona fide news interview" program:

[W]here a program is and has been regularly scheduled for an appreciable period of time, follows the usual program format, which along with content and production, is under the control of the station and features individuals who have been chosen to appear on the program on the basis of their newsworthiness, that program would be deemed to constitute a bona fide news interview program. (*Davis for Congress*, 1976, p. 1604)

If a program "looks and feels" like one of the well-established news interview programs, e.g, *Meet the Press*, etc., then it must be a bona fide news interview program. Congress expressly mentioned several weekly news interview programs during the 1959 debates on the news exemptions to Section 315, such as *Meet the Press*, *Face the Nation*, and *Youth Wants to Know* (*Congressional Record 105*, 1959, pp. 17779, 17829). Many of the subsequent decisions by the FCC also mentioned the same programs and often used these programs as yardsticks for other news interview programs where requests for equal time were in dispute. These specific examples of programs are probably what are referred to in the FCC's 1976 *Davis* decision just quoted with the words "the usual program format." If a program looked and sounded like *Meet the*

Press or *Face the Nation*, it would probably not trigger a complaint. But in the *Davis* case, the program, called *Panorama*, was a daily, not weekly, and was produced by a local station, not a network. The petitioner in *Davis* argued that *Panorama* was not a news program but was "merely a 'talk program'" (*Davis for Congress*, 1976, p. 1605). The FCC disagreed, saying that the program was regularly scheduled and had a consistent day-to-day format that consisted of an emphasis on "news-oriented interviews which are conducted by 'full-time newsman' Maury Povich, who, along with other members of the Panorama staff, selects guests on the basis of their newsworthiness" (*Davis for Congress*, 1976, p. 1605). With the enumeration of these specific characteristics, the FCC began to define the distinctive characteristics of "news interview" programs: temporal consistency; format consistency; autonomous journalistic control; and newsworthiness. The first two of these characteristics could be described as being descriptors along a methodological dimension. Autonomous journalistic control is linked to the idea that journalism is a specific kind of political knowledge (impartial and objective) designed for a specific function (to inform). It is a descriptor, therefore, along epistemological and functional dimensions. The final characteristic, "newsworthiness," is an epistemological characteristic. But it was a problem to implement because it required regulators to "do journalism"—that is, to make decisions about newsworthiness.

Later in 1976, the FCC ruled that a similar program, NBC's *Tomorrow*, was not a bona fide news interview program. In this case, the Socialist Worker's Party (SWP) asked the FCC to tell NBC to give their candidate equal time on *Tomorrow* because the program had interviewed another presidential candidate. SWP argued that *Tomorrow* was similar to "*Tonight* and the *Merv Griffin Show*, which it characterized as variety and talk shows" (*National Broadcasting*, 1976, p. 944). The FCC essentially agreed, saying:

Although there is no dispute that Tomorrow has been regularly scheduled for a period of time and is under the control of NBC, the information in TV Guide supplied by SWP clearly reveals that while some interviews are newsworthy, many are not. Interviewees, as a matter of course, are not selected on the basis of their "public significance or their newsworthiness," i.e. strippers, dream analysts, etc. Thus, while we do not believe it is determinative that Tomorrow includes other types of formats, what is vital and what distinguishes it from Today, 60 Minutes and NET Journal is the fact that its interview format, although obviously often used, cannot be said to constitute a regularly used <u>news</u> interview format. . . . We cannot accept the view that the intermittent appearances of public officials and political candidates indicates that a program is a news interview program. (*National Broadcasting*, 1976, pp. 950–951)

The FCC felt that in order to qualify for a news interview program exemption, that is, to be within the boundaries of journalism, a program must be "newsy" throughout, without an emphasis on entertainment. Interestingly, it relied on program descriptions in *TV Guide* to make its newsworthiness distinctions. It did not consider that the interviews on *Tomorrow* were, as NBC argued, "conducted by Tom Snyder, an experienced journalist employed by NBC News" (*National Broadcasting*, 1976, p. 944). Instead, they seemed more concerned about the newsworthiness of the people Snyder interviewed. The FCC drew an epistemological boundary between the content of entertainment and news programs: If a journalist interviewed people who were not particularly newsworthy—in the FCC's judgment—then the content of the program was entertainment, not journalism. They implied a functional difference between the two types of programs: Entertainment programs entertain, news programs inform—and the blurring of these functions causes the entire program to become entertainment.

In 1981, producers of the *Donahue* show petitioned the FCC to get a news interview program exemption from the equal-time rule. The FCC did not allow it, noting that:

The regular opportunity for audience members to interject personal comments, in addition to the interjection of Mr. Donahue's own comments during the interviewing process, takes the format far from that of programs which Congress noted and which involve a question and answer format such as "Meet the Press," "Face the Nation," and "Youth Wants to Know." (*Multimedia*, 1981, p. 1274)

The FCC evidently felt that the interjecting of personal comments is foreign to news, which is supposed to be an impartial and objective pursuit. This underscores their belief that personal commentary is not impartial, whereas news is fact-based and objective, an epistemological difference. The FCC also did not like the methodology used by Donahue: Members of the audience chosen to ask questions were chosen randomly, and therefore were not chosen based on Phil Donahue's independent "journalistic judgment" (*Multimedia*, 1981, p. 1277). They worried that audience members could ask questions designed to advance the candidacy of a politician being interviewed. The FCC's *Donahue* decision also noted that many of the subjects covered in the program were, in the opinion of the commission, not newsworthy.

Three of the seven FCC commissioners—Joseph R. Fogarty, James H. Quello, and Abbott Washburn—dissented from the decision, preferring the stance that *Donahue* is a bona fide news interview program, even though they agreed that its format was "unconventional."

Commissioner Abbott Washburn wrote a dissenting opinion in which he said he is an avid fan of the *Donahue* program, and in his opinion, many of the segments that the Media Bureau, a fact-finding arm of the FCC, decided were not newsworthy were, in fact, very newsworthy. He cited programs that dealt with inflation, in vitro fertilization, the quality of network television, rights of the mentally ill, and a program called "The IRS and You" (*Multimedia*, 1981, pp. 1279–1280). Washburn noted that Phil Donahue has solid journalism credentials and that Congress left the 1959 amendment general to allow for unconventional program formats:

Mr. Donahue is a broadcast journalist. He is not [an] entertainer like Johnny Carson. He started in Dayton, Ohio eighteen years ago. He has been dealing with news and issues all that time. I think the staff's requirement that these shows must have a strict Question-Answer format is too rigid a reading of what Congress intended. The language of the statute cited "Meet the Press" and "Face the Nation" simply as illustrative examples of news-related programs. The legislators were not expecting the FCC to look at each program and say it's exactly like "Meet the Press" or it *has* to have a Q&A format. (*Multimedia*, 1981, p. 1280)

Later in 1981, the FCC started to loosen its restrictive standards of what is "bona fide news." That year, President Reagan appointed Mark Fowler to chair the FCC. Fowler, who began his broadcasting career as a Florida disc jockey, was now a broadcasting lawyer who had developed a distaste for restrictive broadcast regulations and was an outspoken opponent of the equal-time rule and other measures regulating the content of broadcasting. A *U.S. News and World Report* article said, "He calls broadcasting regulators censors who 'have no place in a democratic, free society.' The best regulator, he adds, is the dial on the television set. 'Good' programming, by Fowler's lights, is what viewers want to see" ("A look at FCC's Fowler," 1985, p. 66). Instead of calling for broadcast deregulation, Fowler wanted "un-regulation" (Flannery, 1995, p. 199), and in fact targeted Section 315 for repeal ("Fowler's First Year," 1982, pp. 47–48). He was more interested in letting market forces rule than in constructing boundaries between different types of broadcast programming.

In a 1983 decision, after some major personnel changes within the commission,[3] the FCC advocated a new stance on the Section 315 exemptions more consistent with Fowler's goal of "unregulation":

A reading of the legislative history and court decisions makes it clear that Congress has conferred upon the Commission wide discretion in interpreting and applying the Section 315 exemptions. We believe the Commission should exercise that discretion by broadening its interpretation of Section 315(a)(4), thereby affording broadcasters greater flexibility in their news programming determinations and promoting political education of viewers and listeners. (*In re Henry Geller*, 1983, p. 1255)

In 1984, Multimedia again petitioned the FCC to designate *Donahue* a bona fide news interview program within the meaning of the Section 315 exemptions. This time it was successful, due, no doubt, to those personnel changes within the FCC.

The 1984 *Donahue* ruling notes that the FCC believed that they were in error in their 1981 *Donahue* decision when they ruled that Mr. Donahue was not in control of the program when he let random audience members ask questions (*Multimedia*, 1984, p. 146). They note that Mr. Donahue's approach to interviewing is unique and innovative and that such innovative formats should not be discouraged just because they are unlike "programs mentioned by Congress over twenty-five years ago" (*Multimedia*, 1984, p. 146). The ruling also notes:

An exhaustive review of the legislative history does not explain how Congress would define news. Nor are currently accepted definitions of news conclusive. However, while Congress did not specifically define news for purposes of the exemptions, it is clear that in enacting the exemptions Congress envisioned increased news coverage of the political process. It would seem elemental that Congress contemplated interviews with elected officials and candidates for elected office as newsworthy subject matter. (*Multimedia*, 1984, p. 147)

Considering the jurisdictional implications of the ruling regarding the FCC's perception of the boundaries of journalism, the journalism community was relatively silent on the *Donahue* rulings. *Donahue's* parent company was, after all, an entertainment company. The few articles that were written about the ruling did not comment on the jurisdictional implications of *Donahue* being designated a "news" program and dealt almost exclusively with the facts of the case and the commentary contained within the ruling. An article in *Broadcasting*, the premiere industry news weekly, briefly quoted Mr. Donahue's reaction to the ruling: "He said he had told the commission the show presents 'more news more often than any other daily syndicated show and that while it presents fashion shows, I hope you don't penalize us for those fashion shows'" ("FCC Grants," 1984). An article in the *New York Times* published the comments of an entertainment executive who seemed to imply that Mr. Donahue, in applying for the news designations, was trying to make a metamorphosis from entertainment to news:

Joseph Bleeden of "The Tonight Show" said Johnny Carson had interviewed political candidates but that the commission's ruling did not interest the Carson staff. "This is an entertainment show," Mr. Bleeden said. "It has always been an entertainment show and we have no desire for it to become anything else." (Prial, 1984)

The *Times* reporter, Frank Prial, in seeking comments about the *Donahue* ruling from the Carson show staff, seemed to imply that in his mind the two programs were similar—and that they were entertainment.

Later in 1984, the *Larry King Show*, a syndicated radio broadcast, was also given a bona fide news interview exemption to Section 315, citing the precedent of the 1984 Donahue ruling (*Mutual Broadcasting*, 1984).

In 1987, the FCC relaxed its standards even further, allowing the news interview "segments" of variety (news and entertainment) programs to qualify for the "bona fide news interview" exemption. The agency reasoned that certain parts of CBS's *The Morning Program* were news:

Candidate appearances on the news interview segments of "The Morning Program," a weekday morning news and entertainment program of CBS, are exempt from the equal opportunities rule as "bona fide news interviews." Although numerous other interviews and features presented on the program may be of an entertainment nature with little or no news value, that fact has no bearing on the issue of whether news interview segments are worthy of the Section 315(a)(2) exemption. (*CBS*, 1987)

No longer did a news program have to be "newsy" throughout. The FCC seemed to be saying that its previous notion—that entertainment and news functions must be strictly separated—was out.

A 1988 FCC ruling on the news value of *Entertainment Tonight* and *Entertainment This Week* contained language attempting to define "genuine news value," a term useful for the FCC for determining whether a program is a bona fide news program (*Paramount Pictures*). The rhetoric in this ruling reflects a desire of the FCC to focus on the format and methodology used in the production of the program, and to introduce a new way of dealing with the problem of determinations of newsworthiness.

The principal consideration . . . is whether the format of ET and ETW can be reasonably treated as bona fide newscasts. . . . Such a determination should not be predicated on the subject matter reported on, but rather should be judged on a basis of whether the program reports news of some area of current events. . . . Our approach seeks to avoid any assessment of the relative merit of the subjects reported on by ET and ETW, and indeed, seeks to determine if these programs report about some area of current events, in a manner similar to more traditional newscasts.

There is no indication that either program does anything but report and air commentary concerning current events and stories related to various aspects of the entertainment industry. Paramount indicates that it produces ET and ETW utilizing the same methods and journalistic guidelines typical of traditional newscasting. We also note that, by comparison, the more familiar local and national newscast formats do include news of the entertainment industry, as well as other specialized areas such as business, sports, and religion. (*Paramount Pictures*, 1988, p. 601)

Any discussion of "some area of current events" now qualified as news—so in other words, a show examining practically any topic could now qualify as a bona fide news program. However, also contained in the *ET & ETW* ruling is the implicit endorsement of the notion that a program that uses certain standard journalistic methods deserves special consideration as a bona fide news program. In a footnote, the ruling notes:

The credentialing of ET's news-gathering staff is handled in the same manner as the credentialing of any other news organization. ET news reports are governed by the 'double-source' rule used throughout the journalism field, and an extensive research library is used to crosscheck every statement of fact contained in ET's reports. (p. 600ff)

Thus, by 1987, the FCC had completely retreated from its 1976 *NBC* decision, making it clear that they would no longer rate the relative newsworthiness of the topics covered by a program—the epistemological dimensions of the boundary—and instead would rely on the judgment of journalists to make these choices. The FCC did not want to appear to be telling broadcasters what they can and cannot say in their programming, nor did they want to appear to be partial to certain kinds of news content. They did however, imply that the boundary between news and entertainment could be distinguished through methodological characteristics. Thus, although the commission was reluctant to say which mass-communicated messages deserve classification as news, it *was* prepared to consider whether a program used legitimate journalistic methods, such as verification of facts from multiple sources (the "double-source rule," popularized by Woodward and Bernstein of Watergate fame), and using research libraries to check facts. Interestingly, in 1987, ET and ETW were programs owned and produced by Paramount Pictures Corporation, an entertainment company, and some of the star "anchors" of the shows had little, if any previous experience in journalism. For example, *Entertainment Tonight* anchor Mary Hart's credentials include: actress, singer, and former Miss South Dakota. Anchor John Tesh, however, worked in broadcast journalism for several years before going to *ET* (*Newsmakers 88*, 1989,

p. 172; Steele, 1993). The FCC essentially said that entertainers who use journalistic methods in programs about entertainment become journalists.

In a 1990 ruling, the FCC declared the syndicated nightly tabloid television program *Hard Copy* a "bona fide newscast" (*Paramount Communications*, 1990). In this ruling the FCC made it even clearer that it did not want to weigh the relative merits of the topics covered by a program:

The Commission [in past rulings] has thus specifically declined to evaluate the relative quality or significance of the topics and stories selected for newscast coverage, appropriately relying instead on good faith news judgment. . . . We have no basis for believing that the stories covered by Hard Copy are selected for any reason other than their genuine newsworthiness. (p. 1653)

In other words, without solid evidence to the contrary, the FCC is extremely reluctant to say that a particular program does not use "good faith news judgment" when selecting stories.

A 1991 ruling on the *Sally Jessy Raphael Show* also cited the need to rely on the judgment of broadcasters in determining the newsworthiness of topics covered by their programs. By declining to say that the *Sally Jessy Raphael Show* was not a news program, the FCC implied that "it must be news if they say it is," and granted the producers a "bona fide news interview" exemption to Section 315 (*Multimedia*, 1991).

By January 1992 the FCC had liberalized the Section 315 exemptions even further, ruling that equal time obligations were only triggered when a program "is controlled, sponsored or approved by the candidate" (*Herbert*, 1992). Interestingly, these were the same guidelines held by the FCC before its *Lar Daly* decision, 33 years before.

CONCLUSIONS

Members of Congress found it difficult to define news, though they did note that news programs have a temporal consistency (are regularly scheduled), and must be under autonomous journalistic control. Sensing that this vague definition was insufficient, Congress then decided that the FCC was far more qualified to make these kinds of distinctions because of its close association with broadcasters.

The FCC decided that it could distinguish news programs by examining the methodological, functional, and epistemological characteristics of programs. Once they started comparing the functional and epistemological differences of programs, however, they discovered it to be a difficult task because it required them to act as journalists—they had to make determinations about the functions of news programs in society, and they had to make determinations of newsworthiness. Later, they settled on the idea that methodological characteristics were the best way to distinguish news from other programs.

But a year or so after that, the FCC finally came back to where they started—the agency realized that trying to demarcate news by analyzing what journalists do is impossible, because journalists decide what news is, and journalists alone decide how to do journalism. The way to determine who deserved a bona fide news exemption depended not on what journalists did but on whether politicians were involved in the journalistic process. Defining news turned out to be an impractical matter for those outside of journalism simply because of the socially-constructed nature of news itself. Governmental thinkers attacked this issue with an essentialist sword, determined to penetrate to the essential elements of news and journalism. They discovered this weapon to be of very little use on a moving, amorphous target.

The government ran into difficulty when it could not resist the temptation to generalize on the essential characteristics of all journalism, including the periphery. If they had stuck to the uncontested areas of journalism, they would have had an easier time. But, of course, that is not where jurisdictional disputes occur. All of the boundary disputes examined here (except perhaps the *Lar Daly* case) occurred on the periphery of journalism, and that is why they occurred. This explains the journalistic uproar about the *Lar Daly* case, and the lack thereof in the other cases. Journalists did not like the idea that the government could determine the content of regular news programs when they covered political candidates, but they were conspicuously silent about such restrictions on programs like *Donahue* and *Entertainment Tonight*, programs they would just as soon cede to the entertainment realm. The FCC, however, treated such disputes seriously.

For the most part, the rhetoric examined here was from outsiders to journalism; it is instructive for journalists to think about how others conceive the cultural landscape, to see where others think journalism fits in. Journalists want the cultural authority to define their role in society and to make day-to-day decisions about what is news and how it should be gathered and presented. They accomplish this as an *interpretive community* of journalists, "united through their collective interpretations of key public events. The shared discourse that they produce is thus a marker of how they see themselves as journalists" (Zelizer, 1993, p. 223). In the end, even the government agrees that being a journalist means more than just being able to define what is newsworthy, it also means the right to self-definition.

NOTES

1. Although some cases concerning Section 315 of the Communications Act of 1934 were appealed to the judiciary, courts never reversed any of the decisions of the FCC in the area of law examined here.

2. For instance, President Eisenhower's press secretary James Hagerty called the decision "ridiculous" in a press release. During congressional debates on the equal-time exception legislation, many representatives and senators referred to the ruling as ridiculous, as did the many columnists and news editorials that denounced it.

3. Reagan appointed deregulation-minded commissioners Mary Ann Dawson, Mark Fowler, and Henry Rivera in 1981, Stephen A. Sharp in 1982, and Dennis R. Patrick in 1983. Deregulation opponent Abbott Washburn left in 1982. Congress cut the number of commissioners from seven to five in 1983, dropping Sharp and liberal member Joseph R. Fogarty (Flannery, 1995, pp. 172–204).

Protecting the Cultural Authority of Journalism by Sanctioning Deviance

> Journalists should take the lead in embarrassing other journalists who screw up.
>
> —Stephen Brill
> "NBC Fraud Shows Media Double Standard"

INTRODUCTION

This chapter is an ethnographic analysis of the process whereby anomalous journalists who are perceived to be a threat to the institution are ritually "relocated" to the outer edges of the boundaries of journalism. It is an examination of a case of journalistic misconduct that was discussed in great detail within the institution of journalism. Dateline NBC, a network news division-produced weekly news-magazine, broadcast a story in 1992 about General Motors pickup trucks; it contained a fiery simulated crash scene, which was staged by the program's producers. This staging was not disclosed to the audience. Michael Gartner, then president of NBC News, was held responsible for the misconduct, which was labeled an act of journalistic fraud. The rhetoric by journalists that followed this example of journalistic deviance resembles what Harold Garfinkel (1956) calls a successful status degradation ceremony, whereby deviant members are expelled from an institution (in this case, the institution of journalism) in order to minimize harm to the institution as a whole.

Garfinkel has had a profound impact on sociological theory. As the founder of the ethnomethodology movement, his social constructivist emphasis on the way members of a group "make sense of, find their way about in, and act on the circumstances in which they find themselves" (Heritage, 1984, pp. 3–4) has opened up a vast new territory within sociology. This chapter utilizes Garfinkel's theory and methods to examine one way in which journalists demarcate the realm of journalism within the cultural landscape.

This rhetorical analysis scrutinizes the naturally occuring[1] discourse among journalists following the *Dateline* broadcast, focusing attention on the elements of status degradation ceremonies described by Garfinkel. This is an examination of the rhetorical strategies of journalists reacting to accusations that the NBC News division used fraudulent methods in presenting the news and that Michael Gartner failed his profession by allowing it to happen.

Deviance in American journalism is defined and confronted by the official agents and apologists of the institution of journalism—namely, other journalists who discuss the practices of journalism as an *interpretive community* (see Fish, 1980; Schrøder, 1994; Zelizer, 1993). This chapter is an examination of how members of a public institution produce cultural meaning and reproduce social structures by engaging in rhetorical discourse designed to map out the cultural space of a social institution.

The "universe" sample for this chapter included all the articles listed in the NEXIS database containing the words "Dateline NBC" and "General Motors" appearing in major American newspapers, magazines, and wire services between November 1, 1992, and June 30, 1993 (some 521 articles). Also examined: a videotape of a conference of journalists who examined the *Dateline* scandal; a lawyer's report commissioned by NBC and released March 21, 1993; as well as some earlier articles about Gartner and NBC News that were examined for historical context.

SOME BACKGROUND ON THE *DATELINE NBC* / GM "EVENT"

Dateline NBC was a weekly network newsmagazine program that began in April 1992. On November 17, 1992, *Dateline NBC* broadcast a report entitled, "Waiting to Explode?," which criticized the design of General Motors full-size pickup trucks built between 1973 and 1987, alleging that they were more susceptible to dangerous explosions when involved in side-impact vehicle collisions. The news report included a powerful visual demonstration of the problem: footage described as an "unscientific crash demonstration," which included a fiery explosion. General Motors Corporation investigated the charges made in the story and then filed a defamation lawsuit against NBC. GM took the unprecedented step of announcing their lawsuit via a two-hour globally televised press conference on February 8, 1993. During the press conference, GM lawyers alleged that *Dateline*'s producers allowed "incendiary" or "sparking devices" (model rocket engines) to be attached to the underside of the trucks to ensure that any gasoline spilled during the simulated accident would ignite—and that *Dateline* then failed to publicly disclose this fact in the program. NBC responded with an on-the-air apology the next night, read by *Dateline* anchors Jane Pauley and Stone Phillips. GM dropped its lawsuit shortly after the apology. Michael Gartner resigned on March 2, 1993. Three producers responsible for the GM pickup story segment were forced to resign on March 19, 1993. NBC President and CEO Robert Wright publicly apologized to viewers and to GM on March 22, 1993.

The news media covered the story of NBC's fraud in detail, and many journalism critics discussed it in various newspapers, magazines, professional journals, and on television programs. The Poynter Institute for Media Studies in St. Petersburg, Florida, sponsored a conference entitled "When Good Journalists Do Bad Things: Truthtelling and the Public Trust." The conference included a two-hour discussion of the *Dateline* scandal by professional journalists and journalism professors, which was televised live on C-SPAN on April 15, 1993, recordings of which Poynter now sells on videocassette.

RESPONDING TO DEVIANCE

The very public outcry by journalists and journalism critics in this case—people who believed they were part of the "mainstream" American journalism institution—was a signal that a boundary line was crossed by *Dateline NBC*. The line was described as an epistemological boundary between different kinds of knowledge (truth and fiction), as a functional boundary between news and entertainment, and as a methodological boundary between disinterestedness and agency. The *Dateline* story was portrayed as a violation of professional norms that threatened the distinction between mainstream and tabloid journalism, or between news and entertainment. This public discourse served several purposes:

1. To distance the methodology, content, and apparent function of the *Dateline* episode from commonly accepted journalism standards and to signal that this kind of behavior is deviant.

2. To reassure the public that professional journalists are able to police their ranks.

3. To maintain the social boundaries between journalism and entertainment (or between mainstream and tabloid television news) by showing that deviant behavior that results in products that resemble these other genres of communication will not go unpunished.

To demonstrate the contours of the boundaries of journalism, Gartner and his associates were labeled as deviant journalists. There are both costs and benefits to revealing deviant behavior: "the basic dilemma of social control: to publicize or not to publicize deviant behavior" (Merton & Gieryn, 1982, p. 124). Such publicity is negative and can serve to undermine public confidence in the institution—especially in the short term. A pattern of unpunished violations of norms, however, could be more damaging to the perceived integrity of the profession in the long run.

Durkheim (1984) says the public sanction of deviance is a healthy exercise for a group or institution because it helps to show group members how to recognize the area between acceptable and unacceptable behavior. In his study on the sociology of deviance among the Puritan settlers of America, Kai Erickson (1966) notes that "the interactions which do the most effective job of locating and publicizing the group's outer edges would seem to be those which take place between deviant persons on the one side and official agents of the community on the other" (p. 11). The official agents of the journalistic community are fellow journalists, who operate together as an interpretive community, "united through their collective interpretations of key public events. The shared discourse that they produce is thus a marker of how they see themselves as journalists" (Zelizer, 1993, p. 223). One of the distinctive aspects of turmoil within the institution of journalism (probably much like turmoil in other institutions) is that those within the institution "strive to maintain discursive control over such turmoil. Among other things, this helps to consolidate and legitimate professional practices and identity (by) . . . retain(ing) definitional control of the field, its problems and potential solutions" (Dahlgren, 1992, p. 2).

The site of this chapter is in the symbolic actions of journalists— their communicative acts—as they respond to threats to the cultural authority and boundaries of the institution of journalism in America. These rhetorical actions are interpreted and evaluated as components of a successful status degradation ceremony. Such a ceremony consists of "communicative work directed to transforming an individual's total identity into an identity lower in the group's scheme of social types" (Garfinkel, 1956, p. 420). The individual in this case is Michael Gartner, former president of NBC News. The other three *Dateline* workers who were fired over the controversy—executive pro-

ducer Jeff Diamond, senior producer David Rummel, and field segment producer Robert Read—were also denigrated somewhat by their
peers, but Gartner received the major blame for the controversy because he was ultimately responsible as head of the NBC news division.
Because he served as a lightning rod for criticism, most of the attention here will be given to Gartner and the rhetoric directed at him. It
is clear that—to his detractors—Gartner symbolized everything that
was wrong with NBC News and everything that was wrong with
American television journalism.

SOME BIOGRAPHICAL NOTES ON GARTNER

Throughout the 1980s and 1990s, Michael Gartner was one of the
most well-known and outspoken personalities in the journalism profession. Gartner—with his trademark bow tie—was an icon for First
Amendment absolutism. A third generation journalist, his father and
grandfather both worked at newspapers in Iowa ("Michael Gartner,"
1989). Some of his previous accomplishments include: page one edi-
tor, *Wall Street Journal*; editor and co-owner, Ames, Iowa, *Daily
Tribune*; general news executive, Gannett Co.; president, Des Moines
Register and Tribune Co.; editor, *Louisville Courier-Journal* and
Louisville Times; member, Pulitzer Prize board; and president,
American Society of Newspaper Editors. A New York University Law
School graduate, Gartner is known as a strict interpreter of First
Amendment press rights. For instance, Gartner once argued that
"there is no right to privacy—except from the government" (Roper,
1987, p. 52). This stance led to some controversial decisions, such as
NBC's decision to identify the alleged rape victim in the William
Kennedy Smith trial. Gartner is also known among journalists for his
strict stand on the use of anonymous sources. He says it is wrong for
reporters to use anonymous sources "in all but the most delicate of
stories," because it damages the credibility of all journalism (Stein,
1987). Gartner is also known for his business and financial expertise.
In 1984, he managed to get the Gannett Co. into a bidding war for
control of *The Des Moines Register*, and reportedly pocketed more than
$3 million from the deal ("Breaking into Broadcast," 1988).

THE STATUS DEGRADATION CEREMONY

Garfinkel (1956) theorized that there are eight sequential stages of
a successful status degradation ceremony, consisting of specific
"effects that the communicative tactics of the denouncer must be designed to accomplish" (p. 422ff). These eight types of arguments must
be put forward by people within a community or institution that

wants to banish deviants and at the same time, minimize harm to the institution itself. The eight stages of this rhetorical ceremony are

1. Both the event and the perpetrators are made to look unusual.

2. The perpetrators are compared to bad stereotypes—implying that they are not just accidentally bad.

3. The denouncers show that they belong to the community and that they are speaking for the community or institution, not just as private individuals.

4. The denouncers show that the values of the community are salient, and that they are correct and justified.

5. The denouncers show that they speak for these values.

6. The denouncers show that they have support from the community.

7. The deviants are banished.

8. The deviants are ritually separated from the community so that the community may go on as before.

Next is a detailed examination of each of the steps in the status degradation ceremony. Journalists made arguments before, during, and after the *Dateline* fiasco that seem to resemble each of the stages described by Garfinkel 40 years ago.

Stage 1: Both the Event and the Perpetrators Are Made to Look Unusual

The charges against NBC first came to light when GM staged its global press conference to announce its lawsuit. Harry Pearce, executive vice president and general counsel of General Motors Corp., said: "We now face a poisoned environment spawned by the cheap, dishonest, sensationalism of NBC's program 'Waiting to Explode?' and its aftermath." GM's attack was quickly reported by journalists who seemed shocked that NBC had apparently used "other than standard" newsgathering techniques. Journalists argued that *Dateline* used methods journalists don't normally use—they hired a biased subcontractor who staged a news story. NBC had hired The Institute for Safety Analysis (TISA) as a subcontractor to conduct the "unscientific crash demonstration." TISA is commonly hired to provide evidence for plaintiffs in personal injury lawsuits. GM argued that the Institute had an agenda to promote, and *Dateline* did not disclose this fact, nor did it attempt to balance TISA's views with those of disinterested sources. It appeared that *Dateline* had crossed an epistemological and methodological boundary into the realm of agency, fiction, and entertainment. The information was gathered using entertainment-style methods, so it was fictional—designed to shock or entertain.

NBC was also charged with stonewalling—for not quickly admitting guilt but instead trying to rationalize its methods and its story. Stonewalling is one thing journalists particularly despise—but love to publicize (Brill, 1993a; Ettorre, 1993; Hall, 1993c). Eventually, Gartner realized that he should come clean: "I realized that we were just plain wrong. . . . We were stonewalling them, using all kinds of excuses and rationalizations. What we had done was just plain dumb, and wrong. And I was raised to admit you're wrong when you're wrong" (Brill, 1993a, p. 5). Gartner did not come to this realization, however, until after GM initiated its multimillion dollar lawsuit.

Michael Gartner, *Dateline NBC*, and NBC News were made to appear strange, and their offenses were made to look like elementary violations of common sense. Howard Rosenberg (1993) of the *Los Angeles Times* delivered a potent insult: "A high school journalism student knows that staging or faking or fabricating or falsifying news is, under any circumstances, absolutely forbidden. The big lie, the ultimate corruption. Sweep that ethic under the rug, and a news organization becomes morally barren"(p. 10). Rosenberg's rhetoric implies that *Dateline's* producers were not journalists at all because they apparently did not receive (and do not reproduce) the methodological training common to all journalists (even high school journalists); they were made to seem unusual.

Even before the *Dateline NBC / GM* event, critics charged that NBC was unable to launch a successful newsmagazine or other types of news programming, implying that NBC had an inferior network news division (Hiltbrand, 1992). NBC News was also criticized for inadequate checks on accuracy and journalistic standards. Peter Herford, a 26-year veteran broadcast journalist from CBS, said the *Dateline NBC / GM* event would have never happened at ABC, where someone is in charge of standards. Herford, who now heads the broadcasting program at Columbia University Graduate School of Journalism, said,

At ABC, they had a full-time person, a vice president for news standards, who had a staff, who did nothing but review every investigative piece that went on the air, every major magazine piece that went on the air. He read all the scripts, etc., etc., etc. . . . At ABC, that ['Dateline'] piece never would have gotten past him. (Zurawik & Stoehr, 1993, p. 28)

Thus, the NBC News division was portrayed as an unusually inferior organization, with no one doing the normal task of enforcing journalistic standards.

In some of the rhetoric following the event, Gartner was portrayed as an outsider to broadcast journalism. For instance, Jonathan Alter (1993) noted that a few years before he went to work in broadcast journalism Gartner once told some ABC News producers that he thought

TV News is nothing more than a "shallow comic book" . . . a superficial medium incapable of complex ideas. Today Gartner is in danger of being fired as president of NBC News, in essence for living down to his low expectations for the medium in which he works. . . . Ultimately he looked down his nose a bit at what he did for a living—and it showed. That both loosened his own standards and left him without allies below him. (p. 49)

Alter thus argues that Gartner's outsider attitude toward television journalism carried on during his tenure at NBC News and could be one of the causes for this scandal. Alter also criticized Gartner for being more of a money manager than a journalist (Alter, 1993). This is a familiar charge among journalists who bristle at the thought of money managers—"bean counters"—invading their ranks (penetrating their jurisdictional boundaries) and controlling journalistic output (Underwood, 1993). It is an attempt by journalists to equate the journalist/manager organizational boundary with a "good" journalism/"bad" journalism boundary.[2]

In the rhetoric examined here, Gartner, NBC News, and *Dateline*, were all made to seem unusual—as deviants who lacked knowledge of basic journalistic standards and thus operated outside the realm—the boundaries—of journalism.

Stage 2: The Perpetrators Are Compared to Bad Stereotypes— Implying That They Are Not Just Accidentally Bad

One of the ways journalists made sense of the *Dateline NBC* / GM event was to stereotype it as similar to other well-publicized instances of journalistic deviance. The 1980 Janet Cooke/*Washington Post* scandal and the 1989 scandal following ABC News's re-enactment of the Felix Bloch suspected spy case were mentioned by several journalists as examples of similar lapses in journalistic standards. In the infamous Janet Cooke case, a *Washington Post* reporter fabricated a story about an eight-year-old heroin addict and then passed the fiction off as reality (Cooke, 1980; see also Green, 1981). In the Felix Bloch case, ABC's *World News Tonight* showed a tape that it identified as suspected spy Felix Bloch, passing a briefcase of secrets to a Soviet spy. The people in the video were actually actors hired by ABC, and the video was doctored to make it look like a surveillance tape (Huff, 1989).

By stereotyping the practices of *Dateline NBC* as similar to those of other well-known journalistic scandals, journalists were able to quickly make sense of the event, understand its significance, and formulate responses to it. Four authors mentioned the Cooke scandal and one mentioned the Bloch scandal as stereotypical examples of the same kind of fraud.[3]

Another author implies that the *Dateline NBC* / GM event is stereotypical of news values used in other countries where simulations, staging, and nondisclosure are not taboo in journalism:

If NBC is looking for some consolation, it can find plenty of company in Japan. Staging the news is so commonplace that the Japanese have a word for it: *yarase*.

"In America, it's the exception rather than the rule," says *Newsweek's* Tokyo Bureau Chief Bill Powell. "Here, it's just standard operating procedure. There is much greater latitude given to producers to set things up if it doesn't work out." Adds Dorian Benkoil, an Associated Press editor who researched Japanese media on a Fulbright journalism fellowship: "In the U.S. the lines between entertainment and news are blurring recently. In Japan they never developed." (Frey, 1993, p. 30)

The implication of this rhetorical claim is that the way *Dateline NBC* operates is completely foreign (literally and figuratively) to American journalists.

Another of the rhetorical claims made by journalists following the *Dateline NBC*/GM event was that the "unscientific crash demonstration" was methodologically similar to things done on tabloid television programs, and that there were organizational similarities between *Dateline* and the tabloids (Hall, 1993c; Rosenberg, 1993). Others noted that some of the people who worked on the *Dateline NBC* program had previously worked at the tabloids (Diamond, 1993).

Ironically, tabloid producers used the *Dateline NBC* event as an opportunity to argue that their standards were higher—if anything—than NBC's network news standards. John Terenzio, executive producer of *A Current Affair*, was quoted in a *New York Times* article: "We would not have re-enacted a car crash using little rockets to blow up the car. . . . We would have felt that was not correct, and our legal department would not have allowed it" (Kolbert, 1993). Terenzio thus delivers the fatal rhetorical blow to *Dateline NBC*: Its standards are even lower than those of tabloid television programs. Rosenberg (1993) makes a similar point about NBC News's standards when he notes that none of the tabloid shows identified the alleged rape victim of William Kennedy Smith, though NBC's *Nightly News* did.

Stereotyped as anomalous, Gartner, NBC News, and *Dateline NBC* are rhetorically "moved" outside the realm of journalism to the cultural space where tabloid television, "reality-based programming," and entertainment television programs reside.

Stage 3: The Denouncers Show that They Belong to the Community and that They Are Speaking for the Community or Institution, Not Just as Private Individuals

Journalists demonstrated that judgment on Gartner and the *Dateline* scandal was only to be passed by fellow journalists—who understood the nuances of journalism—and who alone had the jurisdiction to police their ranks and control the boundaries of their profession. The Poynter Institute conference in which the actions of NBC in the GM truck incident were debated was filled almost exclusively with members of the journalism community—reporters, editors, producers, and journalism professors ("When Good Journalists," 1993). Lawyers were notably absent from the field of invited participants. Lawyers did get involved when NBC hired "outside" counsel, Robert Warren of Gibson, Dunn & Crutcher in Los Angeles, and Lewis Kaden of Davis, Polk & Wardwell in New York, to conduct an investigation of how the exploding truck story came to be broadcast. This concerned some journalists who felt threatened by the fact that people from outside the institution of journalism were going to judge the performance of journalists:

Some NBC News staffers have questioned why the network hired lawyers to investigate the case rather than . . . asking a respected journalist to conduct an internal inquiry. NBC's [spokeswoman Peggy] Hubble said that management felt outsiders would provide the most impartial investigation. [But] . . . one source speculated that hiring attorneys may be in part to protect lawyer-client confidentiality and to protect the network [from] lawsuits. (Hall, 1993b)

In the final analysis, journalists quickly assumed the role of jury in this case, undercutting any attempts by General Motors to have the trial go to a real court. Later, at the Poynter conference, Michael Gartner said that he wanted to settle the case quickly and get it behind them, and this is why the on-air apology was broadcast the day after GM filed its lawsuit ("When Good Journalists," 1993). He also said that he had complete authority on the wording of the apology, and whether to accept the conditions of it or not. Gartner's rhetoric was a reassurance to the journalists present at the conference that journalists were in control of the outcome of this case, and were thereby maintaining cultural authority—and jurisdictional control—

over the settlement. GM's swift acceptance of the apology and drop-ping the suit indicates that the lawsuit was probably intended as a public relations move designed to provoke media criticism and the embarrassing public apology from NBC.

Stage 4: The Denouncers Show that the Values of the Community Are Salient, and that They Are Correct and Justified

For many years, television news was accepted as a money-losing venture for the networks, who accepted the burden of news as a part of the "public service" requirements required by the FCC (Paley, 1979, p. 118; Schoenbrun, 1989, p. 78). By the late 1980s, television newsmagazines like *60 Minutes* had proven to be quite profitable for the networks, so they all launched new newsmagazine programs de-signed to make money and to win ratings periods (Zurawik & Stoehr, 1993).

Several broadcast news critics sounded alarms when they heard that John F. Welch, Jr., the president of General Electric (which bought RCA and its subsidiary NBC in 1985), wanted to make the NBC News division profitable. (Auletta, 1991; Lieberman, 1988). After all, they argued, NBC's entertainment division was way ahead of the other networks in prime-time ratings points, so NBC had a com-fortable profit margin; and besides, they argued, News was tradition-ally an unprofitable division. In August 1988, former news division president Lawrence Grossman was fired for not cooperating in GE's quest to make the division profitable; and Michael Gartner was hired in his place, partly because of his devotion to the idea that news busi-nesses should make money (Auletta, 1988, pp. 22–23, 482–484). In a 1992 interview, Gartner said, "You can't be journalistically vigorous unless you're financially strong. You just don't want to lose money—you don't want to be walking around with a tin cup. It is a news busi-ness and you want to be successful in both worlds, news and business" ("NBC's Gartner," 1992, p. 56).

The altruistic mission of journalism to inform the citizenry does not always mesh well with the business mission to make money and profits for stockholders. This is a perennial dilemma for journalism organizations, which must remain in business if they are to serve the public. To be true to the social mission of journalism means that one must appear to be suspicious of profit-centered motives. Gartner was not clearly on the side of altruistic motives, and his critics used this as ammunition in their arguments portraying him as an outsider who was not completely devoted to the social functions of journalism.

Stage 5: The Denouncers Show that They Speak for These Values

In 1989, television journalism critic Jonathan Alter attacked the bottom line ethic of NBC:

Instead of feeling liberated by their entertainment success to spend more of their riches on serious journalism, G.E.'s managers have downgraded the news division. . . . Lacking the ratings benchmarks of (NBC's) hits like "L.A. Law" and "Cosby," the other networks don't expect as much ratings success from news, and have more air time to devote to it. At CBS, news is still the jewel in the crown. At ABC, now loaded with talent, news is practically the crown itself. At NBC, it's a fancy belt buckle. . . . What really matters is proving (NBC is) a company with a commitment to something beyond the bottom line. (p. 86)

Alter was echoing a familiar theme in newsrooms: Journalism is a public service that should not be concerned with profits. Clearly, the profit motives of Gartner, the NBC network, and its parent GE seemed foreign to some journalists.

Evidence also surfaced that NBC allowed its Entertainment Division to have control over news promotions—deciding which programs and segments would be mentioned during self-promotion advertisements (Warren & Kaden, 1993, p. 14). This connection between entertainment and news is not a healthy one, according to Reuven Frank, former president of NBC News. Frank (1993) notes that as news has become profitable, and as news employees—journalists—become concerned with profit, they naturally want these kinds of self-promotions to help increase the ratings for their programs:

Since TV magazines have achieved the status conferred by profit, they . . . get promos now. But the nabobs of entertainment continue to determine what will be hyped. This gives them veto power over the choice of topics in news division programs. A smart executive [news] producer will pick up topics likely to appeal to West Coast show business executives. (p. 20)

Entertainment executives were probably thrilled when they saw the sensational crash footage from the "Waiting to Explode?" segment. Frank's argument shows a concern that the boundary between news and entertainment divisions became blurred at NBC, raising questions about the authority and independence of journalism at the network. Journalists seemed dismayed that NBC News did not maintain strict boundary separation and autonomy from the other branches of the network.

Once the guilt of *Dateline NBC* had become a foregone conclusion, journalists came up with a variety of explanations of personnel and structural problems and other factors that pressured *Dateline* and Gartner into the climate that would allow such behavior. One of these explanations was that business pressures were affecting the journalistic product. Diamond (1993) argued:

NBC News has been in disarray . . . because (1) GE has been trying to sell the network, thus contributing to a "Who cares?" atmosphere, and (2) the severe staff layoffs of the past few years, ordered by GE and executed by Gartner, have cut into the quality of the newsgathering. Further, it's said, *Dateline NBC* has pushed the boundaries of accepted journalism because of the unrelenting need to create a successful magazine show like CBS's *60 Minutes* and ABC's *20/20.* (p. 18)

One unidentified NBC News producer said profit motives and competitive pressures were the keys to why the event occurred: "The tenor of the creation of 'Dateline' was that the profit of the news division rested on this show. In an atmosphere where there is such intense pressure for ratings, something like the 'Dateline' incident was bound to happen" (Hall, 1993c, p. 13).

Gartner had approved massive cost-cutting measures at the news division, including layoffs of seasoned journalists. "There is a feeling among many here that the thrust of the present management is on ratings and that many of the people who have been pushed out had higher standards than some of those who are now in charge of these prime-time shows" (Hall, 1993c, p. 13).

The denouncers of Gartner and NBC showed that they were suspicious of values that were other than purely journalistic.

Stage 6: The Denouncers Show that They Have Support from the Community

Although Gartner's detractors did not claim to be speaking for the journalism community, the preponderance of rhetoric critical of Gartner-the-individual indicates that they did. Only one or two came to his defense, signaling that his denouncers were supported by the journalistic community. Another way *Dateline's* and Gartner's critics demonstrated their support from the institution of journalism was by building an "us versus them" mentality between the institution of journalism and the NBC News organization, accomplished primarily through professional solidarity.

Gartner was portrayed in many articles as a "prickly" manager who was easy to dislike (for example, Alter, 1993; Gay, 1989; "Michael Gartner," 1989; Roper, 1993), signifying that his position was probably not permanent, and Gartner himself seemed to acknowledge as

much (Gay, 1988). Being known as unlikable certainly made him easier to banish from television news, but not all television critics
thought that his personality was relevant. Some seemed to indicate
that it was an unfair attribute upon which to base his expulsion:

Pressure for Gartner's ouster had been fueled by criticism from editorialists and
columnists. "Gartner has become a bit of a sacrificial lamb for the media, the
fall guy for all of television's problems," said Jon Katz, a media critic and
former CBS producer. . . .
    "Michael has an uncanny ability to [anger] any audience of two people he
encounters; he projects arrogance," said Eric Bremner, former head of King
Broadcasting in Seattle and former chairman of the NBC affiliates. But, he
said, "You have to respect some of his accomplishments." (Kurtz & Carmody,
1993)

The banishment of Gartner and the three *Dateline* producers was
supported by all those who engaged in published discussions of the
event. Their unanimity proves that, perhaps unwittingly, they discovered that the way to fix the problem was through professional solidarity and ritual banishment.

Stage 7: The Deviants Are Banished

Gartner and individual journalists responsible for the *Dateline* story
on GM were ritually banished from journalism through rhetoric designed to remove them from the cultural space of journalism. They
were also banished by the company, NBC, which made a clean
sweep—signaling that it was going to recover from this setback by up-
grading the quality of its personnel. Michael Gartner resigned from
NBC—under pressure—on March 2, 1993. Three other producers,
executive producer Jeff Diamond, senior producer David Rummel,
and field segment producer Robert Read were forced to resign March
18, 1993. The accused were "made strange" compared to the rest of
the institution of journalism—so that the institution would survive.
And survive it did.

Stage 8: The Deviants Are Ritually Separated from the
Community So that the Community May Go on as Before

Statements from NBC after the incident reflected the idea that the
way to fix the news division was to sweep out the old and to find a
good replacement for ousted president Michael Gartner. An NBC
News executive said the ideal candidate would be a "top TV journalist who is a terrific communicator and has a squeaky-clean reputation

for integrity" (Hall, 1993a). Diamond (1993) notes that one of the conditions for Gartner's replacement was that the person had to come from within the television industry: "Newspaper people need not apply," he said. The implication of this rhetoric is that one of Gartner's problems was that he lacked broadcasting experience, his lack of experience may have been a contributing cause of the event, and he was always considered an outsider to broadcast journalism.

A few months after the event, Gartner's replacement declared that all was better at NBC News:

Andy Lack, president of NBC news said it took just three weeks for the news magazine *Dateline NBC* to bounce back in the ratings after the fiasco of a doctored test on General Motors pickup trucks.

Lack said those who produced the questionable report "risked their credibility."

But he said he believed the show bounced back so quickly and was again accepted by viewers because NBC "handled the issue professionally, straightforwardly, as openly and honestly as you would expect . . . and the audience said 'OK, we get it, let's move forward.'" (Engstrom, 1993)

Others within the company also made arguments that the setbacks from the event were temporary. NBC *Nightly News* anchor Tom Brokaw described the temporary nature of the damage:

The incident on 'Dateline' was a mistake. . . . I don't think it's fair to say we've been permanently scarred, any more than CBS was permanently scarred by the [lawsuit filed by Gen. William Westmoreland over a 1982 "CBS Reports" documentary] or the *Washington Post* was permanently scarred by Janet Cooke. (Hall, 1993a, p. 2)

By emphasizing the temporary nature of the setback and by citing some classic examples of other journalism outlets surviving scandals, NBC executives showed they were confident that NBC News would survive the mistakes of a few deviant individuals.

Others within the NBC News division expressed a positive attitude about the effects of the event. Knight-Ridder entertainment columnist Gail Shister (1993) wrote that Stone Phillips, a co-anchor of *Dateline NBC*, believed the consequences of the event would be good for the profession and the NBC News institution:

NBC's strength will come from the news division's newly instituted system of internal checks and balances, Phillips says. That system is the silver lining in the Dateline cloud.

"Industrywide, there has been a re-examination of how newsmagazines go about doing their work. That's always healthy. Nobody wants to be the broadcast that hurts the over-all credibility of the whole medium. When there's a mistake of this magnitude, it hurts us all. Hopefully, some good will come out of it." (p. C2)

Again, expressions of optimistic rhetoric within NBC News in the aftermath of the ceremony reflect the attitude that the institution will fix itself and become stronger because of the negative experience. More than just a public relations ploy for outsiders, this kind of rhetoric also helps boost employee morale—making it a self-fulfilling prophecy. NBC News used the *Dateline* fiasco as a justification to make changes and fix problems, hoping that the experience would strengthen them. As Hemingway (1929) wrote in *A Farewell to Arms*, "The world breaks everyone and afterward many are strong at the broken places."

CONCLUSIONS

Definitions of journalism matter to those working in the profession and institution of journalism. These definitions are a way for journalists to make sense of what they do and who they are. Definitions help them determine who belongs in journalism and helps to delineate the contours of the cultural space of journalism.

The status degradation ceremony serves as a warning to journalists to follow the rules and stay within the boundaries of journalism or be cast out as a deviant. In this case, journalists defined their profession/institution as one that does not permit fabrications or fictions. In an act of social control, journalists ritually removed Gartner and several other deviants from the institution.

Sociological "strain" and "interest" theories help explain how and why the journalism institution produces boundary-work rhetoric like this status degradation ceremony. Clifford Geertz (1973) says in strain theories, people "flee anxiety," and in interest theories, they "pursue power," and they probably will do both at the same time, or do one as a result of the other (p. 201). It could be argued that in the rhetoric surrounding this event, journalists attempted to flee the anxiety of the public disgrace of a well-publicized example of fraudulent practices; and at the same time they attempted to pursue the power of the authority of journalism—accomplishing both by sanctioning the perpetrators. Perhaps they were fleeing from Gartner himself, a man who, with his strange ideas about privacy and profitability, had often been a source of anxiety for journalists. More than three years later, Gartner was still considered an outcast by many journalists. After the Society of Professional Journalists announced that Gartner would be the keynote speaker for its Fall 1995 annual convention, several members argued against his selection. "Making someone the keynote speaker is an honor. And Gartner, for all his journalism accomplishments, forfeited the right to that honor because of his ethical lapses at NBC," wrote SPJ member Jonathan Salant. "[We] must hold ourselves accountable and ferret out ethical violations within our profession" (Case, 1995, p. 12).

Although the rhetoric in this status degradation ceremony did not precisely match all the stages itemized by Garfinkel 40 years ago, it is obvious that the responses to this threat to the authority of journalism demonstrate how the boundaries of a social institution are drawn by those who consider themselves inside the institution, and that it is up to the members of a social institution to enforce its boundaries.

Garfinkel theorized that the status degradation ceremony is accomplished in order to deflect attention away from the structural or organizational defects of an institution. That did not happen throughout this case. For instance, conflict over the business/journalism boundary was mentioned by Gartner's accusers as an underlying motive for the misconduct, which tends to move the blame from the individual—Gartner—onto the organization—NBC. In Stages 1 and 2, the NBC News organization was frequently blamed as the underlying cause of the scandal. By March 1993, however, criticism of the organization as the cause of the scandal had virtually disappeared, and the blame was set squarely on Gartner's shoulders. Most of the later articles about the *Dateline* scandal (in Stage 8) focused on how Gartner and the producers responsible for the episode were banished from the organization. This tended to shift attention away from the structural and organizational flaws that made the scandal possible, and implied that the real problem was a few individuals, most notably Gartner. One reason for this discrepancy is that many of the denouncers in Stage 8 were people within the NBC News organization who clearly had a motive for shifting blame to the banished individuals and for seeing that the organization was again trusted as credible and able to produce quality, truthful journalism.

The concept that truth (and, implicitly, a social institution that practices full disclosure) will prevail in times of controversy descends from the seventeenth-century self-righting principle expressed by John Milton (1644): "Let [Truth] and falsehood grapple; who ever knew Truth put to the wors[e], in a free and open encounter?" (p. 34). Clearly, in the rhetoric critical of NBC, Gartner, and *Dateline*, the critics believed that their criticism would sensitize journalists to these issues and, therefore, prevent this from happening again. This rhetoric is also designed to stake out a cultural space in mass communications—programs produced by network news divisions.

In the cultural space between journalism and other things like entertainment, some boundaries are sharper than others. In this instance, journalists sought to sharpen a boundary by expelling one of its prominent members who they perceived had an ambivalent attitude toward questionable behavior. The strength of their rebuke demonstrates how seriously they took the threat.

NOTES

1. Discourse data gathered using interview, survey, focus group, and participant-observer methods can be tainted because they are produced by "unnatural" groups (Schrøder, 1994, p. 341).

2. Gieryn (1992) examines a similar scientist/management boundary.

3. Diamond (1993), Hall (1993a), Johnson (1993), and McCarthy (1993) mention the Cooke scandal. Zurawik & Stoehr (1993) mention the Bloch scandal.

The Clinton and Flowers Story: Too Good to Pass Up

Across the front page of our minds: TABLOIDS SEIZE CONTROL, RUIN PRESIDENTIAL ELECTION. That's the headline that haunts journalism and the political process, and the rest of the media have no one to blame but themselves.

—Jonathan Alter
"The Cycle of Sensationalism"

INTRODUCTION

Many journalists consider journalism a profession, and just as others who produce a product, they devise rules distinguishing acceptable from unacceptable practices and product content. In this chapter, I examine how journalists attempted to refine and reshape the boundary of legitimate journalism produced during one phase of the 1992 presidential campaign. According to many journalism critics, the range of acceptable topics of journalistic coverage of political candidates and the professional practices of journalists have drastically changed in the past few decades (for example, Ornstein, 1991; Sabato, 1991; Wines, 1987). American journalists who consider themselves part of the "mainstream" social institution of journalism (as opposed to the institution of "tabloid" journalism) say they find it difficult to determine the limits of acceptable journalism, but they insist that it is an important distinction in order to maintain professionalism. For instance, if a journalist goes too far in exposing details about a candidate's private life, or uses techniques or methods commonly associated with tabloids, that journalist might be accused of practicing tabloid journalism.

Journalists who consider themselves mainstream say tabloid journalism makes decisions about the newsworthiness of a story based on entertainment value, while they imply that they make, or should make, decisions about newsworthiness solely on informational or news value. As ABC News correspondent Sam Donaldson notes, "I'm for interesting television news presentations. But it seems to me that too often we put on a story or a feature . . . or go after an interview because we think we can promote it and entice a greater number of people to watch our broadcasts rather than because of an honest belief that it has an intrinsic news value" (Donaldson, 1987, p. 326). The epistemological difference between these two kinds of knowledge is often described as the difference between information that the public "wants" and what they "need." Mainstream journalists purport to give citizens true information they need to make informed choices— to make the democracy work. They also claim that they are different from tabloid journalists who merely give people *interesting but unimportant* stuff. Obviously there are types of information that interest tabloid and mainstream journalists alike. See Figure 6.1 for one way in which this seems to be conceptualized by journalists.

Figure 6.1
Two Epistemological Dimensions of the Content of Journalism

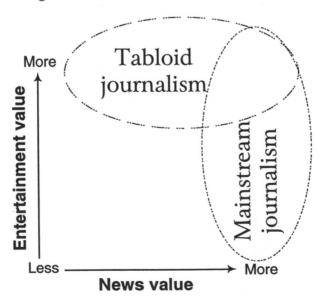

According to many journalists, the boundary between tabloid and mainstream journalism has noticeably blurred and moved during recent political campaigns. Allegations of the marital infidelities of candidates were not mentioned by most journalism outlets for many years of American presidential politics, but were fairly common in tabloids. Then in the past decade, several instances of allegations of infidelity were mentioned and investigated by so-called "mainstream" journalism institutions. These investigations have been both defended and condemned by journalists and journalism critics—a sign that a boundary is in dispute.

In this chapter, I analyze the rhetoric in published articles critical of the journalism institution following news reports during the 1992 presidential campaign of allegations by Gennifer Flowers of marital infidelity in Bill Clinton's past. The rhetoric is also compared to the rhetoric critical of news media coverage of allegations of marital infidelity that dogged Gary Hart during the 1988 presidential campaign. The critical rhetoric analyzed here is the symbolic action of journalists and others who decided that the issue of news coverage of the private lives of presidential candidates warranted discussion as an issue of professionalism. The rhetoric demonstrates that journalists felt that the airing of the Flowers allegations expanded the range of acceptable news topics and news sources, and thereby threatened professional boundaries. Some journalists justified the change, while others demanded a retreat to earlier standards.

In 1988 the issue received much attention when presidential candidate Gary Hart was discovered to be having an adulterous affair with Donna Rice after challenging reporters to "tail" him. By 1992 the criteria used to establish the newsworthiness of candidates' private relationships changed to fit the story: Some journalists argued that it was now acceptable for mainstream journalists to grill presidential candidates about unsubstantiated rumors of marital infidelity in their past, even though they were not current infidelities and no challenges to find wrongdoing were issued by the candidates to reporters. These journalists argued for an enlargement of the cultural space of legitimate journalism. The discourse among journalists about the Clinton/Flowers scandal and the apparent contradiction of the "professional rules" set down in 1988 after the Hart/Rice scandal shed light on the ways journalists adjust professional boundaries as they adjust their perceived roles in society.

Journalism critics argued that epistemological, functional, and methodological differences between tabloid journalism and mainstream journalism were vanishing because mainstream journalism outlets repeated allegations first aired by tabloids. The rhetoric demonstrates an awareness by journalists that a boundary was changing or blurring, and that this change was a threat to the perceived jurisdiction of the mainstream institution of journalism. The analysis also shows that journalists believed that this threat could be dealt with in two distinct ways: through rhetoric arguing for a return to traditional rules governing practices and content—designed to maintain perceived boundaries; and through rhetoric arguing for new professional rules and jurisdictions—designed to change perceived boundaries to "fit" the new circumstances.

DRAMATISTIC ANALYSIS

My analysis of this rhetoric utilizes Kenneth Burke's dramatistic analysis method to describe the underlying themes and motivations. Burke's theories and methods have been lauded by modern rhetoricians for their interpretive thoroughness and parsimony (Golden, Berquist, and Coleman 1989; Madsen, 1993; Nichols, 1952; Larry Smith, 1987). His theory is particularly appropriate for this work because of his emphasis on the rhetoric of *identification*, "a key concept because men [sic] are at odds with one another, or because there is 'division'" (Nichols, 1952, p. 136). In this chapter, I examine how journalists identify themselves by defining some of the divisions, or boundaries, of legitimate journalistic work. Dramatistic analysis consists of three phases, which, when used together in a recursive analysis, serve as mutual correctives (Conrad, 1984). The first phase is a *statistical analysis*, which involves uncovering the major themes of a given body of rhetoric. The second is the selection of a *representative anecdote*, a story or subplot that is representative of the essence of the entire work under analysis. Barry Brummett says a representative anecdote is identified by asking, "If this discourse were based on a story, an anecdote, what would the form, outline, or bare bones of that story be?" (Brummett, 1984). The third phase of Burkean dramatistic analysis is *pentadic analysis*, an analysis of the "ratios," or relationships between the five main constitutive elements of rhetoric: act, scene, agent, agency, and purpose. Burke (1968) explains some of these ratios:

A "purpose-agency ratio," for instance, would concern the logic of "means se-lecting," the relation of means to ends (as the Supreme Court might decide that an emergency measure is constitutional because it was taken in an emergency situation). An "agent-act ratio" would reflect the correspondence between a man's character and the character of his behavior. . . . Insofar as men's actions are to be interpreted in terms of the circumstances in which they are acting, their behavior would fall under the heading of a "scene-act ratio." But insofar as their acts reveal their different characters, their behavior would fall under the heading of an "agent-act ratio." For instance, in a time of great crisis, such as a shipwreck, the conduct of all persons involved in that crisis could be expected to manifest in some way the motivating influence of the crisis. (p. 446)

A "scene-act ratio" is the relationship of an action to the situation in which it takes place. And in many cases, according to Burke, an "agent-act ratio" exists in conjunction with a "scene-act ratio" (Golden, Berquist, and Coleman, 1989, p. 333). This can be illus-trated in this chapter by thinking about how a particular journalist or newspaper (the agent) works to sharpen a boundary (the act) between journalism and other mass communication when faced with a sensa-tional story about a presidential candidate (the scene). Boundary-work rhetoric is designed to delineate boundaries for specific reasons, such as the consolidation of professional power and prestige associ-ated with certain jurisdictions. Burke's dramatistic analysis offers a range of tools to dissect and understand how this kind of rhetoric op-erates.

To present the statistical analysis phase, I examine the history of the Clinton/Flowers drama, then I identify the primary themes of ar-guments put forward by journalists discussing the media coverage, particularly regarding perceived changes in professional rules. To pre-sent the representative anecdote phase, I examine how journalists de-scribed the uncontrollable nature of sensational political/sexual news items, resigning to the inevitability of news coverage once these kinds of stories are broken. To present the pentadic analysis phase, I exam-ine several of the ratios in this drama—such as scene-act, agency-pur-pose, and agency-scene—in several different ways.

The sample for this analysis was gathered using an on-line NEXIS search of "major American news sources" for articles published and television programs broadcast within a year of the initial breaking of the story (January 23, 1992), and containing the search terms "Bill Clinton," "Gennifer Flowers," and "news media."[1] This search re-vealed several hundred articles, many of which had to be discarded because they dealt only superficially with the issue, often in year-end-review-type articles. All the articles that examined the boundaries of acceptable journalistic topics (or implied that there were boundaries) were included in the analysis. The final selection for analysis included the full texts of 94 newspaper and magazine articles and the transcripts of two television programs. In addition, many articles and books dealing with the media coverage of the Hart/Rice scandal in 1987 were examined for the pentadic analysis.

STATISTICAL ANALYSIS: "THE BOUNDARIES, THEY ARE A-CHANGIN'"

In mid-January 1992 presidential candidate Bill Clinton, campaigning in New Hampshire for that state's important early primary, was dogged by rumors of past marital infidelity. Bill Clinton and his wife, Hillary Rodham Clinton, admitted to reporters early in the campaign that although there had been past indiscretions, they were now happily married and considered questions on this issue to be inappropriate. Even so, the questions were raised. On January 18 a local New Hampshire television reporter asked Clinton, "Have you ever had an extramarital affair, Governor?" Clinton responded, "Well, if I had, I wouldn't tell you" ("Tabloid Prints," 1992). The same day, Hillary Rodham Clinton told reporters, "In any marriage there are issues that come up between two people who are married that I think are their business" ("Tabloid Prints," 1992).

The next night, ABC News' Cokie Roberts, moderating a debate between Democratic contenders, asked Clinton, "There is concern on the part of members of your party that these allegations of womanizing, that the Republicans will find somebody and that she will come forward late and that you would lose the all-important-to-Democrats women's vote." Clinton responded, "I think it is highly unlikely, given the competitive environment in which I've been in, that you have anything to worry about on that score" ("Tabloid Prints," 1992). In other words, the Clintons, in their equivocal responses, signaled that although he had a history of this kind of behavior, it was now over, and now it was a private matter between them.

On Thursday, January 23, publicists from the *Star*, a supermarket tabloid owned by the same company that publishes the *National Enquirer*, faxed advance copies of a story from its upcoming edition (due in supermarkets on Monday, January 27) to major news organizations and to the Clinton campaign (Rosenstiel, 1992). The story detailed allegations by Arkansas state employee Gennifer Flowers of a 12-year affair with Bill Clinton—an affair that Flowers said ended several years earlier. Jim Wooten, covering the Clinton campaign for ABC News, asked Clinton to comment on the allegations contained in the *Star* story. Clinton told reporters that day,

I read the story. It isn't true. And I told her over and over, I said, "Just tell the truth. Tell the truth." If we had just walked away from our marriage [that is, gotten a divorce], I could be up here running for president and you would not be here tonight talking to me about this (Balz & Kurtz, 1992; Rosenstiel, 1992; "Tabloid Prints," 1992).

Most major news organizations appeared to be unsure of whether—and if so, how—to report the allegations. Of the three major networks, only NBC mentioned them on its evening newscast that night. ABC News, however, examined the story in detail during its *Nightline* program later that evening. All the networks sent video clips of the story that afternoon out to their local affiliates, which, according to *Newsweek* reporter Jonathan Alter, operate on "looser" standards regarding the substantiation of rumor, hearsay, and allegation (Alter, 1992; Rosenstiel, 1992).

Most news outlets entered the story this way: They told their audiences that there was a sensational story that was causing anguish among journalism outlets over how to cover it. In journalist's parlance, it was a "media story." This allowed journalists to move the boundary to include these kinds of discussions as legitimate journalistic topics, while denying that there had been any movement. ABC's *Nightline*, which devoted its entire half-hour to the story on January 23—the same day as the advance of the *Star* story was released, justified its coverage that way. ABC's Jeff Greenfield introduced the story to *Nightline* audiences:

Here we go again. A major contender for high public office is confronted by charges of private wrong-doing. . . .
    When is private conduct relevant to the judging of public officials? Unlike the Hart case, these allegations lack independent substantiation. . . . So the mainstream press has held back. Of the major networks, only NBC mentioned the new allegations on tonight's evening newscast and then only glancingly. CBS and ABC ignored the story. So did CNN. ("Tabloid Prints," 1992)

Greenfield ignored the apparent contradiction of his statement— that his network's evening news program decided not to mention the allegations, yet here he was reporting them. Greenfield's rhetoric appears to be designed to show that the boundary is holding steady—"the mainstream press has held back"—yet it ignores the fact that reporters from his organization (ABC's Jim Wooten and Cokie Roberts) had earlier in the week asked Clinton about the allegations of womanizing, and now Greenfield himself was repeating them.

Guests on the *Nightline* program that night blasted Ted Koppel and ABC for covering the story:

MANDY GRUNWALD, Political Consultant: "This is the first program that Nightline has done on any topic relating to the Democratic presidential candidates. . . . Here we are just a couple weeks before the New Hampshire primary. People are about to go out there and vote. . . . And you're choosing with your editorial comment by making this program about some unsubstantiated charges that . . . started with a trashy supermarket tabloid. You're telling people something that you think is important. That's not context. You're setting the agenda and you're letting the Star set it for you."

TED KOPPEL: "Up until the time that Governor Clinton was prepared to come on the broadcast tonight, or if not this one, to come on PrimeTime Live, up until it became quite apparent that the campaign fully intends to address this issue, we, I must tell you, were not going to run this broadcast as we are running it tonight." ("Tabloid Prints," 1992)

In this exchange we see Grunwald—a political consultant who was well-connected with the Clinton Campaign—arguing that the so-called mainstream news media are taking their cues about what are the important stories of the day from supermarket tabloids. Koppel argues that the topic became legitimately newsworthy when Clinton announced his intention to answer the tabloid's allegations.

Thus, although the mainstream news media consider the tabloids to be different from them and not particularly newsworthy, they consider responses—or the stated intent to respond—to tabloid allegations newsworthy.

GRUNWALD: "I think you would want to check out the story a little bit more before you devote a half hour to it."

KOPPEL: "You're an—well, we're not devoting a half hour to the story itself. We're devoting a half hour to precisely the kind of discussion—"

GRUNWALD: "But that's just a neat little way to get at the story."

KOPPEL: "Well, if that's what we were doing, then we'd be talking about different aspects of it."

JONATHAN ALTER, *Newsweek*: "Where Mandy might be right is that we all
  do, and I'm partially guilty of this myself, essentially get the details
  through customs as a media story. It is a media story, but we are also
  a little bit hypocritical in not admitting that we are, in fact, spreading
  it even when we discredit it." ("Tabloid Prints," 1992)

Some journalists, like Jonathan Alter, admitted the circular reason-
ing and hypocrisy of repeating tabloid allegations within media stories
about how the allegations are handled by the media. Later that week,
Paul Friedman, executive producer of ABC's evening newscast, also
admitted, "I suppose that we're all guilty of some sort of circular
phenomenon here. . . . Because other people treat it as a story, you
don't have any choice but to do it" (Kurtz, 1992b). ABC News producers publicly denounced this type of campaign coverage yet had
their reporters asking Clinton about womanizing rumors in the weeks
before the Flowers allegations surfaced. When the allegations did surface in the *Star*, ABC was quick to devote its *Nightline* news program
to the topic. Journalists seemed to be saying that this kind of information is not within the bounds of legitimate journalism, but "it's aw-
fully close." Their actions indicate the belief that if they could get
Clinton to admit to something through repeated inquiries, this might
bring the story within the bounds of journalism. If not, "media stories" examining how other journalists handled the allegations were
one way to pull it within the bounds of journalism.

The next day, January 24, daily tabloid newspapers in the
Northeast, such as the New York *Daily News*, the New York *Post*,
New York Newsday, and the *Boston Herald American* ran the allegations
as the top story of the day (Alter, 1992; Diamond, 1992). *New York
Newsday* and the *Daily News* even had the same banner headline:
"Sex, Lies and Audiotape." In the following days, Clinton made more
denials, and soon the entire institution of American journalism was
caught in the dilemma of how to report the accusations and denials.

To answer the charges more fully, Clinton and his wife, Hillary
Rodham Clinton, scheduled an interview on CBS's *60 Minutes* to be
broadcast immediately following the Super Bowl, on Sunday, January
26, 1992. Clinton's advisers wanted him to reach the largest potential
audience, and *60 Minutes'* producers were happy to oblige (Matalin &
Carville, 1994, pp. 102-114). The day after the Clintons' appearance
on *60 Minutes*, Flowers and the *Star* held a press conference in New
York's Waldorf-Astoria Hotel, to introduce Flowers' allegations to
the mainstream news media and to refute the Clintons' denials. This

event was broadcast live on CNN. An estimated 350 reporters from various journalism outlets showed up to cover the press conference. Clinton adviser James Carville complained later that 350 reporters would not have shown up if someone had discovered a cure for cancer (Matalin & Carville, 1994, p. 114). Some news organizations waited until Clinton responded to the press conference, then said that the scandal became news as soon as Clinton acknowledged it through denial. Others said it became a news story as soon as Clinton announced his date on *60 Minutes*. Still others decided the rumors were newsworthy as soon as Clinton responded to the advance on the *Star* story, on January 23. Despite the disagreement about when the story entered the boundaries of what is considered to be "legitimate news," most, if not all, American news outlets eventually ran stories about the allegations.

As Howard Kurtz (1992b) noted, "Many newspapers have displayed a sort of split personality. While their news columns are filled with stories on Clinton and Flowers, their editorial and op-ed pages have denounced the coverage." Kurtz notes that there was widespread disagreement among journalists about the contours of this boundary. Although editors and campaign reporters seemed to feel that the allegations were news, editorialists—who often serve as media critics—complained that a boundary was being compromised.

Most of the complaints centered on the theme that because the tabloid *Star* paid Gennifer Flowers for her story, it was unobjective and suspect—that is, people will say anything if you pay them enough. By publicizing Flowers' allegations, the so-called mainstream news media were "following the lead of a tabloid" and giving unsubstantiated rumor the respectable mantle of "news."

Flowers had audiotapes of telephone conversations with Clinton, but according to one audio expert who analyzed the recordings about a week after the initial allegations were made—and the story was dying down—they were inconclusive and were probably edited together to sound like conversations (Lauter, 1992). And the conversations didn't contain any mention of sexual dalliances. Furthermore, according to some sources, Flowers' credibility was questioned because she made several verifiably false statements within her allegations. For instance, a *Newsweek* article used a lot of space to list inconsistencies in her accounts:

Gennifer Flowers . . . has credibility problems. Among them:

- Flowers says she met Clinton when covering a political story for KARK-TV, a Little Rock station where she says she worked for two years. But a KARK spokesman says Flowers only covered fluff stories, not politics and not Clinton. Records indicate she worked there less than a year.

- Flowers claims she met Clinton at the Excelsior Hotel in 1979 or 1980. The hotel didn't open until late 1982.

- Flowers claims Clinton called her on Dec. 11, 1991, and told her to call him after 11 p.m. at the Governor's Mansion. But records show that Clinton was campaigning in Chicago and Florida that day and spent the night in Washington.

- Flowers claims to have been a part of an opening act for Roy Clark's band and to have joined the band's U.S. and European tours. But her own booking agent says she exaggerated her role.

- Flowers claims in Arkansas newspaper profiles to have worked on the TV show "Hee Haw" as one of the cleavage-baring "Hee-Haw" girls. But a "Hee-Haw" spokesman says she wasn't on the show.

- Flowers claims to have taken 50 hours of classes at the University of Arkansas. There is no record of her having attended the school.

- Flowers claims to have been Miss Teen-Age America, 1967. She wasn't—that year or any other. (Alter et al., 1992)

For *Newsweek*, it was evidently very important to expose every crack in Flowers' story, as a method of undermining her credibility and the credibility of the account published in the *Star*. This was a way for them to say that the story was not worthy of journalism because the source was not credible. Other journalists also took great pains to poke holes in Flowers' allegations. For instance, *Washington Post* columnist Amy E. Schwartz (1992) argued that Flowers' "body language" indicated she was lying. Others analyzed the conversations on Flowers' tapes to undermine her story:

It took Jimmy Breslin, Queens populist and tab-newspaper reporter . . . [to pick up] on a key exchange, the moment when Flowers said to Clinton, "Do you remember what I said to you?" Breslin, thanks to the time he spends around the courts in Kew Gardens, recognized the cue—as any eighteen-year-old thief would. It's the "lead sentence of the rodent. Always the 'do you remember' is said in the presence of recording equipment or a stool pigeon." But Clinton, Yale lawyer, Rhodes scholar, candidate to lead the Free World, answered, "No what'd you say?" (Then followed some dirty talk by Flowers). (Diamond, 1992)

Another *Washington Post* columnist, Judy Mann (1992), also listened carefully to the tapes:

Clinton's accuser has had enough holes punched in her biography to sink a candidate for dogcatcher. I don't care whether she was lying about being on "Hee-Haw" or not. My personal red light went off when I read the transcript of the audio tape and found the Arkansas governor identifying himself on the telephone as "Bill Clinton." Are we to believe that people who have had an affair for 12 years don't recognize each other's voices?

Clearly, many journalists were uncomfortable with the *Star's* story and tried to undermine its credibility, and the credibility of its star witness, Gennifer Flowers. By attacking the credibility of Flowers, they "moved" the story outside the boundaries of legitimate journalism.

The Exclusion versus Adjustment Debate

Two camps developed during the debate about the Clinton story: those who felt that the Flowers story was within the bounds of legitimate journalism, and those who did not.

The major argument for *exclusion* of the story—advanced by those who felt that the story was outside the bounds of legitimate journalism—was that it constituted a violation of the "Gary Hart rules" set down four years earlier. During the 1988 presidential campaign, news coverage of Gary Hart's relationship with Donna Rice was justified by some journalists as a legitimate news topic because: It was a current, on-going affair; Hart publicly and vehemently denied being engaged in adulterous affairs, and extolled the sanctity of his marriage; and Hart issued a challenge to reporters to catch him cheating (Cramer, 1992; Germond & Witcover, 1989; Randolph, 1987). Some condemned the coverage of the Hart/Rice affair because it was irrelevant to the candidate's fitness for leading the country, it invaded his privacy, and it was chosen as a news topic solely because of its sensational nature (that is, its entertainment value). Most journalists, however, eventually concluded that Hart's actions were compulsive and self-destructive, and his continued denials in the face of mounting evidence made the actions newsworthy because of what this said about his "character." Thus, to some, the Hart/Rice scandal did not start out as clearly being within the bounds of legitimate or "mainstream" journalism, but after continued investigation revealed corroborating evidence—and the focus of the stories became trained on the deception, not the af-fair—it became clearly within the bounds. Credible evidence of infi-delity and lying came to be broadly identified as a "character issue." After the Hart/Rice scandal, journalists never formally codified "rules" about when and how such character issues were to be handled in the future, but many took this episode to be precedent setting. Later jus-tifications of the coverage of Hart implied that certain types of pri-vate conduct rightly concern the public—such as current, on-going deceptions that can be substantiated through investigation. Still, these boundaries were left somewhat blurry after Hart, which meant that journalists faced with the Flowers allegations had to rethink about where the boundaries had been or where they should be—a dif-ficult proposition for a craft operating under daily deadlines. These determinations were complicated in the Clinton/Flowers story by other factors such as the reliability of the origins of the story and in-creased competition among different kinds of news media.

Many critics of the news coverage of the Flowers story argued that the mainstream media now follow the lead of tabloid journalism in determining the importance of certain news stories. This highlights one of the major differences between the Hart and Clinton controver-sies: With Hart, the story was first uncovered or "broken" by a main-stream newspaper, the *Miami Herald*. With Clinton, the story was broken by a supermarket tabloid, the *Star*. It was easy for journalists to rationalize that the Hart story was within the boundaries of jour-nalism because it was uncovered by fellow journalists. But journalists saw the Clinton story as a trap set by the tabloids: If journalists re-ported the allegations, they would be legitimizing the story as journal-ism and opening themselves up to criticism for being sensationalistic; if they ignored the allegations, they would be accused of suppressing the news, or worse, coddling the candidate.

Two major themes flow through the rhetoric of those who justified the *adjustment* of the boundaries of legitimate news to include the Flowers allegations:

1. The boundaries should change because this is a legitimate story (or it be-came a legitimate story) because several vital conditions were met.
2. Journalists cannot control the boundaries of journalism.

The following lists of arguments are examples of how journalists—through analytical and critical rhetoric—maintain and adjust profes-sional boundaries.

Arguments for exclusion

- The Clinton/Flowers story is different from the Hart story because:
    —The journalistic source of the story is a tabloid (Carman, 1992; Clift, Fineman, and Carroll, 1992).
    —The main source, Gennifer Flowers, is suspect: was paid, has changed her story, has lied about other aspects of her life, is tied to the Republican opposition, is a former nightclub singer (Alter et al., 1992; Campbell, 1992; Clift, Fineman, and Carroll, 1992; "Old News," 1992; Page, 1992).
    —There were no pictures (Schorr, 1992).
    —There was a denial (Haithman, 1992).
    —Clinton's wife and campaign workers are not victims (Haithman, 1992; Schorr, 1992).
    —This is not a current affair (Malone, 1992; Scattarella & Ortega, 1992; Schorr, 1992).
    —Clinton didn't challenge journalists to catch him cheating (Cooper, 1992; Scattarella & Ortega, 1992; Schorr, 1992).
    —We don't know whether Clinton lied, but we know that Hart did (Schorr, 1992).
    —Clinton never claimed purity (Cooper, 1992; Gerzon, 1992).

- Therefore, because this case is unlike the Hart case, Clinton should be treated easier (Gersh, 1992; Gerzon, 1992; Scattarella & Ortega, 1992; Schorr, 1992).

- The "Gary Hart rule"—that old affairs (non-current ones) are off-limits to news coverage—is out ("Clinton flap," 1992).

These arguments for exclusion of the story from the bounds of legitimate journalism note several distinguishing characteristics of the boundaries of legitimate journalism:

1. "True" journalism stories are first publicized (or broken) by mainstream journalism outlets, not by supermarket tabloids. Journalists are supposed to break political stories—that is journalism's function in society; and journalists are the only ones who use the kind of careful, deliberate, investigative methods designed to uncover these kinds of stories. (Methodological and functional differences.)
2. Stories like this are not "bought" from apparently biased sources. Journalistic information is believable because it is untainted by selfish motivations. (Methodological and epistemological differences.)
3. Journalists must conform to previous rulings concerning the sorts of information that are in the public interest to know, whereas tabloid journalists can publish whatever they feel like and whatever they think will sell papers. (Functional and epistemological differences.)

Arguments for adjustment of the boundaries

Many proponents of the adjustment side of the debate argue that the Clinton/Flowers story was, or became, a legitimate news story.

- Flowers' allegations became a legitimate news story when
  —Clinton responded to—didn't ignore—questions by reporters about the allegations and rumors. This is called the "circular defense," because it ignores the fact that if Clinton didn't respond, journalists were likely to say that he was stonewalling (Evans & Novak, 1992; Gitlin, 1992; Hines, 1992; Kurtz, 1992b; Lamb, 1992; Page, 1992; Rosenstiel, 1992).
  —Papers such as New York's daily tabloids started publishing stories about the *Star's* story, so it moved from supermarket tabloids to metropolitan tabloids (Alter, 1992; Evans & Novak, 1992).
  —Clinton announced that he was going on *60 Minutes* to address the allegations (Freeman, 1992; Gailey, 1992; Jones, 1992; Lamb, 1992; Lambro, 1992; Rosenstiel, 1992).

- News coverage of a presidential candidate's extramarital affairs
  —is nothing new. Take Grover Cleveland, for example (Clayton & Thurston, 1992; "Clinton Agonistes," 1992; Stepp, 1992).
  —is warranted because it is important as an aspect of a candidate's character (Beck, 1992; Alan Bernstein, 1992; Connell, 1992; Ladowsky, 1992; Lamb, 1992; Lambro, 1992; Malone, 1992; "Questions about Clinton," 1992; Reinken, 1992).

- Rumors of Clinton's infidelity had been common knowledge among reporters for years, so it was only a matter of time before we shared these rumors with the public (Applebome, 1992; Daley, 1992; Evans & Novak, 1992; Freeman, 1992; Gailey, 1992; Hines, 1992; Lamb, 1992; Lambro, 1992; Rosenstiel, 1992; Schreiner, 1992; Sloyan, 1992).

- Journalists should admit that the tabloids did a great job getting this story—it's an example of great "enterprise" reporting—digging up and putting the pieces of a story together (Ladowsky, 1992; Lamb, 1992; Schreiner, 1992).

- Mainstream news organizations have paid for interviews in the past, so why make such a fuss about the *Star*? (Diamond, 1992; Lamb, 1992; Schreiner, 1992).

- A symbiotic relationship exists whereby mainstream journalists depend on tabloid journalists to do the dirty work of delving into the private lives of celebrities. After stories like this are broken, mainstream journalists blush over the work of the tabloids, then sanitize it (analyze it) for their readers (Jones, 1992; Lamb, 1992).

These arguments for inclusion of the story within the bounds of legitimate journalism deny some of the previously mentioned distinguishing characteristics of journalism, and give their own take on the boundary between news and entertainment:

1. The Flowers allegations became legitimate news through customs as a "media story"—implying that there are no epistemological boundaries between news and entertainment when a sensational story concerns a presidential candidate (all is fair in love and politics). Another implication is that media stories are always legitimate news.
2. Rumors of infidelity by presidential candidates should be considered legitimate journalism because they say something about the person's character—implying that the epistemological importance of this information justifies a violation of standard journalistic methodology—not repeating rumors.
3. The tabloids used our methodology—digging-up and researching the story, and even paying for it—so it is epistemologically the same as the kind of information we provide. (denial of methodological and epitemological differences)

Proponents of the *adjustment* side of the debate also argue that journalists cannot control the boundaries of journalism.

*   Don't blame us for the changes in the boundaries of news coverage of presidential campaigns because:
    —The candidates control them (Kolbert, 1992).
    —Television news programs control them (Carman, 1992; Gelfand, 1992; Kolbert, 1992; Kurtz, 1992a; "Old News," 1992).
    —The market (that is, consumer demand) controls them (Black, 1992; Gelfand, 1992; Jones, 1992; Kolbert, 1992; Ladowsky, 1992; Rosenstiel, 1992).
    —Tabloids control them ("Clinton turns," 1992; Lamb, 1992; Merry, 1992; Roberts, 1992; Scattarella & Ortega, 1992).
    —The standard of privacy has changed (Kolbert, 1992).

These arguments for justifying the inclusion of the story within the bounds of legitimate journalism deny some of the distinguishing characteristics of legitimate journalism and also deny the cultural authority of journalism to set boundaries or to control the flow of information. Instead, these authors imply that journalistic media are influenced by political candidates, by market influences, and by tabloid competitors. They seem to imply that the coverage of sensational political stories is uncontrollable or inevitable because they become "media stories," which means that journalists end up spreading the very gossip and innuendo they deplore. Once the Flowers allegations had received widespread attention, there was no reason to refrain from repeating them if it was in the context of a media story. In other words, the story had a life of its own, essentially uncontrollable.

This uncontrollable nature of sensational political stories is not accidental, according to some critics, who argue that the so-called "mainstream" journalism institution allows tabloids to set the agenda and substance of campaign coverage, just so that they can "cash-in" on sensational tales. As David Lamb of the *Los Angeles Times* noted:

"My colleague Margaret Carlson calls it tabloid laundering," said Dan Goodgame, White House correspondent for *Time*. "You let the tabloids go out and pay people for stories and do the dirty things Establishment journalists hold themselves above. Then you pick up and cover the controversy, either directly or as a press story. You write: 'Oh, how horrible the press is.' Then you go into the details." (1992)

In the following section, I examine how journalists seemed resigned to the fact that the Clinton/Flowers story was a Pandora's Box; after it was revealed, the coverage was inevitable—it had an unstoppable momentum all its own.

REPRESENTATIVE ANECDOTE: "SENSATIONAL NEWS IS LIKE A RUNAWAY TRAIN"

Brummett (1984) says Burke's "representative anecdote" is a particularly appropriate method for analyzing mass media:

The representative anecdote is a critical tool especially well-suited to analysis of the media, first, because of their "anecdotal" nature. Television, newspapers, film, popular magazines, etc., mediate reality to people by recasting the chaotic, disjointed world into "story exposition forms," presenting the world to audiences in the brief, one-half to two hour dramas of newscasts, articles, sitcoms, limited series, etc. . . .
    The representative anecdote is a particularly *representative* tool for media analysis because it resonates with the anecdotal, representative, dramatic form of the media, and because the content carried by that form is used by millions as equipment for living. . . . [It] taps what a culture *most* deeply fears and hopes, and how that culture confronts those concerns symbolically. (pp. 165–166)

As noted before, a representative anecdote is really an articulation of a central theme, or plot, through which a drama unfolds. In this situation, much of the rhetoric analyzed ponders the question: "Who controls political campaign news these days, tabloids or mainstream news media?" Many have previously argued that news has a momentum all its own and is uncontrollable. For instance, Timothy Crouse noted in 1972 that presidential campaign journalism suffers from peculiar relationships between the press and the candidate: "A group of reporters were assigned to follow a single candidate for weeks or months at a time, like a pack of hounds sicked on a fox. Trapped on the same bus or plane, they ate, drank, gambled, and compared notes with the same bunch of colleagues week after week" (p. 7). Crouse details the group dynamic of news reporters moving en masse to follow a campaign—all on the same vehicle, writing the same leads to the same stories (p. 22). Exclusive stories were seen as being unfaithful to the rest of the pack of reporters, and after a story was started, it spread like wildfire throughout the pack (p. 347). In a metaphorical sense, Crouse explains that the "bus" of news coverage is driven by journalists—aided by campaign managers, the candidate, and his unforeseen problems—but after a story is unleashed, it becomes uncontrollable, with a momentum all its own.

Larry Sabato, in his 1991 book on news coverage of political scandals, *Feeding Frenzy*, talks about how, when stories of political scandal are "broken," they tend to spark an uncontrollable feeding frenzy, like a group of sharks attacking prey:

If one newspaper prints, or one broadcaster airs a story, however questionable or poorly documented it may be, other media outlets will then publish or broadcast the news without verifying it. This abdication of journalistic responsibility encourages the purveyors of campaign smut to search out the weak media link. (p. 58)

Sabato's use of the "weak link in the chain" metaphor is particularly telling—he sees news media as a barrier, a chain boundary, between private and public information. Sabato interviewed many campaign journalists and editors for his book on the journalistic coverage of political scandal. One reporter, Michael Oreskes of the *New York Times*, gave this explanation for why mainstream journalistic outlets seem more eager to run questionable stories these days:

When we refuse to publish it, someone else publishes it. Then the fact that they published it becomes a story, so it still gets into our paper even though we originally decided it wasn't worth publishing. So you really lose control over your role as the gatekeeper. . . . On account of this some people begin to weaken their standards and say, "Well, it's going to get published anyway, so I'll go ahead and publish it first." (p. 58)

Oreskes blames not market fragmentation but the unity of the political economy of the contemporary mass media marketplace—and its great diversity of media voices—for lowering the standards of journalism. Journalism outlets like the *New York Times* are businesses after all, and if they believe that their competitors include supermarket tabloids like the *Star* and the *National Enquirer*, then they must do whatever is necessary to remain competitive—including watching supermarket tabloids to see what is newsworthy. As Paul Friedman, executive producer of ABC's evening news program said after the initial breaking of the Flowers story, "We're all worried about the *Star's* next issue" (Kurtz, 1992b). Worried, yes, but no doubt also watching it for clues about how the story will evolve.

This, of course, refutes the idea that the fragmentation of the mass media marketplace results in a diversity of media voices serving different publics and different roles. Instead, it is a resignation to the realization that the public perceives the news media as a monolithic block. As *Newsweek's* Jonathan Alter noted during the *Nightline* discussion about the allegations, "People tend to think the press is one thing. It's many news organizations. A lot of people think Geraldo is the press. So you're dealing with an essentially uncontrollable situation" ("Tabloid Prints," 1992).

Matthew Robert Korbel, in a recent book that analyzes television coverage of the 1992 presidential campaigns, calls stories that do not tell anything about the candidate's stand on substantive issues of government "nonissues," and he shows how such nonissues can crowd out the discussion of more-substantive issues (pp. 24–25). He also notes how the Flowers allegations essentially burned out of control:

For a brief period while it was unresolved, the Clinton-Flowers fiasco moved from a nonissue about alleged infidelity to a nonissue about the media problems caused by the nonissue. . . .

In general the nonissue firestorm will burn if it produces a media conflict that invites process coverage, if fueled by new allegations or new facts substantiating old charges, or if not overpowered by the emergence of a different (read: interesting) nonissue. On this latter point, the Gennifer Flowers matter was inevitably drowned out by the Vietnam draft item (a fact that provided little solace to the embattled candidate), and other nonissues later followed suit. (p. 68)

In Clinton's 1992 presidential campaign, the Flowers story careened out of control. It was a story put on the national agenda by a supermarket tabloid. As the campaign correspondents for the British news weekly, *The Economist*, noted:

The days when you could work out what the story of the day was by reading the front pages of the *Washington Post* or the *New York Times*, or by watching the network news, have gone for ever. In their place is something more messy, more partisan (but partisan for everyone and nobody), more modern, more controlled by the consumer—and more fun. ("Old News," 1992)

Many of the articles concerning the Clinton/Flowers scandal and its news coverage questioned the control journalists have over the boundaries of journalism, lamenting the influences of tabloids, political operatives, and the prurient interests of audiences. For instance:

"I'm continually impressed with how little we can do about the tone of a campaign," said Tom Hannon, political director for the Cable News Network. "The tenor seems beyond the control of any news organization. The process moves along; the media are essentially passive, despite appearances to the contrary." . . .
While once the major newspapers and the network television news programs set the agenda for the campaign coverage, this year the newspapers and the networks often seemed to be responding to supermarket tabloids and television talk shows. . . .
"The day of the network news being the horse that pulls the cart is over," said Lane Venardos, executive producer of special events for CBS. "We're either being pulled, or at best we're running alongside." (Kolbert, 1992)

Lou Gelfand (1992), the reader representative at the Minneapolis *Star Tribune*, seemed concerned about the way Clinton was being treated. He polled journalists and politicians about the 1992 presidential campaign news coverage, asking them why campaign journalism seems so often concerned with less-than-substantive issues. Many blamed television and the prurient curiosity of the public:

[*Star Tribune* National editor Roger] Buoen says "it's because we have moved from a print culture to an electronic culture. Sixty percent of U.S. households didn't buy a book last year. Adults now watch an average of more than 4 1/2 hours of television a day. In short, we have become a society less interested in reading and more interested in watching TV. And with this transformation has come a change in certain values. TV news is overwhelmed by the entertainment mission, and it's showing up in mainstream newspapers. Fearing a loss of viewers and readers, news producers and editors search for interesting (entertaining) stories. One result has been more emphasis on a candidate's personal life, often at the expense of serious issue-dominated pieces."

Journalists seemed ashamed that their profession was taking its leads from tabloids, completely losing control over the boundaries of legitimate journalism.

It isn't surprising that a supermarket tabloid like the Star prostituted itself by paying cabaret singer Gennifer Flowers an undisclosed amount of money to loosen her tongue.

But when a publication of such easy virtue is setting the journalistic standard for the national press, then we're all in trouble.

Otherwise respectable publications were eager to jump into bed with this story, all for cheap thrills. Grabby headlines. Titillation in an otherwise lackluster campaign.

No thought to whether a little caution now might have helped prevent a big embarrassment later. No thought to whether promiscuously spreading an unsubstantiated story might give them the equivalent of a social disease: vanishing credibility. (Scattarella & Ortega, 1992)

Thus, in the Clinton/Flowers saga, it became easy for journalists to blame the uncontrollable momentum of news for the way the Flowers allegations became news. The newsworthiness of stories—and hence, the boundaries of campaign journalism—are no longer controlled by major "elite" newspapers or even the network news divisions. Now campaign journalism is an essentially uncontrolled, open market, subject to fluctuations by any sort of social force. The primary dimension of the market's uncontrollable nature is that the mainstream news media can no longer "put the brakes" on stories they perceive as not newsworthy or as stories that race beyond the bounds of traditional journalism. In fact, they no longer have complete control over determinations about which stories are newsworthy and therefore belong within the realm of legitimate journalistic enterprise. Instead, they use some of the tools at their disposal to rank the relative reliability and newsworthiness of stories they would rather not run. In the next section, I examine how journalists use these tools to give readers clues about newsworthiness and reliability. They may not be able to stop the runaway train that some stories become, but they can certainly try to slow them down or minimize their impact.

PENTADIC ANALYSIS: RANKING THE RELIABILITY OF NEWS

Rhetoric is symbolic action. In the actions analyzed here, journalists pondered the boundaries of legitimate political journalism, and in so doing, revealed several rhetorical strategies. One of the strategies has been to criticize stories that do not fit into traditional standards in an attempt to make distinctions between news- and entertainment-based journalism.

In this section of the chapter, I look at how journalists attempted to rank the reliability of news stories by inserting some subtle and not-so-subtle clues, and by weighing the relative importance given to different stories. I compare the coverage given by one newspaper to the Hart/Rice scandal with the coverage it gave to the Clinton/Flowers scandal to see if this group of journalists felt the two stories deserved different treatment based on the circumstances (the scene). I also examine how journalists (agents) raised questions about the veracity of Gennifer Flowers by adding subtle clues (agency) to their descriptions of her.

A pentadic analysis examines how act, scene, agent, agency and purpose relate to one another in an unfolding drama. In the dramas examined here, the purpose-agency, scene-act, and scene-agency ratios were used by authors seeking to distinguish the boundaries of journalism.

The *Washington Post:* A Case Study in Sharpening Boundaries

When the Clinton/Flowers story emerged in the nation's news media, journalists criticized changing the rules they had established following the publishing of allegations of the marital infidelities of Gary Hart in May 1987. The purpose-agency ratios, the relation of means to ends, in these two instances were quite different. The Hart story was broken by the *Miami Herald*, not by a tabloid, and this made it seem more reliable in the eyes of many journalists, even though the *Herald's* reporters used some questionable investigative techniques—snooping outside Hart's Washington townhouse.

Rumors about Hart's marital infidelity had been rampant among reporters during his short bid for the Democratic presidential nomination in 1984, and those same rumors again surfaced in 1987 after he declared his candidacy for a second try. Journalists agonized over how they would deal with the allegations. According to an unnamed reporter at the *Washington Post*, the paper's executive editor, Ben Bradlee, had

"declared a statute of limitations" on probes of Hart's personal behavior: nothing before the last presidential election was relevant to considerations of his character. "My feeling," the reporter says, "was that if Hart cleaned up his act for the second run, that was fine with me. I was astounded to find out that he hadn't." (Wines, 1992, p. 19)

Once the *Miami Herald* broke the story on Sunday, May 3, 1987, the rest of the nation's news media unleashed a flood of stories mentioning the earlier rumors, using the *Herald* story as the backdrop for airing them. The *Washington Post* covered the Hart story in great detail throughout the controversy; it was featured on page one for six consecutive days (May 4–9, until Hart had dropped from the race) and dominated the news even though there were other very important events happening in Washington during this period. For instance, the Iran-Contra hearings began on Capitol Hill on May 5, 1992, the same day that William Casey, head of the CIA, died. Attorney General Edwin Meese was implicated in the Wedtech scandal a few days later. During the week following the initial story about Hart & Rice, published on May 4, the *Post* ran 42 more articles, columns, and editorials about the scandal (see Table 6.1).

An editorial on May 5 defended the *Miami Herald's* coverage because it appeared that Hart was up to something "looking pretty fishy" ("The Gary Hart Dispute," 1987). The same day, Ben Bradlee defended the coverage because "He challenged the press to do what he is now complaining they did" (Vobejda, 1987). Bradlee (1995), in his recent autobiography, says the Hart/Rice scandal was one of the most difficult situations he faced as an editor, but it was made easier by his knowledge that Hart was lying about the state of his marriage (pp. 479–484). The *Post* was obviously confident about its coverage and about Hart's guilt: It ran a satirical column on May 5 that made fun of the candidate's problems (Mansfield, 1987), and the next day ran a story about how the Hart scandal was becoming a popular topic for comedians (Kastor, 1987).

Table 6.1
Articles Published in the *Washington Post* on the Hart/Rice Scandal (during the week after it was broken)

May 4:   Dickenson, James R., and Paul Taylor. "Newspaper Stakeout Infuriates Hart," pp. A1, 4.

May 5:   Taylor, Paul. "'Outraged' Hart Prepares Rebuttal," pp. A1, 10; Edsall, Thomas B. "Model-Actress Was Hart's D.C. Visitor," pp. A1, 9; Vobejda, Barbara. "Ethical Questions Arise on Reporting The

Private Life of a Public Figure," pp. A6–7; Walsh, Edward. "Well-Connected Lawyer Advises Hart Campaign," p. A9; Dickenson, James R. "Hart Weekend: Conflicting Stories," p. A10; "The Gary Hart Dispute," (unsigned editorial) p. A18; Shields, Mark. "Gary Hart and the Arrogance of Indifference," p. A19; Mansfield, Stephanie. "Satire: Ringing In With The Rice Merchants," pp. D1, 8; McCombs, Phil. "Sex and Power: An Age-Old Intimate Relationship," pp. D1, 8.

May 6:   Peterson, Bill, and T. R. Reid. "Hart Says His Judgment, Not Conduct, Was Flawed: Many Supporters Keep Own Counsel," pp. A1, 14–15; Taylor, Paul, and James R. Dickenson. "Candidate Assails 'False' News Stories," pp. A1, 12; Johnson, Haynes. "The Stench of Scandal," p. A2; Romano, Lois, and Marc Fisher. "Donna Rice Declines Limelight, Canceling News Conference," p. A12; Kinsley, Michael. "The New Honesty in the Press," p. A19; Yoder, Edwin M., Jr. "'Totalitarian Journalism,'" p. A19; Raspberry, William. "Victimized . . . by Himself," p. A19; Kastor, Elizabeth. "The Jokers Take Hart," pp. B1, 9; Mann, Judy. "Terminal Stupidity," p. C3.

May 7:   Taylor, Paul. "Hart Defends His Account of Weekend," pp. A1, 22; Reid, T. R. "Lee Hart Breaks Silence to Defend Her Husband," p. A23; Goodman, Ellen. "The Importance of Hart's Character . . ." p. A27; Cohen, Richard. ". . . And the Things He Finds Unimportant," p. A27; Romano, Lois. "The Miami Herald's Go-Ahead," p. C1, 8; Gilliam, Dorothy. "Unacceptable Behavior of Barry and Hart," p. D3.

May 8:   Taylor, Paul. "Hart to Withdraw From Presidential Campaign," pp. A1, 14; Maraniss, David. "The Character Issue: A Bomb Waiting to Burst," pp. A1, 15; Broder, David S. "Democrats' 1988 Contest Wide Open," pp. A1, 14; Reid, T. R. "Dreams of a Hart Administration Die With Call: 'We've Got Another Problem,'" p. A15; "A Candidacy Ends," (unsigned editorial) p. A22; Broder, David S. "Another Unexpected Disclosure," p. A23; Will, George F. "The Wolf Factor," p. A23; Shales, Tom. "The Season of Scandal," pp. D1, 4.

May 9:   Randolph, Eleanor. "The Press and the Candidate: Hart Sex Life Was Longtime Focus of Rumors," pp. A1, 10; Reid, T. R. "Biting Attacks Leveled on Media, Process of Selecting U.S. Leaders," pp. A1, 11; Peterson, Bill. "Dinner, Discussion, Decision," pp. A1, 10; "'This Campaign Cannot Go On,'" (transcript of Hart's withdrawal statement) p. A11; MacPherson, Myra. "Trials of the Political Wife," pp. G1, 2.

May 10:   "Gary Hart: The Aftermath," (unsigned editorial) p. B6; Laitin, Joseph. "Politics, Sex And Drugs," p. B6.

May 11:   "Tipster Said She Was Donna Rice's Friend," p. A3; Greenfield,
            Meg. "Private Lives, Public Values," p. A13; Raspberry, William.
            "What About The Miami Herald?" p. A13.

On Wednesday, May 6, 1987, the *Post* ran several opinion columns
on the Hart coverage, most of which defended the newsworthiness of
the story. Columnist William Raspberry said,

Hart stands convicted of abominable judgment, at best, and, at worst, an un-
presidential recklessness.
    "I've been victimized," he told the Denver Post yesterday. It's true; he has
been. But less by the Miami Herald, which broke the story, than by himself.
    If you are already at pains to refute persistent rumors of womanizing . . .
the last thing you want to do is bring a young model to your house while your
wife is out of town.

Columnist Michael Kinsley said "Anything that keeps a politician
humble is healthy for a democracy" (1987). Edwin M. Yoder, Jr.,
however, was critical of the new direction journalism was going; he
said that even though Hart should not have dared reporters to "put a
tail on me. . . . One can well imagine politicians daring newspapers to
do all sorts of things they shouldn't do, even on a dare" (1987).
    In a book recounting the coverage of the story, *Post* reporter Paul
Taylor (1990) says that the paper received many calls from sources
who knew of other women who had had affairs with Hart, one of
whom supplied the paper with photographic evidence (pp. 48–49).
Armed with the knowledge of this evidence, Taylor was emboldened
to ask Hart during a nationally televised press conference in New
Hampshire on May 6, "Have you ever committed adultery?" Taylor
says he was subsequently pilloried by other members of the press who
deemed the question inappropriate. Four columnists at the *New York
Times* criticized him for lowering the level of political discussion. He
responded in a letter to the editor that was published a few weeks
later:

Anthony Lewis wrote that I was responsible for the "low point" of the news
coverage of a story in which "reporters and editors salivated in their zeal to
learn all and tell all." William Safire said that I was "demeaning" my profession and that "titillaters" in the press like me needed to be stopped. A.M.
Rosenthal, quoted in another newspaper, said he found the question
"nauseating.". . .
    It is not the job of a journalist to win plaudits for civility (though it's
certainly nicer when we do). Nor is our job to pry into the most private

matters—except when public figures, in conducting and discussing their private affairs publicly, force our hand. Sometimes this job demands that we raise questions we'd rather not ask. Your columnists suggest I broke some kind of gentleman's code. . . . What I did was ask Gary Hart the question he asked for. (Taylor, 1987a)

Later on the night of May 6, Taylor told Hart aides about the *Post's* evidence, in hopes of getting an exclusive interview with the candidate. Instead, Hart pulled up stakes and flew back to Colorado in the middle of the night with his wife and a handful of top aides. The *Post's* threat to expose another past affair had forced Hart to withdraw from the race. Later, the *Post* seemed to be proud of its role in getting Hart to drop out of the race, and this may account for its defense of the coverage. In the second paragraph of the top story of its May 8 issue, the paper told its readers of its political influence: "He decided to drop out early yesterday morning, hours after *The Washington Post* presented a top campaign aide with documented evidence of a recent liaison between Hart and a Washington woman with whom he has had a long-term relationship" (Taylor, 1987b). This statement seems to indicate that the *Post* had a vested interest in the political effect of the Rice story. One analysis of the *Post's* involvement charged that it "engaged in high-stakes political poker rather than journalism," because it used its information on other Hart dalliances primarily to force the hand of the candidate, not to enlighten readers (Judis, 1987, p. 25).

On May 9, a *Post* reporter argued to readers that "It was Gary Hart's past . . . that transformed his sex life, rarely a public concern in presidential politics, into the 'character issue' that quickly came to dominate Hart's 1988 campaign. . . . Indeed, the 'womanizing' issue had been simmering for almost 15 years" (Randolph, 1987). Journalists familiar with the rumors about Hart and his denials felt that the coverage was justified and were quick to believe that Hart was involved with Rice.

After the story first broke, Hart struck back by condemning the ethics and credibility of journalism. This angered Ben Bradlee, who said, "Much more than the Miami thing was his speech at the publishers' association and at [former *New York Times* executive] Sidney Gruson's [fundraiser], where he said he was being stabbed in the back by the press" (Judis, 1987, p. 23). Journalists wanted to show that they were right and Hart was lying. The most-cited justification of the intense media investigation of Hart's private life was that he insisted that he was a happily married man, and that he held himself to a "high standard of public and private conduct," while journalists knew his reputation as a womanizer (Taylor, 1987a). Journalists could not stand the hypocrisy, and many clearly felt confident in telling the story. The ends—of exposing his lying—justified the means—asking him humiliating private questions. In contrast, the Clinton/Flowers story was one that most journalists seemed reluctant to report.

The *Washington Post* first covered the Clinton/Flowers story on Friday, January 24, the morning after the *Star* advance was released, in a lengthy neutral article on page 8 which highlighted Clinton's denial of its truthfulness, and the lack of credibility of the source (Balz & Kurtz, 1992). The *New York Times* also ran the story that day, but it was run even smaller and further back in the paper, in an unsigned article at the bottom of page 14, again highlighting Clinton's denial and noting the unreliability of the source ("Clinton Denounces," 1992).

Within the next week (January 25–31), the *Post* published 23 more articles, opinion columns, and editorials on the scandal, 20 of which criticized the news media coverage of the Flowers allegations, principally by disparaging the tabloid media origins of the story (see Table 6.2).

Table 6.2
Articles Published in the *Washington Post* on the Clinton/Flowers Scandal (during the week after it was broken)

Jan. 25:   Kurtz, Howard. "Clintons Agree to Do '60 Minutes,'" p. A10.

Jan. 26:   Maraniss, David. "Clinton's Life Shaped by Early Turmoil," pp. A1, 16; Von Drehle, David, and Thomas B. Edsall. "Clinton Accuser to Drop Bid on Reviving Lawsuit," p. A16; Quinn, Sally. "Tabloid Politics, the Clintons and the Way We Now Scrutinize Our Potential Presidents," pp. C1–2.

Jan. 27:   Balz, Dan. "Clinton Concedes Marital 'Wrongdoing,'" pp. A1, 6; and "I Have Absolutely Leveled with Voters," [transcript of Clinton's *60 Minutes* appearance] p. A6.

Jan. 28:   McGrory, Mary. "Flowers and Dirt," p. A2; Kurtz, Howard. "Five Days from Tabloid Tattle to Front-Page Fare," p. A8; Von Drehle, David. "Clinton Accuser Defends Story, Plays Tapes," p. A8; "The Clinton Controversy," [an unsigned editorial] p. A20; Broder, David. "Odd Way To Choose a President," p. A21; Shales, Tom. "Campaign '92: The Muck Starts Here," p. E1; Span, Paula. "The Bright & Slimy Star," p. E1.

Jan. 29:   Maraniss, David. "Weary From Scrutiny, Looking Over His
            Shoulder; Clinton's Campaign Isn't Exactly Back to Normal, but
            There Are No Signs It Is Reeling," p. A9; Schwartz, Amy E. "Endless
            Questions," p. A21.

Jan. 30:   Kurtz, Howard. "Reports on Clinton Pose Quandary for
            Journalists," p. A14; Schwartz, Maralee. "Gov. Clinton's Remarks
            'Offensive,' Kerry Says," p. A14.

Jan. 31:   Balz, Dan. "Clinton's Foes Say No News Is Bad News; Lack of
            Coverage Frustrates Democrats," p. A10; Hoagland, Jim. ". . . Over
            Democratic Party Activists," p. A19; Krauthammer, Charles. "The
            Press Confronts Its Power," p. A19; Mann, Judy. "The Incredible
            Gennifer Flowers," p. E3. Trueheart, Charles. "Little Rock, Still Soft
            on Clinton," pp. G1–2; Romano, Lois. "Gary Hart Redux in
            Tinseltown?" p. G3.

One of the three articles uncritical of the news coverage of the
Flowers story was a lengthy and largely complimentary biographical
profile of Clinton (Maraniss, 1992b). Another was a gossip column
that speculated on the effects of the allegations on Clinton's support
among Hollywood celebrities, and that compared Clinton's fate to
that of Hart (Romano, 1992). The third was a campaign digest that
reported candidate Bob Kerry's unhappiness with the content of the
taped conversations between Flowers and Clinton (Schwartz, M.,
1992).

The *Post* was not involved in breaking the Flowers story, and, sensing the scene-agency differences between this tabloid-generated story
and the Hart story (that is, the situation and the reasons for running
it), chose to discuss the Flowers story in ways that questioned its
truthfulness, and therefore, questioned whether the story was within
the epistemological bounds of journalism. Although it devoted a fairly
large amount of editorial space to the scandal, it was not featured
nearly as prominently as the Hart story had been, and almost all of
the articles it published included implicit warnings about its reliability. The Clinton/Flowers story only made it to the front page on one
day, the day after Mr. and Mrs. Clinton appeared on *60 Minutes*.
Some at the *Post* questioned why the story was used at all, because of
the unsubstantiated nature of the allegations. But, as noted earlier, it
became newsworthy for all the news media once it gained momentum
as a media story. Robert Kaiser, managing editor of the *Washington
Post*, noted that tabloids have the power to "make" political news
happen, by virtue of getting people interested in them:

"One of our functions in life is to keep our readers abreast of political news, and the *Star* is one of many megaphones in the world that do appear to have the power to make something happen in politics," Kaiser of the *Post* said. "It would be foolish to deny that there are lots of forces in society, some of which are more reputable than others, that have that power." (Rosenstiel, 1992)

By airing the Flowers allegations, the news media acknowledged that mass media forces outside the mainstream news media have the power to affect politics and, therefore, to receive mainstream news coverage. The mainstream news media cannot control what becomes news, but they can do things to minimize the impact of unsavory stories.

The differences in the ways the two scandals were reported can be explained by examining some of the relevant pentadic ratios of the two dramas:

1. The purpose-agency ratios (or relationship of ends to means) of the reporting of the two stories were completely different. With Hart, reporters wanted to expose someone who they knew was lying. With Clinton, tabloid journalism seemed to force the story onto the agenda for a monetary purpose: in the money paid to Flowers, and collected at supermarket checkout stands by the *Star*, which counted on increased sales. Hart had challenged reporters to catch him cheating, and it was common knowledge to many reporters that he was lying about his supposed "rock-solid" marriage. Clinton had issued no challenges, and admitted that he had engaged in "wrongdoing" in his marriage but insisted that he was reformed.

2. With the Hart story, a disinterested (unpaid) source corroborated the story.[2] With the Flowers allegations, no one could corroborate her story, she seemed to have problems telling the truth, and her audiotapes seemed inconclusive. The agent-scene ratios of the two stories were vastly different. For the Hart/Rice scandal, the *Miami Herald* sent journalists to confirm the allegations made by a tipster who did not ask for money but just claimed to be fed up with the lies. Many of the facts offered by this tipster proved correct. For the Clinton/Flowers scandal, no corroborating evidence was found by the many journalists who followed up on Flowers' allegations.

3. Hart's offenses were current. Clinton's offenses were alleged by his accuser to have ceased four years earlier. The scene-act and agent-act ratios of the way these stories played-out were different. When journalists (agents) revealed (act) that Hart and Rice had gone on an overnight boating trip to Bimini together about a month before being found at his D.C. townhouse (scene), it pretty well sealed his fate to be labeled a womanizer. Journalists (agents) investigating (act) Clinton could not find evidence of any current behavior (scene) to suggest he was a womanizer.

By minimizing the credibility of the Flowers story, the *Post* held on to some remnants of a boundary—these subtle clues informed readers about the relative importance of the story—demonstrating that it really belonged outside the boundary of journalism. Even so, they could not ignore it completely.

Many of the ways in which journalists handled the Flowers allegations give clues about how they perceived them to be less than reliable and not deserving to be included within the boundaries of legitimate journalism. In the following section, I examine how journalists' descriptions of Flowers were calculated to cast doubts on her veracity. I interpret these instances as attempts by journalists to place the Flowers story outside the bounds of legitimate journalism, even though they felt powerless to ignore it.

Gennifer Flowers As Former Singer or Former Journalist?

The descriptions of Gennifer Flowers' occupation in the articles analyzed demonstrate the way journalists use subtle rhetorical clues to raise doubts about the veracity of a source and, therefore, the reliability of a piece of information. Flowers had worked as a reporter at a television station in Little Rock, KARK-TV, then worked sporadically as a nightclub singer before she began working as an administrative assistant for the Arkansas Appeal Tribunal, the state unemployment appeals board.

In the articles and transcripts analyzed, Flowers was *much* more often called a "former singer" than a "former TV reporter" or "state employee."[3] Usually the term "singer" followed a term for a drinking establishment, such as "cabaret," "nightclub," or "saloon." And a few of the authors cast doubt on her singing ability, with phrases such as "a nightclub singer of questionable ability and desperate for money," "failed C+W singer," or "onetime cabaret singer," implying that she was not talented. Her hair color was mentioned in many of the articles, usually as a "dark-roots blonde," implying that she was a fake. One article called her a "homewrecker," and wondered what kind of a woman who claims to love a man would then want to put him through this kind of "trial by media." To many journalists, her motives were obviously selfish, and the media attention her allegations received was unwarranted.

Flowers' previous job as an entertainer was a perfect character fit for the dramatic theme of the stories most journalists wrote about her. It helped bolster their arguments that her story was more entertainment than news, closer to fiction than reality, and that she was not only an entertainer but an untalented one who operated with less-than-honorable motives. The vast majority of articles conveniently neglected to mention that she had once worked as a journalist at a so-called "mainstream" journalism outlet, sparing the authors from confronting the ultimate irony of the situation: a former "legitimate" journalist becoming a story source for an "illegitimate" tabloid journalism outlet. One story that did mention her journalism credentials called her a "journalistic dropout." Another called her a "smoking bimbo."

Clearly journalists were uncomfortable with the Flowers story because it seemed beyond the cultural space of journalism. Yet they felt forced to write about it—either because their editors asked them to, or because the uncontrollable force of the "media story" made it impossible to ignore, or they wanted to chastise their colleagues for covering it. Many journalists—through acts of commission or omission—inserted clues about the reliability of a story about which they felt compelled to comment. In this way they held on to the remnants of a boundary they felt once existed—by discrediting a story they felt powerless to kill.

SUMMARY

Political candidates in America become celebrities, and like all celebrities, they lose some of their privacy because of public curiosity. The sex lives of celebrities interest readers and viewers but are not necessarily newsworthy. "News" about deviance in the sex lives of politicians is frowned upon by journalists, generally with statements about how such information does not tell much about how the person would govern. This epistemological boundary between "interesting" (entertaining) and "newsworthy" (important and verifiable) information was one with which journalists struggled in the cases examined here. Although journalists who think of themselves as "mainstream" purport to avoid stories about the private lives of political candidates, clearly they do not refrain from telling them if they perceive that the public is curious about them. Instead of maintaining strict separation between styles of political discourse in different kinds of media—such as "tabloid" scandal-based news discourse and "mainstream" issue-based news discourse—the American news media as a whole have decided to carry on a single discourse that borrows from many styles. It is, as the article in *The Economist* noted, "more messy" this way, but more equal too. The central problems this raises for journalists deal with jurisdiction and authority—who covers what, and who is in control of the media agenda.

Tabloid and mainstream journalists are equally interested in stories that are newsworthy and entertaining at the same time. Such stories, particularly if they involve political celebrity scandal, tend to take on a life of their own after they are broken, and become practically uncontrollable. Journalists imply that they are helpless in these situations because they cannot control the boundaries of news. The evidence seems to show that some journalists have consciously decided to abandon the enforcement of certain boundaries because those boundaries have historically prevented them from covering certain popular (profitable) stories.

So-called "mainstream" journalists do what they can to discredit and minimize the importance of stories they dislike even as they feel compelled to report the details of them. This is an uncomfortable position for a profession which used to save the best (read: the juiciest scandals) for private conversations between colleagues. Before, they felt that they could control the agenda of the news, and they ignored tabloid headlines. Now they fear what tabloids are going to do with a story because they believe they are all competitors—partners in the mass media industry, all vying for ever-smaller pieces of one ever-larger pie.

The rhetoric analyzed here shows how journalists perceive their redefined role in society—such as that of defining the reliability of certain stories, and of making things happen in the democracy. When politicians such as Gary Hart tell lies about their private lives, those private lives become worthy of public scrutiny. And some journalists get distracted with making things happen—such as forcing liars to drop out of political campaigns—rather than performing their often-declared function in society: informing the citizens or informing the debates of citizens. The functional boundaries of journalism have become distorted. For instance, dubious accusations are now newsworthy for the sole reason that they can have a newsworthy effect on candidates. The mainstream news media now publish rumors (along with sufficient discrediting commentary) if they believe that these rumors might have a newsworthy effect on a candidate's political future. In this way the news media become the story themselves, as they try to make things happen in the democracy—again without really informing the citizens of so-called "substantive issues." Clearly, journalists believe that the functional roles or boundaries of journalism are shifting. Although journalists may have at one time thought of their function as that of messenger or megaphone for society, they now perceive their function to be more proactive, particularly in politics. If a story can have a newsworthy effect—no matter how true or false it is—then it must be news.

In addition, journalists now seem relatively unsure about what counts as important, newsworthy information versus what is merely entertaining—an epistemological distinction. The "rules" mainstream journalists cited in justifying their coverage of the Hart drama were also cited in many of the articles critical of the coverage of the Clinton/Flowers drama. Some journalists defended the Clinton/Flowers story as legitimately within the bounds of journalism, which, in light of the "Hart rules," can be interpreted as an attempt to reshape certain boundaries to fit particular situations. For instance, one of the justifications of the Hart story was that it provided evidence that proved the candidate was lying—it proved that his contention that he was happily married was a falsifiable claim. Proving someone to be a liar says something about the person's "character." With Flowers, there was no such hard evidence—just a "her word against his" contention; that is, merely "allegations." In other words, the information upon which the two stories were based was epistemologically different: In one case, there was hard evidence, in the other, questionable allegations. *The Star* paid Gennifer Flowers for her allegations—some said she was paid to change her story, because she had publicly and vehemently maintained for several years that rumors of a romantic relationship with Clinton were false. In other words, the motivation for breaking the Clinton story appeared to be monetary. In the Hart case, an acquaintance of Donna Rice decided that she did not like the way Hart kept saying he was a faithful husband when she knew he was having a relationship with Rice, so she tipped off a reporter who had just argued in an editorial that the media should believe Hart and leave him alone. In other words, the breaking of the Hart story appeared to be motivated—in the reporter and the tipster—by a desire for the truth to be told.

The apparent motivations for the two stories were radically different, implying that there were epistemological differences in the kind and value of the information the stories contained. On the one hand, the Flowers story was almost certain to be biased, and on the other, the Hart story was almost certain to be unbiased. Yet some journalists claimed that there were no differences between the two. They justified using the Flowers story with arguments that the two stories were essentially the same. Both of the stories were sensational—people were curious about them. In the end, for some journalists, the only thing that really mattered was giving the public what they seem to want.

The disagreement about whether these stories were within the bounds of legitimate journalism demonstrates that the boundaries were blurred, that it was a contested area, and that efforts to sharpen these kinds of boundaries are difficult to enforce or even define when journalists see supermarket tabloids as competitors who operate within a common space.

I suspect the boundary between tabloid and mainstream is probably most evident in a "self-critical" dimension. It appears that tabloids do not expend editorial energy criticizing themselves for covering stories like these or for breaking boundaries. (I cannot empirically confirm this suspicion, however, because tabloid news media are neither collected nor indexed at research libraries, which in itself highlights another interesting dimension of the boundary between tabloid and mainstream.)

By telling readers that certain information is "trashy" and should be digested with a fair amount of skepticism, the so-called mainstream news media signal to their audiences that they are aware that what they are doing is questionable and that they are uneasy about their new role—of spreading rumor and innuendo. In that regard they at least maintain control over the conscience of their medium, even as they abdicate the cultural authority to maintain some of its boundaries.

NOTES

1. The NEXIS database—like nearly all scholarly research resources—virtually excludes the texts of the so-called "tabloid" mass media. The texts and arguments analyzed here belong to those who consider themselves part of the "mainstream" American journalism community.

2. Cramer contends that Lynn Armandt, a friend of Donna Rice, secretly gave tips about Rice and Hart's relationship to Tom Fiedler of *The Miami Herald* (Cramer, 1992, p. 432). Fiedler says that it was someone else (Germond & Witcover, 1989, p. 185).

3. Flowers' former occupation as a "singer" was mentioned in 28 stories, "TV reporter" was mentioned in 9 stories, and "Arkansas state employee" in 13

stories. Six of the stories mentioned all three. The rest of the stories did not mention her occupation or simply called her "an Arkansas woman."

Conclusions

When the goal is expansion of authority or expertise into domains claimed by other professions or occupations, boundary-work heightens the contrast between rivals in ways flattering to the ideologists' side; when the goal is monopolization of professional authority and resources, boundary-work excludes rivals from within by defining them as outsiders with labels such as "pseudo," "deviant," or "amateur"; when the goal is protection of autonomy over professional activities, boundary-work exempts members from responsibility for consequences of their work by putting blame on scapegoats from outside.

—Thomas F. Gieryn
"Boundary-work and the demarcation of science from non-science"

A REEXAMINATION OF CHAPTERS 3, 4, 5, AND 6

Chapter 3—The Evolution of Television Journalism, the First Two Decades

Early television journalism could not help being influenced by its medium, a medium that evidently looked like a great teaching tool to the first naïve observers. To those who held the purse strings—and who controlled television programming—television appeared to be the greatest advertising medium of all time. Soon, it became a requirement that all television programming be designed to draw the largest possible audience. This quest for profits put pressures on television journalists to adopt techniques that seemed less than faithful to the truth and less than faithful to the traditions of journalism, in some critics' opinions.

Television journalism began as a field in which few journalists wanted to get involved. It was seen as a professional ghetto, a place that any self-respecting journalist would avoid. A few respected journalists, like Edward R. Murrow, were able to enter television journalism and lend it a degree of respectability. They did this by bucking the trend of allowing advertisers and network money managers to influence content. Murrow and Friendly's *See It Now* openly rebelled against the idea of advertiser or even network influence on their journalistic judgment. Most other television journalists, however, did not maintain such a hard line stance on the separation between journalism and outside interests.

Chapter 4—Governmental Definitions of News

In Chapter 4, I examined how government regulators and legislators confronted the issue of staking out the cultural space of legitimate journalism by formulating definitions of news and newsworthiness. Members of Congress discovered the difficulty of defining the role of a self-defined profession that jealously guards its cultural authority to decide when something is news, and when journalism is legitimate. This autonomy was recognized by legislators as one of the hallmarks of journalism—an organizational distinction or dimension of the boundary of journalism's cultural space. As long as journalists are independently calling the shots—and political candidates are not involved in producing news about themselves—then it must be assumed that the product is journalism.

In addition, legislators concluded that legitimate journalism programs about political candidates are regularly scheduled—a methodological distinction of the boundary of journalism. Beyond these characteristics, Congress was unable to identify any other essential characteristics of journalism. Many legislators seemed unsatisfied with the vague nature of these definitions, so they asked that the Federal Communications Commission undertake the task of clarifying the boundaries and definitions of journalism. They felt that the members of the FCC, through their close association with broadcasters, were far more qualified to embark on the politically-sensitive task of formulating a concrete definition for a field that practices autonomous self-realization and self-conception. Congress seemed to imply that the FCC, because many of its members had strong ties to broadcasting or were former broadcasters themselves, were the most qualified agents of the government to engage in this endeavor.

The FCC had asked for the jurisdiction to make these definitions, but after they got it, they discovered that it was not an easy task. Instead of making firm pronouncements on the essential elements of journalism, the FCC frequently deferred to the apparent intent of

Congress contained in the published debates of the legislation initiated to "correct" the *Lar Daly* decision. At one point, the FCC decided that it could identify some essential elements of journalism by distinguishing it from other types of communication along several dimensions: An epistemological dimension (journalism examines issues of "public significance"); a methodological dimension (journalism programs utilize a "regularly used news interview format"); and a functional dimension (journalism programs are designed to inform rather than entertain, and are not designed to "advance the candidacy" of a particular candidate) (*Davis*, 1976; NBC, 1976; Multimedia, 1981).

Within a few years, however—in the early 1980s—the FCC concluded that methodological distinctions were the only ones it was qualified to make, because epistemological and functional distinctions could only be made by journalists themselves—these were elements of "doing journalism"—making decisions about who is newsworthy, what deserves coverage, and what journalism should do for society. This doctrine—of relying solely on methodological distinctions—led to several interesting decisions, such as those defining *Entertainment Tonight* and *Sally Jessy Raphael* as "bona fide" news programs. Perhaps realizing the folly of defining the essential characteristics of news, the FCC eventually reverted to its original stance—that to qualify as journalism, programs about political candidates must not be controlled by those candidates.

The cultural space of journalism is socially constructed, so attempts to essentialize this space proved to be an impractical matter. It is instructive for journalists to consider how others conceive the cultural landscape, to see where others think journalism fits into our culture. Journalists want the cultural authority to define their role in society and to make day-to-day decisions about what is news and how it should be gathered and presented. In the rhetoric analyzed in Chapter 4, it is apparent that the government eventually agreed that being a journalist means more than just being able to define what is newsworthy, it also means the right to autonomous self-definition.

Chapter 5—Status Degradation of a Deviant Journalist

Part of the process of self-definition of a group includes the process of identifying and punishing deviance. In Chapter 5, I examined how the journalistic community identified a deviant member and then carried out a successful status degradation ceremony to expel the deviant member in a process designed to repair and situate the boundaries of journalism. In the case of *Dateline NBC* and Michael Gartner, the journalistic community defined fabrication, fiction, stonewalling, and undue attention to profit-making as acts of journalistic deviance.

Michael Gartner was identified as a man more concerned with profits than journalistic values, and his personal arrogance and strange ideas about privacy made him someone who was easy to dislike and then banish.

The status degradation ceremony of Michael Gartner was accomplished in a way to cleanse the profession, making it healthy again, as well as to deflect attention away from the structural defects of a journalism institution. Journalists noted that Gartner was responsible for blurring the organizational boundary between television business and television journalism at NBC, and this blurriness at NBC led to a climate that made the misconduct inevitable. Under Gartner, NBC perpetrated a journalistic fraud—and for a while—denied wrongdoing. They stonewalled like crooked politicians—a situation upon which journalists love to pounce. Journalists seem to prefer disclosure and honesty, but Gartner and NBC refused to confess and make amends until faced with a multimillion dollar lawsuit and global press conference from General Motors.

Journalists perceived Gartner as a man who had lost his journalistic bearings during his rise to the top of the profession. He seemed to have an ambivalent attitude about journalistic wrongdoing if it meant increased profits, and he did not defend or even accept the idea that journalism should be primarily be concerned with performing a public service, rather than with profitability.

Chapter 6—Gennifer Flowers and Bill Clinton

In Chapter 6, an examination of criticism of news coverage of politicians' sex scandals, the differences between "newsworthy" and "interesting" information were discussed. Journalists argue that just because some bit of information is interesting to the public, that does not make it news. Critics argued that newsworthy information about the private lives of political candidates must be important in regard to the political process and must be confirmed by independent journalistic investigation, that is, it should not include unsubstantiated allegations or speculation.

One way for journalists to make otherwise non-newsworthy allegations newsworthy was to discuss them in the context of a "media story" about how journalists are dealing with the allegations. This could be interpreted as a way for journalists to stretch a boundary without destroying it—questionable allegations are spread, are identified as questionable, and the spreading of them is criticized as being outside the bounds of journalism—all within the same story. It is a convenient method for satisfying the public's appetite for celebrity sex scandals while maintaining the semblance of a boundary by repeating the questionable allegations in an analytical context.

In the Bill Clinton/Gennifer Flowers story, Flowers' allegations were first broached by a supermarket tabloid, which, in the eyes of many in the so-called "mainstream" news media, made the story different from the Gary Hart/Donna Rice story. Yet the mainstream media found a way to discuss it by placing it in the context of a media story. Both the Hart/Rice and Clinton/Flowers stories provoked volumes of boundary-work rhetoric from journalists and journalism critics, signaling a boundary in dispute.

Rather than maintain separate genres of political discourse—one focused on sensational scandal and one focused on "issues" (and each relinquishing control of the other type)—the so-called mainstream news media appear to want to maintain a unified media marketplace wherein all news media—tabloid and mainstream—compete for stories about political scandal. Tabloids, on the other hand, do appear to have relinquished control of "issue-based" political news to the mainstream news media. The best explanation for this blurring of jurisdictions on the part of the mainstream news media is that it is economically-motivated; journalism organizations, realizing the intense public curiosity for political scandal, want to "cash in" on the intrigue. Another motivation may be to "make something happen" in politics. The analysis of the *Washington Post*'s rhetoric justifying its role in the Gary Hart scandal indicates there was a desire by the *Post* to get Hart to drop out of the race—far from the traditional journalistic role of informing the public.

In the rhetoric examined in Chapter 6, journalists noted that a problem with scandal-based political news is that it tends to take on a life of its own and becomes essentially uncontrollable. Some seemed to recognize that this presented a threat to journalism's cultural authority. They realized they could not maintain control of the news when it was based on scandal and unsubstantiated allegations.

One of the ways they dealt with this dilemma was to use sufficient discrediting information within the stories about the scandals. If they felt compelled to report on the Flowers allegations—either through requests from bosses to get "a piece of the story" or through a desire to comment on it through customs as a "media story"—they almost always inserted specific details intended to discredit the reliability of the allegations and the accuser. In this way they told their readers that although the story may be interesting (read: entertaining), it may also be untrue.

Journalists have always been of the gossipy type; they love to share rumors about public officials. But they used to share these rumors only with each other. That was back when they ignored tabloid headlines and they thought they could (and did) control the agenda of news coverage. Now they watch what the tabloids are doing because they believe that they are all competitors in a unified news media industry. Journalists discovered that rumors can have an impact on the political fortunes of politicians—particularly if they helped spread those rumors. Some journalists justifying the coverage of these scandals argued that anything that affects a politician's chances of surviving a political battle is newsworthy. Unfortunately, this is a self-fulfilling prophecy when it comes to journalistic discussion of allegations of socially deviant sexual behavior, which are always sensational. The news media, when they publish these stories, become the newsworthy "political force" to which the politicians must reckon—and about which journalists must discuss.

Many journalists defended the news coverage of the Hart/Rice scandal on several grounds, which came to be recognized as a threshold of "rules" governing when the private sexual lives of politicians become worthy of public scrutiny. These "rules" were the same ones cited by many journalists critical of the coverage of the Clinton/Flowers drama, yet these rules were fairly ineffective in slowing the momentum of coverage of the Flowers allegations. Those journalists who defended the Clinton/Flowers story as legitimately within the bounds of journalism attempted to rhetorically reshape certain boundaries to fit this particular situation.

Others argued that the publication of the allegations was indefensible—signaling the intention to keep the boundary as they perceived it once was. This disagreement about the boundary shows that it was a contested area. Journalists' efforts to sharpen this boundary proved futile because some within their ranks perceived supermarket tabloids as competitors who operate within the same cultural space. In other words, journalists' lack of consensus about this jurisdiction produced the inevitable consequence: They were ineffective at monopolizing their jurisdiction over this kind of political discussion.

Ironically, the fact that tabloids do not criticize themselves for covering sensational stories like these seems to indicate that their conceptions of their boundaries are clear and distinct. On the other hand, this may just indicate that tabloid journalists do not see their medium as being restricted by any boundaries, or that self-criticism is just not a tradition or norm for tabloid journalism the way it is in mainstream journalism. Either way, tabloids present a problem for journalists. If they sharply define entertainment as their realm, journalists have to explain why they are invading it. If they leave the boundary between tabloids and mainstream journalism fuzzy, then journalists have to find a way to distinguish themselves. Mainstream journalists, through their voluminous self-criticism, indirectly tell the public that they are able to criticize their institution, and that they are uneasy about perceived changes in their role in society. In contrast, people may perceive tabloid journalism as an institution that is unable to conduct self-analysis and that is unconcerned about having boundaries around its role in society.

An Integration of the Findings

Journalism boundary work is done primarily by insiders—those who have the most to lose through the loss of jurisdiction and autonomy over the production of certain kinds of mass communication. The boundary work is accomplished primarily through acts of public self-criticism, wherein journalists attempt to show that certain members of the journalistic community or individual journalism businesses are straying from the accepted standards, goals, and ideologies of journalism. The self-criticism of the institution of journalism—a kind of social control—has both costs and benefits: It makes the public aware of the deficiencies of the institution, but it also proves that the institution patrols itself and attempts to enforce standards. In the rhetoric examined here, journalists seemed acutely aware of the costs of this kind of social control. One of the ways journalists attempted to minimize this cost was through rhetoric that downplayed the significance of boundary breaches that could only be blamed on serious structural defects in the institution of journalism, while accentuating the seriousness of boundary "problems" that appear to be the fault of deviant individuals, to be the fault of outsiders, or to have relatively painless solutions.

For example, Michael Gartner was singled out as the cause of a problem that could actually be traced to pressures coming from the corporate institution of NBC's parent company, GE, or to overall market pressures within the mass media industry. These endemic causes were mentioned by some in the initial explanations of the *Dateline* scandal, but when it became clear to journalists that this kind of criticism would be unproductive, attention shifted to the most visible individual. Losing one deviant individual was not a great cost to the journalism community. Similarly, the news media criticism following the Clinton/Flowers scandal tended to place blame and focus attention on the outsiders in the case—Gennifer Flowers and the *Star*—while downplaying the significant problem of the influence of nonjournalistic motives such as making profits by providing entertainment to the audience.

Much like the boundary-work rhetoric of scientists, journalistic boundary-work distinctions are often couched in dichotomous pairs of terms such as professional versus amateur, responsible versus irresponsible, ethical versus unethical, legitimate versus pseudo, altruistic versus selfish, and mainstream versus tabloid. These distinctions are useful to journalists when they are trying to exclude others but are noticeably absent when they attempt to bring some field of mass communication within their jurisdiction. They use what Abbott (1988) calls *reduction*, reducing the task to an essential element that is already within their jurisdiction (p. 98). For instance, a questionable story of a political sex scandal becomes a "media story."

In all cases, journalistic boundary work serves to strengthen the position of the institution of journalism—either by reinforcing those boundaries that need protection or by manipulating those boundaries that become too restrictive.

A SYNTHESIS OF THE FINDINGS

At this point it is important to revisit some of the questions posed in Chapter 1 to evaluate how they have been answered.

Question 1: How and why have television journalists and others defined "television news" and the goals, norms, and ideologies of television journalism as they have?

Journalists have an interest in making the public believe that of the different varieties of mass media messengers, they alone provide factual information. This gives them credibility—a valuable professional resource. Similarly, journalists have an interest in making the public believe that adjacent professions such as mass media entertainment do not have credibility, and that journalists are the sole legitimate suppliers of important and informative information. Mass media entertainers supply quasi-factual information that is "merely" interesting or entertaining. Journalists supply important information needed by citizens to operate the democracy. This explains the special attention given by journalists to the way political news is handled. Political news is their bread and butter—their bottom-line reason for existence in society. When other mass media communicators—such as tabloid journalists—attempt to provide political information, "mainstream" journalists are quick to try to make the boundaries between journalism and other kinds of political information sharp and distinct.

Vow of Poverty

One way television journalists differentiate themselves from other kinds of television communicators is by noting their lack of interest in profits. By giving the impression that they are motivated solely by altruistic motives—providing a public service to society as purveyors of the truth—they make other kinds of mass media messengers appear less saintly. The public are more likely to trust and believe in an institution that is devoted to such selfless motives. In a sense, journalists take a vow of poverty when they enter the field.

Autonomy, Cultural Authority, and Scientific Method

Television journalists distinguish themselves from other television communicators by noting their independence and freedom from outside influences, such as advertisers and politicians. Autonomy and independence are coupled with the idea that journalists are skeptical of claims made by interested actors, and they employ methods designed to verify the accuracy of information, such as corroborating evidence and the use of multiple sources to reduce the uncertainty of claims. This reliance on methods that resemble those used by scientists and other legitimate kinds of investigators—like detectives—("just the facts, ma'am") again reinforces the public perception that journalism is the sole mass media provider of truthful, factual political information. For instance, in the Gennifer Flowers case, journalists questioned the reliability of information provided by an interested actor that could not be corroborated. Journalists noted that the supermarket tabloid, the *Star*, did not exhibit skepticism when it approached the story, and further, that it destroyed its independence when it paid Flowers, making her story far from a disinterested pursuit.

Self-Criticism

Tabloid and mainstream journalists seem to be equally interested in exposing lies, deceptions, and deviance, particularly if they involve sex and political candidate celebrities. But this also highlights one of the apparent differences between these two kinds of mass media: Journalists expend a considerable amount of space exposing perceived lies, deceptions, and deviance occurring within the journalism community—as the Gartner case illustrates. Journalists follow a norm of self-criticism.

Question 2: How have the boundaries between entertainment and news been constructed and negotiated as they have; and what rhetorical moves do journalists and others make to distinguish between the two?

One of the recurring themes in Chapter 6 was that journalism is unlike entertainment because its reason for existence is a somewhat higher calling: Informing people rather than amusing them. Mainstream journalists seemed to have a somewhat holier-than-thou attitude when comparing themselves to the tabloid industry, whose mission seems superfluous by comparison. This flattering appraisal of the importance of journalism was intended to contrast with entertainment and to give advantages to journalism.

In Chapter 4 we saw how the FCC found it difficult to decide where the line should be drawn between news interview and entertainment/variety programs, because they both often feature the same political celebrity guests. During the 1992 presidential campaign, for example, Bill Clinton appeared on MTV and Arsenio Hall, as well as on the standard journalism shows. To distinguish between entertaining variety programs and journalism programs, the government relied on some strange criteria, such as whether the program was regularly scheduled. Eventually the government realized that the sole distinguishing feature of journalistic programs was that journalists were in charge of and in control of them. This rhetoric did just what journalists really wanted: an acknowledgment that journalism is autonomous—it is whatever journalists say it is—and only journalists are qualified to define journalism. It was a governmental acknowledgment of the cultural authority of journalism.

In the data examined in Chapter 6, many journalists note that journalism (usually) does not pay sources for news but does employ techniques that—unlike entertaining tabloid journalism—attempt to eliminate bias through balancing sources. Entertainment programs that resemble news programs—such as some of the variety and tabloid programs mentioned in Chapter 4—often use techniques borrowed from fictional programs. For instance, they hire actors to make dramatic reenactments of news events. Journalists argue that they are more careful about the truth, that they are more skeptical about the motives of sources, even in the stories about which tabloids and mainstream media both report. Tabloids are characterized as reckless and sloppy, with little regard for the actual truth.

Question 3: What are the differences in the uses of distinguishing characteristics between those within the journalism profession and those outside the profession? In effect: Who does boundary work, and how do different groups do it differently?

In Chapter 4, I noted how the government found it hard to distinguish between "newsworthy" and "merely interesting" information. To make these kinds of distinctions required them to do journalism work. Journalists are the only ones qualified to make this kind of epistemological distinction, and the FCC seemed to realize that it was unqualified. They decided that their best hope of distinguishing journalism from other pursuits was by examining the newsgathering process—the methods used in gathering and producing the news. By the mid-1980s the FCC settled into a plan of evaluating the methodologies of purported news programs to see if standard journalistic methods were being used. A few years later they realized that this procedure allowed entertainers to become journalists simply by employing a few journalistic methods. The FCC eventually came to the conclusion that journalism is whatever journalists say it is—it is a self-defined field. To qualify for a "bona fide news exemption" to Section 315, the program had to be *controlled* by journalists, not by politicians or other interested outsiders, affirming the importance of the independent and autonomous nature of journalistic work.

Question 4: How do the interests and strategies of boundary-work rhetoric along the news/entertainment boundary compare to the interests and strategies of rhetoric uncovered along other boundaries, such as science/non-science; and what is it about the news/entertainment boundary that makes these strategies different—or similar?

Much of this study could be seen as an attempt to replicate the work of sociologist Thomas F. Gieryn, who has studied the boundary-work rhetoric of scientists as they carve out their niche in the cultural landscape. Gieryn developed the *sensitizing concept* of boundary-work rhetoric—as a pursuit designed to consolidate the professional power of a group—watching the boundaries of science. I have used the boundary-work concept as an interpretive tool for understanding the boundaries of journalism in two specific areas: the boundaries of television journalism and the area where journalism and entertainment intersect.

Gieryn's first published paper on boundary work laid out the premise that boundary-work rhetoric takes on special characteristics depending on the specific situation it is designed to affect (Gieryn, 1983). He identified three motives for boundary-work rhetoric (listed in the quote at the head of this chapter): *expansion* of authority; *monopolization* of authority; and *protection of autonomy*. Each of these motives elicits a specific kind of boundary-work rhetoric, and all of these were seen in the sites analyzed here. The evolution of television journalism was a ripe source of rhetoric arguing for an expansion of authority into the new medium. The cases of political scandal journalism were the site of some rhetoric that attempted to monopolize the authority of journalism over political news by denying the jurisdiction of tabloids in political news. The case of the government trying to define the essence of journalism is an example of rhetoric arguing for the protection of the autonomy of journalism—the authority to define itself. The Gartner case also demonstrated how autonomy and authority are maintained by imposing sanctions against deviance.

Gieryn's next paper on boundary work (a collaborative effort with Bevins and Zehr) analyzed the public rhetoric of scientists and lawyers during two public trials dealing with the teaching of evolution in public schools (Gieryn, Bevins & Zehr, 1985). During the 1925 Scopes trial in Tennessee, scientists who were recruited as witnesses for the defense made public statements that created the perception of a boundary between science and religion. In their analysis of this rhetoric, Gieryn, Bevins, and Zehr identified five characteristics that scientists and lawyers used to distinguish science from religion: *ontological differences*—science interprets a physical realm, religion interprets a spiritual realm; *epistemological differences*—science makes literal, empirical observations of reality, whereas religion is poetical and allegorical, that is, non-literal; *methodological differences*—science makes tentative claims, religion makes timeless claims; *functional differences*—science helps technological progress, religion gives spiritual and moral guidance; and *social differences*—scientists reach public consensus over scientific facts, theologians forever squabble about sectarian differences, making religious belief a kind of private opinion.

In my analyses, there was no mention of ontological differences between news and entertainment, because they both reside in the physical realm. Journalists and other interested actors did use epistemological differences to distinguish between different kinds of knowledge produced by journalism and entertainment (fact and fiction). Agents of the government bureaucracy, however, discovered that making epistemological distinctions was the equivalent of "doing journalism"—they had to make decisions about what topics are newsworthy. Instead, they found it easier to distinguish between news and non-news television programs by citing methodological differences—that is, one group gathers news this way, the other gathers information another way, so is it still news? The trouble with relying on this as the sole distinction is that entertainers or politicians using journalistic methods can very easily become journalists.

I also found that functional differences were often cited as a distinguishing characteristic of the boundary between entertainment and journalism. Whereas entertainment serves the function of amusing viewers with fantasy and fiction, journalism is a more sobering influence, giving them the facts of the day. Television news was also differentiated from other types of journalism on a functional dimension—because television news is short and directed to lower socioeconomic classes, it serves more of a headline source, a "lite news," rather than full strength news. In addition, broadcast news serves a different function than entertainment for the broadcasting industry—it is a price they pay for a government franchise.

I also found that there are social differences between so-called "mainstream" journalism and tabloid journalism. Mainstream journalism engages in a great deal of self-flagellation and criticism every time it senses a boundary between news and entertainment has been crossed. In contrast, there does not seem to be a norm of self-criticism within the social institution of tabloid journalism.

Gieryn, Bevins, and Zehr discovered that during the 1981–1982 McLean trial in Arkansas, scientists attempted to create a boundary between evolution-science ("real science") and creation-science ("non-science"). Four aspects of this boundary were identified:

[1.] Science is the domain of experts, whose specialized training and accomplishments enable them *alone* to decide the validity of knowledge about nature. . . . "Professional" scientists have passed various gatekeepers at the boundaries of science by publishing in technical journals, by gaining employment at mainstream colleges and universities, by learning specialized research techniques, and by having their work favorably reviewed by peers at (for example) the National Science Foundation. . . .

[2.] Genuine scientists are skeptical, tentative and cautious about claims to knowledge. . . .

[3.] Scientists reach consensus over facts or theories that are accorded at least the provisional status of "truth." . . .

[4.] Science is the disinterested search for knowledge. (Gieryn, Bevins & Zehr, 1985, pp. 401–404)

Going through these point-by-point, I found the following:

Journalism is not the domain of professional experts. Journalists tend to think of themselves as experts about what is news, but they do not have a lock on making decisions about newsworthiness in today's news media environment where tabloids are lumped into the same heading of "reality-based programming" as conventional news programs are. There are no credentialing requirements for journalists; no required memberships in professional organizations or institution-wide adherence to ethics codes. College courses of journalism study are only informally recognized as important preparation for journalism work. Instead, it often seems that previous experience is the only requirement for journalism work. This often leads to the (some say faulty) impression that journalism is a craft—you can either do it, or you can't—and that it is not something you can learn in school.

Although expert status is informally conferred on the members of some dominant journalism outlets, such as journalists at the *New York Times*, it is a status not recognized by all journalists. In today's journalism environment, anyone with a scoop becomes an expert. Still, most journalists recognize a substantive, structural difference between "mainstream" and other kinds of journalism, even if professionalism sometimes seems elusive. For one thing, tabloid newspapers and television programs do not win Pulitzer Prizes, nor are they even listed in most journalism industry indices, such as the *Editor & Publisher Yearbook*. Clearly, journalists see a difference between tabloid and mainstream.

Journalists seem to rarely earn the status of "expert." Yet, in Chapter 4, we saw government regulators and legislators decide that journalists are the only ones qualified to make journalistic decisions—such as determining who and what is newsworthy and determining the role of journalism in society and the proper work practices of journalists. The government told journalists: "You *are* the experts, and you alone can determine what is news and what is journalism." In Chapter 6, however, we saw journalists saying that they are unable to control who and what becomes news.

Skepticism. Like scientists, journalists are skeptical about truth claims. They follow special procedures to verify information, such as: Check facts with several reputable sources, get balancing quotes when one source is suspected to be biased, do not pay sources for stories or tips because information becomes suspect when not offered freely. Tabloid journalists do not always follow the same rules. In mainstream journalism, the usual standard for running a story is: "Is it true, and is it important?" In tabloid journalism, the usual standard seems to be: "Will it sell papers, and have we covered ourselves well enough to avoid a lawsuit?"

Community consensus. Journalists work together closely on stories and get clues from each other about whether a story is news or not. "Pack journalism" is the term given to the tendency of journalists to all follow the same cues and to pursue the same stories, in apparent consensus. In Chapter 6, I showed how consensus over news can sometimes lead to situations where a story becomes practically uncontrollable, as every journalist in the country pursues the same angle and the same leads. Once the momentum of consensus sets in on a given story, there seems to be little imagination among journalists, and a lot of pack behavior among those chasing it.

Disinterestedness. Journalism is very similar to science in that it purports to be a disinterested quest for the truth, or more precisely, for the facts. Journalists attempt to keep an open mind, independent and unbiased, and operate without favor or preset agenda. This disinterestedness was a trait journalists used to distinguish themselves from biased political news programs that do not deserve equal time exemptions from the FCC, and from tabloid journalism, which operates with preset ideas of stories, and who work with biased sources with an agenda to promote.

Oscillation

Gieryn's first published work on boundary work includes the observation that John Tyndall (1820–1893) "oscillated" between arguing that science is "not religion" to arguing that science is "not mechanics," depending on the needs at the particular time of the argument (Gieryn, 1983, pp. 784–787). This strategy helped Tyndall firm up the perception of boundaries of science by showing that it could be described in relation to two other bounded realms in the cultural landscape. In the rhetoric I analyzed, there seems to be a similar phenomenon: Journalists frequently condemn the motives of those who engage in boundary-blurring activities by attributing them to profit-centered motives instead of the more defensible altruistic or public-service motives. On the other hand, when journalists defend the use of a questionable story or method, they often argue that they should not ignore news, and that because they are businesses, they must remain profitable. In other words, they seem to oscillate between arguing for maintenance of profits and maintenance of respectability, depending on their particular needs at a given time.

EPILOGUE AND SUGGESTIONS FOR FURTHER RESEARCH

The cultural authority of journalism is defended and supported through various acts that reassure the public that journalists are credible, independent, and authoritative. This study has examined some of the ways this cultural authority is obtained through the social construction and maintenance of boundaries between journalism and other forms of mass communication. I have shown that the rhetorical strategies for building and maintaining these perceived boundaries vary according to aspects of the specific situation; the strategies are *contextually contingent*. Depending on the importance of the specific boundary situation, the ramifications of changes to it, the kinds of actors involved, and the specific audience that would be affected, the strategy of boundary-work rhetors adjusts to best solve the particular boundary dispute.

One unexpected finding that deserves further study is that some journalists seem to be less concerned about the integrity of certain boundaries than others, and even seem willing to abandon the enforcement of them. For instance, in Chapter 6 we saw that some journalists were concerned that the tabloid media now have the ability to force some stories onto the public agenda, and that this is a fairly recent change. Other journalists, however, seemed resigned to the fact that this is a reality of the new media marketplace. Why do some journalists sound alarms about this situation—in effect, trying to patch holes in perceived boundaries—while others accept this apparent realignment of the boundaries as a new permanent feature of the mass media industry?

Another area ripe for investigation: the sources of journalism's cultural authority. Although journalists perceive that certain of their policies and procedures contribute to a perception of credibility and authority, the public may reach conclusions about this in vastly different ways. One phenomenon that has almost reached the level of fact in certain circles is that publicity and name recognition are always good, no matter how bad the content of the publicity. Bill Clinton's opponents in the Democratic primary in 1992 complained that he was getting all the publicity—even though it was "bad" publicity—and that this hurt them. Even his campaign advisers admitted that his name recognition soared because of the Flowers episode.

More-recent episodes illustrate this phenomenon, such as actor Hugh Grant's arrest for soliciting a prostitute in Los Angeles in the summer of 1995, which translated into increased box office revenues for a film in which he starred when it was released at about the same time.

Director Oliver Stone explored this phenomenon in his movie "Natural Born Killers," where the most vile members of society reach celebrity status precisely by being the most vile.

For the news media, does this mean that the most vile news medium becomes the most watched news medium? What is the relationship between ratings points and cultural authority—or between popularity and credibility? Is there a point of diminishing returns for raising the ante (or lowering the standards) in terms of sensationalism? In the second half of 1995, some television stations around the country announced that they were dropping certain afternoon talk shows (like *The Jenny Jones Show* and *The Ricki Lake Show*) because the programs reached a low point of prurience that became revolting to viewers. Do people believe that these shows are a style of news delivery medium, lumping all "reality-based programming" into a monolithic block?

In short, this study has answered many questions about how journalists perceive the boundaries between what they do and what others do. Someone should now examine how audiences perceive these same boundaries, and how the public confers cultural authority on journalists and other mass communicators. We now know a bit more about how journalists perceive their space in the cultural landscape—where they see themselves fitting into society and their roles in it. Perhaps now we should also examine how audiences perceive the same features of the boundaries between journalism and entertainment, and perhaps how people who identify themselves as entertainers perceive the boundary between journalism and entertainment.

References

A candidacy ends [Editorial]. (1987, May 8). *Washington Post*, p. A22.

A look at FCC's Fowler: Apostle of the free market. (1985, May 13). *U.S. News & World Report*, p. 66.

Abbott, Andrew. (1988). *The system of professions*. Chicago: University of Chicago Press.

Agency credits TV for Saran Wrap's shift from a slow seller to a fast moving item. (1954, March 29). *Advertising Age*, pp. 2, 6.

Allen, Spencer. (1953). Producing the local television newsreel. In Baskett Mosse and Fred Whiting (Eds.), *Television news handbook* (pp. 45–54). Evanston, IL: Medill School of Journalism, Northwestern University.

Alter, Jonathan. (1993, March 8). On the ropes at NBC News. *Newsweek*, p. 49.

Alter, Jonathan. (1992, January 27). The cycle of sensationalism. *Newsweek*, p. 25.

Alter, Jonathan. (1989, October 16). Behind the NBC News blues. *Newsweek*, pp. 86–87.

Alter, Jonathan, Carroll, Ginny, Fineman, Howard, & Talbot, Mary. (1992, February 3). Substance vs. sex. *Newsweek*, p. 20.

Applebome, Peter. (1992, March 8). Bill Clinton's uncertain journey. New York Times, Sec. 6, p. 26.

AP's Kramp urges more stress in news. (1959, June 22). *Broadcasting*, p. 70.

Auletta, Ken. (1991). *Three blind mice: How the TV networks lost their way*. New York: Random House.

Balz, Dan. (1992, January 31). Clinton's foes say no news is bad news; Lack of coverage frustrates Democrats. *Washington Post*, p. A10.

Balz, Dan. (1992, January 27). Clinton concedes marital 'wrongdoing.' *Washington Post*, pp. A1, 6.

Balz, Dan, & Kurtz, Howard. (1992, January 24). Clinton calls tabloid report of 12-year affair 'not true.' *Washington Post*, p. A8.

Barnouw, Erik. (1982). *Tube of plenty* (Rev. ed.). Oxford, England: Oxford Books.

Barnouw, Erik. (1970). *A history of broadcasting in the United States. Volume III, The image empire; from 1953*. New York: Oxford University Press.

Barnouw, Erik. (1968). *A history of broadcasting in the United States. Volume II, The golden web, 1933–1953*. New York: Oxford University Press.

Barrett, Edward W. (1964, Summer). Editorial notebook. *Columbia Journalism Review*, p. 18.

Beck, Joan. (1992, January 30). Voters are right to weigh rumors of infidelity. *Chicago Tribune*, p. 23.

Bennett, W. Lance, Gressett, Lynne A., and Haltom, William. (1985, Spring). Repairing the news: A case study of the news paradigm. *Journal of Communication, 35*(2), 50–68.

Benton, William. (1953). Three roads to TV's salvation. In Herbert L. Marx, Jr. (Ed.). *Television and radio in American life* (pp. 173–178). New York: H. W. Wilson Co.

Bernstein, Alan. (1992, February 2). Whatever the issues, trust factor always crucial with voters. *Houston Chronicle*, p. C2.

Bernstein, Carl. (1992, June 8). The idiot culture. *The New Republic*, pp. 22–25, 28.

Best, Joel. (Ed.). (1989). *Images of issues: Typifying contemporary social problems*. New York: Aldine De Gryter.

Bird, S. Elizabeth. (1992a, September). Travels in nowhere land: Ethnography and the 'impossible' audience. *Critical Studies in Mass Communication, 9*, 250–260.

Bird, S. Elizabeth. (1992b). *For enquiring minds: A cultural study of supermarket tabloids*. Knoxville, TN: University of Tennessee Press.

Bird, S. Elizabeth.(1990). Storytelling on the far side: Journalism and the weekly tabloid. *Critical Studies in Mass Communication, 7*, 380–385.

Bird, S. Elizabeth, and Dardenne, Robert W. (1990, Summer). News and storytelling in American culture: Reevaluating the sensational dimension. *Journal of American Culture, 13*, 33–37.

Bird, S. Elizabeth, and Dardenne, Robert W. (1988). Myth, chronicle, and story: Exploring the narrative qualities of news. In James W. Carey (Ed.). *Media, myths, and narratives* (pp. 67–86). Newbury Park, CA.: Sage.

Black, Eric. (1992, May 17). We get it all—but substance. *Star Tribune*, p. A1.

Blumer, Herbert. (1954). What is wrong with social theory? *American Sociological Review, 19*, 3–10.

Bogart, Leo. (1991). *The American media system and its commercial culture* [Occasional Paper Number 8]. New York: Gannett Foundation Media Center.

Bogart, Leo. (1980). Television news as entertainment. In Percy Tannenbaum (Ed.). *The entertainment functions of television* (pp. 209–249). Hillsdale, NJ: Lawrence Erlbaum Associates.

Bradlee, Ben. (1995). *A good life*. New York: Simon & Schuster.

Breaking into broadcast news—At the top. (1988, August 8). *Newsweek*, p. 59.

Brill, S. (1993a, April). Ending the double standard. *The American Lawyer*, p. 5.

Brill, S. (1993b, April 25). NBC fraud shows media double standard. *Chicago Tribune*, Sec. 4., p. 1.

Briller, Bert. (1989). A new television battleground. *Television Quarterly, 24*(1), 67–77.

Broder, David S. (1992, January 28). Odd way to choose a president. *Washington Post*, p. A21.

Broder, David S. (1987a, May 8). Democrats' 1988 contest wide open. *Washington Post*, pp. A1, 14.

Broder, David S. (1987b, May 8). Another unexpected disclosure. *Washington Post*, p. A23.

Brummett, Barry. (1984). Burke's representative anecdote as a method in media criticism. *Critical Studies in Mass Communication, 1*, 163.

Burke, Kenneth. (1969). *A grammar of motives*. Berkeley: University of California Press.

Burke, Kenneth. (1968). Dramatism. In David L. Sills (Ed.). *International encyclopedia of the social sciences, Vol. 7* (pp. 445–452). New York: Macmillan and Free Press.

Burke, Kenneth. (1941). *The philosophy of literary form: Studies in symbolic action*. Baton Rouge: Louisiana State University Press.

Burns, Eric. (1993). *Broadcast blues: Dispatches from the twenty-year war between a television reporter and his medium*. New York: HarperCollins.

Campbell, Colin. (1992, April 8). Gennifer Flowers and Jennifer Fitzgerald and the dawn of the post-Cold War era. *The Atlanta Journal and Constitution*, p. D17.

Carey, James. (1989). *Communication as culture*. Boston: Unwin Hyman.

Carman, John. (1992, April 14). Koppel in the hot seat. *San Francisco Chronicle*, p. E1.

Case, T. (1995, March 11). Controversy follows Michael Gartner. *Editor & Publisher*, p. 12.

CBS, Inc., 63 RR 2d 483 (1987).

Chesebro, James W. (1992, August). Extensions of the Burkeian System. *Quarterly Journal of Speech, 78*, 356–368.

Citizens for Reagan, 36 RR 2d 885 (1976).

Clayton, Andrew, & Thurston, Robert. (1992, October 28). Why bash media? TV makes politics accountable. *Atlanta Journal and Constitution*, p. A13.

Clift, Eleanor, Fineman, Howard, & Carroll, Ginny. (1992, February 10). Character questions. *Newsweek*, pp. 26–27.

Clinton agonistes. (1992, February 1). *The Economist*, pp. 16–17.

The Clinton controversy [Editorial]. (1992, January 28). *Washington Post*, p. A20.

Clinton denounces new report of affair. (1992, January 24). *New York Times*, p. A14.

Clinton flap shows press at its worst. (1992, February 2). *Chicago Sun-Times*, p. 7.

Clinton turns red after accuser's press conference. (1992, January 28). *San Diego Union-Tribune*, p. A7.

Coffin, Thomas. (1955). Television's impact on society. *American Psychologist, 10*, 630–641.

Cohen, Richard. (1987, May 7). . . . And the things he finds unimportant. *Washington Post*, p. A27.

Cohen, Stanley, & Young, Jock (Eds.). (1981). *The manufacture of news* (Rev. ed.). London: Constable.

Collins, Harry M. (1991, Spring). Captives and victims: Comment on Scott, Richards, and Martin. *Science, Technology & Human Values, 16*, 249–251.

Columbia Broadcasting System (Lar Daly), 18 RR 238, recon. den., 18 RR 701 (1959).

67 *Congressional Record—Senate* 12503–12505 (July 1, 1926).

105 *Congressional Record—House* 16225 (August 18, 1959).

105 *Congressional Record—House* 17771–17781 (September 2, 1959).

105 *Congressional Record—Senate* 17832 (September 3, 1959).

Connell, Joan. (1992, January 26). Allegations about Clinton revive fidelity question. *Star Tribune*, p. A18.

Conrad, Charles. (1984, Summer). Phases, pentads, and dramatistic critical process. *Central States Speech Journal, 35*, 94–104.

Cooke, Janet. (1980, September 28). Jimmy's World. *Washington Post*, p. 1.

Cooper, Marc. (1992, February 4). Send us no Flowers. *Village Voice*, pp. 19–21.

Cramer, Richard Ben. (1992). *What it takes: The way to the White House*. New York: Random House.

Crouse, Timothy. (1972). *The boys on the bus*. New York: Ballantine Books.

Dahlgren, Peter, & Sparks, Colin (Eds.). (1992). *Journalism and popular culture*. London: Sage.

Daley, Steve. (1992, February 2). Clinton affair robs campaign of sense of proportion, perhaps a contender. *Chicago Tribune*, Sec. 4, p. 4.

Darnton, Robert. (1975). Writing news and telling stories. *Daedalus, 104*, 175–193.

Davis for Congress Campaign, 36 RR 2d 1601 (1976).

Day, John F. (1968). Television news: Reporting or performing? In Harry J. Skornia & Jack William Kitson (Eds.). *Problems and controversies in television and radio* (pp. 313–319). Palo Alto, CA: Pacific Books.

Diamond, Edwin. (1993, March 15). Auto-destruct. *New York*, p. 18.

Diamond, Edwin. (1992, February 17). Crash course: Campaign journalism 101. *New York*, pp. 28–31.

Diamond, Edwin. (1975). *The tin kazoo: Politics, television, and the news*. Cambridge, MA: MIT Press.

Dickenson, James R. (1987, May 5). Hart weekend: Conflicting stories. *Washington Post*, p. A10.

Dickenson, James R., & Taylor, Paul. (1987, May 4). Newspaper stakeout infuriates Hart. *Washington Post*, pp. A1, 4.

Does tv news need stars? (1962, September 17). *Sponsor*, pp. 32–33.

Donaldson, Sam. (1987). *Hold on, Mr. President!* New York: Fawcett Crest.

Dooley, Patricia L. (1994). Development of American journalistic work in the eighteenth and nineteenth centuries: Politicians, political communication, and occupational boundaries. Unpublished doctoral dissertation, University of Minnesota.

Dooley, Patricia L., & Grosswiler, Paul G. (1995, August). 'Turf wars': Journalists' claims to political communication jurisdiction in the new media age. Paper presented at the annual convention of the Association for Education in Journalism and Mass Communication, Washington, DC.

Downs, Hugh, & Wallace, Mike. (1967). The craft of interviewing. In A. William Bluem & Roger Manvell. *Television: The creative experience* (pp. 164–173). New York: Hastings House.

Dr. Bogart replies to TV news claim. (1964, February 1). *Editor & Publisher*, p. 13.

Durkheim, Emile. (1984). *The division of labor in society*. New York: The Free Press.

Edsall, Thomas B. (1987, May 5). Model-actress was Hart's D.C. visitor. *Washington Post*, pp. A1, 9.

Edward R. Murrow of CBS: 'Diplomat, poet, preacher.' (1953, March 9). *Newsweek*, p. 40.

Engstrom, J. (1993, August 5). Dateline NBC bounces back, executive says. *The* (Toledo) *Blade*, p. 4.

Equal-Time Amendment to Communications Act of 1934. Senate Report No. 562, 86th Congress, 1st Session, July 22, 1959.

Erickson, Kai. (1966). *Wayward Puritans*. New York: Wiley.

Ettorre, B. (1993, December). Was General Motors smart to mobilize the troops? *Management Review*, p. 9.

Evans, Rowland, & Novak, Robert. (1992, January 29). Clinton 'feeding frenzy' stirs some deep-seated resentment. *Chicago Sun-Times*, p. 27.

'Excitement' of news shows lures Gulf. (1960, December 12). *Broadcasting*, p. 34.

Faught, Millard C. (1950, August 26). TV: An interim summing-up. *The Saturday Review of Literature*, p. 8.

FCC grants 'Donahue' section 315 exemption; Commission rules interview program can feature political candidates without having to grant equal opportunities. (1984, May 28). *Broadcasting*, p. 42.

Federal Radio Commission. (1932). *Sixth annual report*. Washington: U.S. Government.

Fentress, Stephen. (1953). Writing and editing the TV newsreel. In Baskett Mosse & Fred Whiting (Eds.). *Television news handbook* (pp. 63–69). Evanston, IL: Medill School of Journalism, Northwestern University.

Ferrell, Robert H. (Ed.). (1983). *The diary of James C. Hagerty: Eisenhower in mid-course, 1954–1955*. Bloomington: Indiana University Press.

Fish, Stanley. (1980). *Is there a text in this class? The authority of interpretive communities*. Cambridge, MA: Harvard University Press.

Flannery, Gerald V. (Ed.). (1995). *Commissioners of the FCC, 1927–1994*. Lanham, MD: University Press of America.

Fowler's first year in review. (1982, May 24). *Broadcasting*, pp. 47–48.

Frank, Reuven. (1993, May 3). Yesterday's sure thing. *The New Leader*, p. 20.

Frank, Reuven. (1991). *Out of thin air*. New York: Simon & Schuster.

Freeman, Gregory. (1992, January 31). Clinton case embarrasses U.S. media. *St. Louis Post-Dispatch*, p. C1.

Frey, J. (1993, April). Faked in Japan. *American Journalism Review*, pp. 30–31.

Friendly, Fred W. (1967). *Due to circumstances beyond our control . . .* London: MacGibbon and Kee.

Fuss, Diana. (1989). *Essentially speaking: Feminism, nature and difference.* London: Routledge.

Gailey, Philip. (1992, February 2). Testing the media's character. *St. Petersburg Times,* p. D2.

Gans, Herbert. (1979). *Deciding what's news: A study of CBS Evening News, NBC Nightly News, Newsweek and Time.* New York: Random House.

Garfinkel, Harold. (1956). Conditions of successful status degradation ceremonies. *American Journal of Sociology 61*: 420-424.

Gary Hart: The aftermath [Editorial]. (1987, May 10). *Washington Post,* p. B6.

The Gary Hart dispute [Editorial]. (1987, May 5). *Washington Post,* p. A18.

Gay, V. (1989, August 9). Mike Gartner reflects on hectic 1st year. *Variety,* pp. 51–53.

Gay, V. (1988, August 8). Gartner's news savvy transmitted to NBC. *Advertising Age,* p. 35.

Gaziano, Cecille, & McGrath, Kristen. (1986). Measuring the concept of credibility. *Journalism Quarterly, 63,* 451–462.

Geertz, Clifford. (1973). *The interpretation of cultures.* New York: Basic Books.

Gelfand, Lou. (1992, May 3). How paper's judged on covering issues, not just spice. *Star Tribune,* p. A23.

Germond, Jack W., & Witcover, Jules. (1989). *Whose broad stripes and bright stars?: The trivial pursuit of the Presidency 1988.* New York: Warner Books.

Gersh, Debra. (1992, February 8). Cash for trash or legitimate news? *Editor & Publisher,* p. 7.

Gerzon, Mark. (1992, January 23). He's no Gary Hart. *New York Times,* p. A23.

Gieryn, Thomas. (1995). Boundaries of science. In Sheila Jasanoff, Gerald Markle, Trevor Pinch & James Petersen (Eds.). *Science, technology and controversy* (pp. 393–443). Newbury Park, CA: Sage.

Gieryn, Thomas F. (1992). The ballad of Pons and Fleischmann: Experiment and narrative in the (un)making of cold fusion. In E. McMullin (Ed.), *The Social Dimensions of Science* (pp. 217–243). Notre Dame: University of Notre Dame Press.

Gieryn, Thomas F. (1983, December). Boundary-work and the demarcation of science from non-science: Strains and interests in professional ideologies of scientists. *American Sociological Review, 48,* 781–795.

Gieryn, Thomas F., & Figert, Anne. (1990). Ingredients for the theory of science in society: O-rings, ice water, c-clamp, Richard Feynman and the press. In Susan Cozzens & Thomas Gieryn (Eds.). *Theories of science in society* (pp. 67–97). Bloomington: Indiana University Press.

Gieryn, Thomas F., & Figert, Anne. (1986). Scientists protect their cognitive authority: The status degradation ceremony of Sir Cyril Burt. In Gernot Böhme & Nico Stehr (Eds.). *The knowledge society* (pp. 67–86). Dordrecht, Holland: D. Reidel.

Gieryn, Thomas F., Bevins, George M., & Zehr, Stephen C. (1985, June). Professionalization of American scientists: Public science in the creation/evolution trials. *American Sociological Review, 50*, 392–409.

Gilliam, Dorothy. (1987, May 7). Unacceptable behavior of Barry and Hart. *Washington Post*, p. D3.

Gitlin, Todd. (1992, April). Media lemmings run amok! *Washington Journalism Review*, pp. 28, 30–32.

Gitlin, Todd. (1980). *The whole world is watching.* Berkeley: University of California Press.

Glasser, Theodore. (1982, Summer). Resolving the press-privacy conflict. *Communications and the Law, 4*, 250.

Goedkoop, Richard J. (1988). *Inside Local Television.* Salem, WI: Sheffield Publishing Co.

Golden, James L., Berquist, Goodwin F., & Coleman, William E. (1989). Kenneth Burke's theory of dramatistic rhetoric. In *The rhetoric of Western thought* (4th ed.). (pp. 318–351). Dubuque, IA: Kendall/Hunt.

Goldenson, Leonard H. (1963, April 1). If I were NAB's keynote speaker I'd say. *Sponsor*, pp. 34-35.

Goldenson, Leonard H., & Wolf, Marvin J. (1991). *Beating the odds.* New York: Charles Scribner's Sons.

Goodheart, Eugene. (1995). The fallacy of constructivism. *Clio, 24*(3), 323–326.

Goodman, Ellen. (1987, May 7). The importance of Hart's character . . . *Washington Post*, p. A27.

Gould, Jack. (1951, June 10). What TV is—And what it might be. *New York Times Magazine*, p. 22.

Gould, Jack. (1947, March 20). The paradoxical state of television. *New York Times Magazine*, p. 34.

Green, Bill. (1981, April 19). Janet's world. *Washington Post*, pp. A1, 12.

Greenfield, Meg. (1987, May 11). Private lives, public values. *Washington Post*, p. A13.

Habermas, Jürgen. (1989). *The structural transformation of the public sphere* (Thomas Burger, Trans.). Cambridge, MA: The MIT Press. (Original work published 1962)

Hagerty shooting for stars in his newscasting program. (1961, January 14). *Editor & Publisher*, pp. 12, 66.

Haithman, Diane. (1992, January 31). Hollywood's party politics; Clinton, Kerrey front-runners on Democratic circuit. *Los Angeles Times*, p. F1.

Hall, J. (1993a, March 12). Mixed mood at NBC News amid Dateline probe. *Los Angeles Times*, p. F2.

Hall, J. (1993b, February 19). Who knew what in question after Dateline apology. *Los Angeles Times*, p. F2.

Hall, J. (1993c, February 15). NBC News: A question of standards. *Los Angeles Times*, p. F13.

Hallin, Daniel C. (1992, Summer). The passing of the 'high modernism' of American journalism. *Journal of Communication, 42*(3), 14–24.

Harris, Julian, & Johnson, Stanley. (1965). *The complete reporter* (2nd ed.). New York: Macmillan Co.

Hearings on H.R. 8301. (1934). 73rd Congress.

Hemingway, Ernest. (1929). *A farewell to arms.* New York: Grosset & Dunlap.

Henry William A., III. (1981). News as entertainment: The search for dramatic unity. In Elie Abel (Ed.). *What's news: The media in American society.* San Francisco: Center for Contemporary Studies.

Herbert, Steven. (1992, February 14). FCC revises 'political programming policy.' *Los Angeles Times,* p. F4.

Heritage, John. (1984). *Garfinkel and ethnomethodology.* Cambridge: Polity Press.

Hiltbrand, D. (1992, June 22). Dateline NBC: Romancing their Stone. *People Weekly,* p. 14.

Hines, Cragg. (1992, January 27). Near miss during interview; Clinton cites marital woes, denies affair; Candidate, wife gamble campaign on TV show. *Houston Chronicle,* p. A1.

Hoagland, Jim. (1992, January 31). . . . Over Democratic party activists. *Washington Post,* p. A19.

Horton, Robert. (1960, April 28). The economic squeeze on mass TV. *The Reporter,* p. 14.

Houseman, John. (1953). Battle over television. In Herbert L. Marx, Jr., (Ed.). *Television and radio in American life.* New York: H. W. Wilson Co. (Original work published 1950)

Huff, R. (1989, July 26). Simulation used in TV piece on Bloch; Device questioned. *Variety,* p. 3.

Hughes, Helen MacGill. (1940). *News and the human interest story.* Chicago: University of Chicago Press.

I have absolutely leveled with voters [Transcript of Clinton's *60 Minutes* appearance]. (1992, January 27). *Washington Post,* p. A6.

In re Henry Geller, 54 RR 2d 1246 (1983).

In the black in 30 days. (1953, September 28). *Broadcasting•Telecasting,* p. 122.

Jab to the nose. (1957, May 6). *Time,* pp. 90–91.

Johnson, Haynes. (1987, May 6). The stench of scandal. *Washington Post,* p. A2.

Johnson, P. (1993, March 23). NBC report details flaws in Dateline procedure. *USA Today,* p. D3.

Johnston, Alva. (1939, May 20). Now what can we do with television?" *The Saturday Evening Post,* p. 107.

Jones, Alex S. (1992, February 9). Meet the press: Dr. Jekyll and Mr. Hyde. *New York Times,* Sec. 4, p. 4.

Judis, John B. (1987, July/August). The Hart affair. *Columbia Journalism Review,* p. 25.

Kaltenborn, H. V. (1968). Radio: Dollars and nonsense. In Harry J. Skornia & Jack William Kitson (Eds.). *Problems and controversies in television and radio.* Palo Alto, CA: Pacific Books. (Original work published 1931)

Kastor, Elizabeth. (1987, May 6). The jokers take Hart. *Washington Post,* pp. B1, 9.

Katz, Jon. (1992, March 5). Rock, rap and movies bring you the news. *Rolling Stone,* p. 33.

Kelly, Frank K. (1960). *Who owns the air?* [Monograph]. Santa Barbara, CA: Center for the Study of Democratic Institutions.

Kendrick, Alexander. (1969). *Prime time: The life of Edward R. Murrow.* Boston: Little, Brown and Co.

Kinsley, Michael. (1987, May 6). The new honesty in the press. *Washington Post*, p. A19.

Kolbert, Elizabeth. (1993, February 14). A tabloid touch in the nightly news. *New York Times*, Sec. 4, p. 1.

Kolbert, Elizabeth. (1992, May 1). As political campaigns turn negative, the press is given a negative rating. *New York Times*, p. A18.

Korbel, Matthew Robert. (1994). *Edited for television: CNN, ABC, and the 1992 Presidential campaign.* Boulder: Westview Press.

Korean Coverage. (1950, September 4). *Newsweek*, p. 48.

Krauthammer, Charles. (1992, January 31). The press confronts its power. *Washington Post*, p. A19.

Kurtz, Howard. (1992a, February 13). Before airing a word, network triggers press furor over Clinton and draft. *Washington Post*, p. A25.

Kurtz, Howard. (1992b, January 30). Reports on Clinton pose quandary for journalists. *Washington Post*, p. A14.

Kurtz, Howard. (1992c, January 28). Five days from tabloid tattle to front-page fare. *Washington Post*, p. A8.

Kurtz, Howard. (1992d, January 25). Clintons agree to do '60 Minutes.' *Washington Post*, p. A10.

Kurtz, Howard, & Carmody, John. (1993, March 3). NBC exec ousted over staged crash; Unpopular at network, Michael Gartner becomes fall guy. *Washington Post*, p. A1.

Ladowsky, Ellen. (1992, March 29). Clinton decries coverage but press treatment anything but tough. *The San Diego Union-Tribune*, p. C4.

Laitin, Joseph. (1987, May 10). Politics, sex and drugs. *Washington Post*, p. B6.

Lamb, David. (1992, February 13). Into the realm of tabloids; Never before has tabloid journalism been such a growth industry; In an age of 'infotainment,' the line separating it from mainstream media often seems a blur. *Los Angeles Times*, p. A1.

Lambro, Donald. (1992, January 30). Clinton episode could hurt other Democrats. *The Atlanta Journal and Constitution*, p. A10.

Lauter, David. (1992, January 30). Expert says Clinton phone tape was 'selectively edited.' *Los Angeles Time*, p. A 20.

Leonard, Bill. (1987). *In the storm of the eye: A lifetime at CBS.* New York: G.P. Putnam's Sons.

Letter to Allen H. Blondy, 14 RR 1199 (1957).

Lewis, Justin. (1991). *The ideological octopus: An exploration of television & its audience.* New York: Routledge.

Lichty, Lawrence W., & Topping, Malachi C. (1975). *American broadcasting; A source book on the history of radio and television.* New York: Hastings House Publishers.

Lieberman, D. (1988, December 5). As NBC cuts costs will it clobber quality? *Business Week*, pp. 137–138.

Loevinger, Lee. (1968). Broadcasting and the journalistic function. In Harry J. Skornia & Jack William Kitson (Eds.). *Problems and controversies in television and radio* (pp. 320–338). Palo Alto, CA: Pacific Books.

Loosbrock, John F. (1948, October). How television covers the news. *Popular Science*, pp. 122–123.

MacNeil, Robert. (1982). *The right place at the right time*. Boston: Little, Brown and Co.

MacPherson, Myra. (1987, May 9). Trials of the political wife. *Washington Post*, pp. G1, 2.

Madsen, Arnie. (1993). Burke's representative anecdote as a critical method. In James W. Chesbro (Ed.). *Extensions of the Burkean System* (pp. 208–229). Tuscaloosa: University of Alabama Press.

Malone, Julia. (1992, February 2). Clinton ignores lessons he should have learned from Hart. The *Atlanta Journal and Constitution*, p. A6.

Mann, Judy. (1992, January 31). The incredible Gennifer Flowers. *Washington Post*, p. E3.

Mann, Judy. (1987, May 6). Terminal stupidity. *Washington Post*, p. C3.

Mannes, Marya. (1957, May 2). The TV pattern: Part 1. Signs of revolt. *The Reporter, 16*, 20.

Mansfield, Stephanie. (1987, May 5). Satire: Ringing in with the Rice merchants. *Washington Post*, pp. D1, 8.

Maraniss, David. (1992a, January 29). Weary from scrutiny, looking over his shoulder; Clinton's campaign isn't exactly back to normal, but there are no signs it is reeling. *Washington Post*, p. A9.

Maraniss, David. (1992b, January 26). Clinton's life shaped by early turmoil. *Washington Post*, pp. A1, 16.

Maraniss, David. (1987, May 8). The character issue: A bomb waiting to burst. *Washington Post*, pp. A1, 15.

Matalin, Mary, and Carville, James. (1994). *All's fair: Love, war, and running for president*. New York: Random House.

Matusow, Barbara. (1986, March). In defense of docudramas. *Washington Journalism Review*, p. 11.

Matusow, Barbara. (1983). *The evening stars: The making of the network news anchor*. Boston: Houghton Mifflin.

McCarthy, C. (1993, February 23). 'Dateline NBC' burns media credibility. *Washington Post*, p. D13.

McClellan, Steve. (1992, September 21). Local TV news directors grapple with smaller budgets, changes in compensation, tabloid TV. *Broadcasting*, pp. 50, 54, 55.

McCombs, Phil. (1987, May 5). Sex and power: An age-old intimate relationship. *Washington Post*, pp. D1, 8.

McGrory, Mary. (1992, January 28). Flowers and dirt. *Washington Post*, p. A2.

McManus, John H. (1994). *Market-driven journalism: Let the citizen beware?* Thousand Oaks, CA: Sage.

Medhurst, Martin J., & Benson, Thomas W. (Eds.). (1984). *Rhetorical dimensions in media: A critical casebook*. Dubuque, IA: Kendall/Hunt.

Menaker, Daniel. (1976). Art and artifice in network news. In Horace Newcomb (Ed.). *Television: The critical view* (pp. 113–119). New York: Oxford University Press.

Merrill, John. (1974). *The imperative of freedom: A philosophy of journalistic autonomy*. New York: Hastings House.

Merry, Robert W. (1992, February 11). The news that's not fit to print. *Chicago Tribune*, p. 15.

Merton, Robert K., & Gieryn, Thomas F. (1982). Institutionalized altruism: The case of the professions. In Robert K. Merton (Ed.). *Social research and the practicing professions* (pp. 109–134). Cambridge, MA: Abt Books.

Michael Gartner: NBC's multimedia newsman. (1989, April 9). *Broadcasting*, p. 95.

Mickelson, Sig. (1957, Summer). Growth of television news, 1946–1957. *Journalism Quarterly, 34*, 304–310.

Milton, John. (1644). *Areopagitica: For the liberty of unlicenc'd printing*. London: Author.

Morse, Margaret. (1986). The television news personality and credibility. In Tania Modleski (Ed.). *Studies in entertainment* (pp. 55–79). Bloomington: Indiana University Press.

Multimedia Entertainment, Inc., 68 RR 2d 1545 (1991).

Multimedia Entertainment, Inc. (Donahue II), 56 RR 2d 143 (1984).

Multimedia Entertainment, Inc. (Donahue), 48 RR 2d 1273 (1981).

Murphy, Raymond. (1994, November). The sociological construction of science without nature. *Sociology, 28*(4), 957–974.

Murrow, Edward R. (1958, October 15). Address to the Radio-Television News Directors Association meeting. Sheraton-Blackstone Hotel, Chicago.

Mutual Broadcasting System, Inc., 56 RR 2d 956 (1984).

National Broadcasting Company., Inc., 38 RR 2d 943 (1976).

NBC's Gartner: A full plate, but no tin cup. (1992, September 21). *Broadcasting*, pp. 56, 58.

Newcomb, Horace, & Alley, Robert S. (1983). *The producer's medium: Conversations with creators of American TV*. New York: Oxford University Press.

News complexity, public knowledge gap widens—Mickelson. (1959, April 13). *Broadcasting*, p. 97.

News is news. (1959, June 18). *Arizona Republic*.

Newsmakers 88. (1989). Detroit: Gale Research.

Nichols, Marie Hochmuth. (1952, April). Kenneth Burke and the 'New Rhetoric.' *Quarterly Journal of Speech, 38*, 133–144.

Nord, David. (1980, Spring). An economic perspective on formula in popular culture. *Journal of American Culture, 3*, 17–31.

Old news deconstructed. (1992, October 31). *The Economist*. p. 23.

Only the title was unchanged. (1964, March 23). *Broadcasting*, p. 80.

Opotowsky, Stan. (1961). *TV: The big picture*. New York: E.P. Dutton & Co.

Ornstein, Norman J. (1991, October). Sexpress. *The Atlantic*, pp. 24–26.

Page, Clarence. (1992, January 26). Feeding frenzy nibbles Clintons. *Chicago Tribune*, p. 3.

Paley, William S. (1979). *As it happened: A memoir*. Garden City, NY: Doubleday & Co.

Paramount Communications, Inc., 67 RR 2d 1652 (1990).

Paramount Pictures, Corp. (ET & ETW)., 64 RR 2d 600 (1988).

Park, Robert E. (1940). News as a form of knowledge. *American Journal of Sociology, 45*, 669–686.

Persico, Joseph E. (1988). *Edward R. Murrow: An American original*. New York: McGraw-Hill.

Peterson, Bill. (1987, May 9). Dinner, discussion, decision. *Washington Post*, pp. A1, 10.

Peterson, Bill, & Reid, T. R. (1987, May 6). Hart says his judgment, not conduct, was flawed: Many supporters keep own counsel. *Washington Post*, pp. A1, 14–15.

Political Broadcasting. Hearings before the Communications Subcommittee of the Committeee on Interstate and Foreign Commerce, United States Senate, 86th Congress, 1st Session, on S. 1585, S. 1604, S. 1858, and S. 1929. June 18, 19, 23, 24, and 25, 1959.

Political Broadcasts—Equal Time. Hearings before a Subcommittee of the Committee on Interstate and Foreign Commerce, House of Representatives, 86th Congress, 1st Session, on H.R. 5389, H.R. 5675, H.R. 6326, H.R. 7122, H.R. 7180, H.R. 7602, and H.R. 7985. June 29, 30, and July 1, 1959.

Powers, Ron. (1977). *The newscasters*. New York: St. Martin's Press.

Prial, Frank J. (1984, May 26). Equal-time exemption to 'Donahue.' *The New York Times*, Sec. 1, p. 24.

Public service responsibility of broadcast licensees. (1946). Washington, DC: Federal Communications Commission.

Questions about Clinton: Charges of infidelity and draft avoidance. (1992, February 13). *San Diego Union-Tribune*, p. B14.

Quinn, Sally. (1992, January 26). Tabloid politics, the Clintons and the way we now scrutinize our potential presidents. *Washington Post*, pp. C1–2.

Radway, Janice A. (1984). *Reading the romance*. Chapel Hill: University of North Carolina Press.

Randolph, Eleanor. (1987, May 9). The press and the candidate: Hart sex life was longtime focus of rumors. *Washington Post*, pp. A1, 10.

Raspberry, William. (1987a, May 11). What about the Miami Herald? *Washington Post*, p. A13.

Raspberry, William. (1987b, May 6). Victimized . . . by himself. *Washington Post*, p. A19.

Ray, William. (1953). Methods of presenting news on television. In Baskett Mosse & Fred Whiting (Eds.). *Television news handbook* (pp. 5–15). Evanston, IL: Medill School of Journalism, Northwestern University.

Reasoner, Harry. (1981). *Before the colors fade*. New York: Alfred A. Knopf.

Reese, Stephen D. (1990). The news paradigm and the ideology of objectivity: A socialist at the Wall Street Journal. *Critical Studies in Mass Communication, 7*, 390–409.

Reid, T. R. (1987a, May 9). Biting attacks leveled on media, process of selecting U.S. leaders. *Washington Post*, pp. A1, 11.

Reid, T. R. (1987b, May 8). Dreams of a Hart administration die with call: 'We've got another problem.' *Washington Post*, p. A15.

Reid, T. R. (1987c, May 7). Lee Hart breaks silence to defend her husband. *Washington Post*, p. A23.

Reinken, Charles. (1992, February 2). Candidates' past still your business. *Houston Post*, p. C3.

Report of the FCC to Congress pursuant to Sec. 307(c) of the Communications Act of 1934. (1935, January 22). Washington: Federal Communications Commission.

Roberts, Jerry. (1992, March 31). New York's tabloids hound Clinton 'A ceaseless drumbeat about his personal life' as primary looms. *San Francisco Chronicle*, p. A 1.

Roe, Yale. (1962). *The television dilemma*. New York: Hastings House.

Romano, Lois. (1992, January 31). Gary Hart redux in Tinseltown? *Washington Post*, p. G3.

Romano, Lois. (1987, May 7). The Miami Herald's go-ahead. *Washington Post*, p. C1, 8.

Romano, Lois, & Fisher, Marc. (1987, May 6). Donna Rice declines limelight, canceling news conference. *Washington Post*, p. A12.

Roper, J. (1987, March 21). Gartner: 'There's no right to privacy'. *Editor & Publisher*, pp. 52, 62.

Rose, Ernest D. (1961, Fall). How the U.S. heard about Pearl Harbor. *Journal of Broadcasting, 5*, 285–298.

Rosenberg, H. (1993, February 15). A tabloid pattern of behavior at NBC. *Los Angeles Times*, pp. F1, 10

Rosenstiel, Thomas B. (1992, January 29). Clinton allegation raises questions on media's role. *Los Angeles Times*, p. A1.

Rowe, Chip. (1992, April). So, when is sleaze news? *Washington Journalism Review*, pp. 30–35.

The rumblings. (1949, February 7). *Time*, p. 70.

Sabato, Larry J. (1991). *Feeding frenzy*. New York: The Free Press.

Salant tells broadcasters to admit they're in business. (1958, April 14). *Broadcasting*, p. 82.

Sarnoff, David. (1941, January). Possible social effects of television. *Annals of the American Academy of Political and Social Science, 213*, 145–152.

Sarnoff, David. (1939, September). The future of television. *Popular Mechanics*, pp. 321–325, 142A–143A.

Scattarella, Christy, & Ortega, Bob. (1992, February 4). Get them here! Cheap thrills! Hot headlines! *The Seattle Times*, p. A6.

Schoenbrun, David. (1989). *On and off the air: An informal history of CBS News*. New York: Dutton.

Schorr, Daniel. (1992, January 13). From adultery to adulthood; Bill Clinton. *The New Leader*, p. 4.

Schreiner, Tim. (1992, April). You can't ignore news . . . and those tabs aren't all from Mars any longer. *Washington Journalism Review*, pp. 33-35.

Schrøder, Kim Christian. (1994). Audience semiotics, interpretive communities and the 'ethnographic turn' in media research. *Media, Culture & Society, 16*, 337–347.

Schudson, Michael. (1978). *Discovering the News*. New York: Basic Books.

Schwandt, Thomas A. (1994). Constructivist, interpretivist approaches to human inquiry. In Norman K. Denzin & Yvonna S. Lincoln (Eds.). *Handbook of qualitative research* (pp. 118–137). Thousand Oaks, CA: Sage.

Schwartz, Amy E. (1992, January 29). Endless questions. *Washington Post*, p. A21.

Schwartz, Maralee. (1992, January 30). Gov. Clinton's remarks 'offensive,' Kerry says. *Washington Post*, p. A14.

Scott, Pam, Richards, Evelleen, & Martin, Brian. (1990, Fall). Captives of controversy: The myth of the neutral social researcher in contemporary scientific controversies. *Science, Technology & Human Values, 15*(4), 474–494.

Seldes, Gilbert. (1954, January 18). The news on television. *New Republic*, pp. 7–10.

Seldes, Gilbert. (1949, March). Television: The golden hope. *The Atlantic*, p. 35.

Shales, Tom. (1992, January 28). Campaign '92: The muck starts here. *Washington Post*, p. E1.

Shales, Tom. (1987, May 8). The season of scandal. *Washington Post*, pp. D1, 4.

Shaw, David. (1985, April 20-26). Danger! Please don't mix facts with fiction. *TV Guide*.

Shaw, Donald L., & Slater, John W. (1985, Winter/Autumn). In the eye of the beholder? Sensationalism in American press news, 1820–1860. *Journalism History, 12*(3–4), 86–91.

Shields, Mark. (1987, May 5). Gary Hart and the arrogance of indifference. *Washington Post*, p. A19.

Shister, G. (1993, March 30). Dateline NBC anxious to win back credibility. *The Toronto Star*, p. C2.

Sloyan, Patrick J. (1992, January 31). A view from Little Rock: Clinton backers having doubts. *Newsday*, p. 6.

Smith, Bernard. (1948, September). Television: There ought to be a law. *Harper's Magazine*, p. 37.

Smith, Larry David. (1987, Fall/Winter). The nominating convention as purveyor of political medicine: An anecdotal analysis of the Democrats and Republicans of 1984. *Central States Speech Journal, 38*, 252–261.

Span, Paula. (1992, January 28). The bright & slimy Star. *Washington Post*, p. E1.

Spector, Malcolm, & Kitsuse, John I. (1977). *Constructing social problems*. Menlo Park, CA: Cummings.

Stark, Steven. (1995, April 29). The loss of standards: Edward R. Murrow, meet Rush Limbaugh. *The* (Toledo) *Blade*, p. 7.

Starr, Paul. (1982). *The social transformation of American medicine*. New York: Basic Books.

Stasheff, Edward, & Bretz, Rudy. (1956). *The television program: Its writing, direction, and production*. New York: Hill and Wang.

Steele, Sandy. (1993). *Official celebrity register, 1993–1994*. Los Angeles: General.

Stein, M. (1987, October 24). Anonymous sources. *Editor & Publisher*, p. 17.

Stephens, Mitchell. (1988). *A history of news: From the drum to the satellite*. New York: Penguin.

Stepp, Carl Sessions. (1992, March 26). Information as entertainment. *Chicago Tribune*, p. 29.

Stevens, John D. (1991). *Sensationalism and the New York Press*. New York: Columbia University Press.

Swislow, William. (1989, March). Mississippi morass: When Hollywood messes with history, everybody stands to lose. *The Quill*, pp. 20–25.

Tabloid prints new Bill Clinton infidelity allegations [Transcript of *Nightline*, an *ABC News* production]. (1992, January 23).

Tarzian, Jean. (1965, March 13). Some candid views on TV news shows. *Editor & Publisher*, p. 58.

Taylor, Paul. (1990) *See how they run*. New York: Alfred A. Knopf.

Taylor, Paul. (1987a, May 22). [Letters to the Editor]. *New York Times*, 22 May 1987, A30.

Taylor, Paul. (1987b, May 8). Hart to withdraw from presidential campaign. *Washington Post*, pp. A1, 14.

Taylor, Paul. (1987c, May 7). Hart defends his account of weekend. *Washington Post*, pp. A1, 22.

Taylor, Paul. (1987d, May 5). 'Outraged' Hart prepares rebuttal. *Washington Post*, pp. A1, 10.

Taylor, Paul, & Dickenson, James R. (1987, May 6). Candidate assails 'false' news stories. *Washington Post*, pp. A1, 12.

Television: A $13,000,000 if. (1939, April). *Fortune*, p. 54.

Television Code (2nd ed.). (1954). Washington: National Association of Radio and Television Broadcasters.

Television in the tavern. (1947, June 16). *Newsweek*, p. 64.

Television news reporting. (1958). New York: CBS News, Inc.

Television stepping up on-the-spot news coverage. (1962, June 30). *Editor & Publisher*, p. 44.

This campaign cannot go on [Transcript of Hart's withdrawl statement]. (1987, May 9). *Washington Post*, p. A11.

Thomas, Bill. (1990, January 19). Finding truth in the age of 'infotainment.' *Editorial Research Reports*, pp. 34–47.

Tipster said she was Donna Rice's friend. (1987, May 11). *Washington Post*, p. A3.

Townsend, Dallas S., Jr. (1963). News on the air. In Edward W. Barrett (Ed.). *Journalists in action* (pp. 284–287). Manhasset, NY: Channel Press.

Trager, James. (1992). *The people's chronology*. New York: Henry Holt and Co., Inc.

Trueheart, Charles. (1992, January 31). Little Rock, still soft on Clinton. *Washington Post*, pp. G1–2.

Tuchman, Gaye. (1978). *Making news: A study in the construction of reality*. New York: Free Press.

Underwood, Doug. (1993). *When MBAs rule the newsroom: How the marketers and managers are reshaping today's media*. New York: Columbia University Press.

Vobejda, Barbara. (1987, May 5). Ethical questions arise on reporting the private life of a public figure. *Washington Post*, pp. A6–7.

Von Drehle, David. (1992, January 28). Clinton accuser defends story, plays tapes. *Washington Post*, p. A8.

Von Drehle, David, & Edsall, Thomas B. (1992, January 26). Clinton accuser to drop bid on reviving lawsuit. *Washington Post*, p. A16

Walsh, Edward. (1987, May 5). Well-connected lawyer advises Hart campaign. *Washington Post*, p. A9.

Warren, R., & Kaden, L. (1993, March 23). Report of inquiry into crash demonstrations broadcast on *Dateline NBC* November 17, 1992. [Unpublished legal brief] New York: NBC News, Inc.

Weaver, David. (1993, June). Personal communication.

Weaver, David, and Wilhoit, G. Cleveland. (1992, November 17). The American journalist in the 1990s: A preliminary report of key findings from a 1992 national survey of U.S. journalists. [Unpublished report]. Bloomington: Indiana University School of Journalism.

West, M. (1994, Spring). Validating a scale for the measurement of credibility. *Journalism Quarterly, 71*, 159–168.

Westin, Av. (1982). *Newswatch: How TV decides the news*. New York: Simon and Schuster.

When good journalists do bad things: Truthtelling and the public trust. (1993, April 15). [Videotaped conference proceeding] St. Petersburg, FL: Poynter Institute for Media Studies.

White, E. B. (1955, February 19). Split personalities. *The New Yorker*.

Wilk, Max. (1976). *The golden age of television: Notes from the survivors*. New York: Dell Publishing Co.

Will, George F. (1987, May 8). The wolf factor. *Washington Post*, p. A23.

Williams, Albert N. (1953). The broadcasters' 'sense of guilt.' In Herbert L. Marx, Jr., (Ed.). *Television and radio in American life* (pp. 103–107). New York: H. W. Wilson Co. (Original work published 1948)

Winch, Samuel P. (1996, May 25). Mission Impossible? When government tries to map the boundaries of journalism. Paper presented at the annual convention of the International Communication Association, Chicago.

Winch, Samuel P. (1994, August 14). The status degradation ceremony of Michael Gartner. Paper presented at the annual convention of the Association for Education in Journalism and Mass Communication, Atlanta.

Wines, Michael. (1987, September). In bed with the press. *Washington Journalism Review*, pp. 16–19.

Winner, Langdon. (1993, Summer). Upon opening the black box and finding it empty: Social constructivism and the philosophy of technology. *Science, Technology & Human Values, 18*(3), 362–378.

Wright, Charles W. (1960). Functional analysis in mass communication. *Public Opinion Quarterly, 24*, 605–620.,

Yoder, Edwin M., Jr. (1987, May 6). Totalitarian journalism. *Washington Post*, p. A19.

Zelizer, Barbie. (1993). Journalists as interpretive communities. *Critical Studies in Mass Communication, 10*, 219–237.

Zelizer, Barbie. (1990). Achieving journalistic authority through narrative. *Critical Studies in Mass Communication, 7*, 366–376.

Zurawik, D., & Stoehr, C. (1993, April). Money changes everything. *American Journalism Review*, p. 28

Index

About the Author

SAMUEL P. WINCH is Lecturer in the School of Communication Studies at Nanyang Technological University in Singapore. His areas of special interest include journalism ethics, visual journalism, and computer-mediated journalism.

ISBN 0-275-95763-2

9 0 0 0 0>

EAN

9 780275 957636

HARDCOVER BAR CODE